D1473641

MAPPING HEGEMONY
Television News Coverage of Industrial Conflict

COMMUNICATION AND INFORMATION SCIENCE

Edited by
BRENDA DERVIN
The Ohio State University

Recent Titles

BOWLING GREEN STATE UNIVERSITY
DISCARDED
LIBRARY

MAPPING HEGEMONY
Television News Coverage of
Industrial Conflict

ROBERT GOLDMAN
and
ARVIND RAJAGOPAL

ABLEX PUBLISHING CORPORATION
NORWOOD, NEW JERSEY

BOWLING GREEN STATE
UNIVERSITY LIBRARIES

Copyright © 1991 by Ablex Publishing Corporation.

All rights reserved. No part of this publication may be reproduced, stored in a retrieval system, or transmitted, in any form or by any means, electronic, mechanical, photocopying, microfilming, recording, or otherwise, without permission of the publisher.

Printed in the United States of America

Library of Congress Cataloging-in-Publication Data

Goldman, Robert, 1949–
  Mapping hegemony : television news coverage of industrial conflict
/ by Robert Goldman and Arvind Rajagopal.
    p. cm. — (Communication and information science)
  Includes bibliographical references and index.
  ISBN 0-89391-697-8 (c1)
    1. Coal Strike, U.S., 1977–1978.   2. Television broadcasting of
news—United States—Case studies.   3. Television broadcasting of
news—Social aspects—Unted States—Case studies.   4. Journalism-
-United States—Objectivity—Case studies.   I. Rajagopal, Arvind.
II. Title.   III. Series
HD5325.M63 1977.U546   1991
070.4′49331892822334′0973—dc20   90-23351
                                                                    CIP

Ablex Publishing Corporation
355 Chestnut St.
Norwood, NJ 07648

Table of Contents

Acknowledgments

I am grateful to the many generous people at Hobart & William Smith Colleges who provided me with a temporary institutional haven when times were bleakest. Thanks to Rick Diehl for the use of his extensive personal archives and his hardnosed perspective on the coalfield political economy. Thanks also to John Wilson, Janet Wasko, David Walls, Steve Papson and Doug Kellner for their feedback after wading through portions of our manuscript in earlier drafts. The Ablex reviewers also provided many useful criticisms and suggestions for improvement. Of all our respondents, we want to express a particular note of appreciation to Ben Franklin of the New York Times who gave generously of his time and memory.

The kernal of this study was done by Arvind as his Master's Thesis. Subsequent expansions and revisions have been my doing. Much of this book was researched and produced in Altoona in 1985-86. In the isolated, depressing, bitterly cold and gray Altoona winter of 1985-1986, rock n' roll was my salvation. To put it bluntly, rock was the kick in the ass that got this book finished. I owe an impersonal debt of thanks to the music, among others, of Jackson Browne, The Clash, Bruce Springsteen, Joan Armatrading, The Who, Dire Straits, Pat Methany, Laurie Anderson, Bob Seger, The Allman Brothers, George Thorogood, Eddie Grant, Los Lobos, John Mellencamp, Talking Heads, Tom Petty, Peter Tosh, Bob Marley, Jimmy Cliff, and Rank & File.

On the personal front, Arvind gives thanks to his parents. I too thank my parents, Sylvia and Hilton Goldman, who have been an unwavering source of support.

Finally, my deepest debt is to Sharon Smith, a common name for a most uncommon woman. The idea for this study was hers. And,

Sharon's wage labor provided the material support for the research and writing done in 1985–86. Without her 'funding' this project would never have been completed. Her professional research skills, performed gratis, have also been an invaluable resource and a chief reason we have been able to pull off a project like this on "no budget." She has throughout this project listened patiently, shown no sympathy, and taken the side of the reader.

Bob Goldman
Spring 1989
Portland, Oregon

PREFACE

Mapping Hegemony? The title refers to our effort to trace, with a detail and specificity we believe has seldom been performed, what it means to speak ^f "hegemonic" broadcast news media. Too often, arguments are made about ideological effect without enough attention to *what* is said and *how* it is said. Addressing these logically prior questions enables us not only to outline the ideologies *produced* by broadcasters, but also to make sense of why they are so plausible, how they reconcile contradictions in a class society, and what position they assume for the audience. That is, we are enabled to show *how* hegemony is constituted.

This book treats television news as public discourse, emphasizing discourse as a form of ideology. If television news has the power to define public images of social reality, then how would we recognize hegemony if we saw it on the television news—if it hit us in the face? By scrutinizing one network's reports on an episode in American industrial conflict, we examine how network television news frames a way of seeing the relations which compose our social, economic and political world. Where better to examine questions about ideology and hegemony than in television news representations of capital-labor conflicts—the prototypical class relation?

The world of television news is today constructed out of such things as "soundbites," "factoids," and "spin control." This may sound more like video games than television news, but it is high-tech, commodity news and these bits of media jargon unintentionally reveal the extent to which the news has been transformed into a mechanically paced object of consumption, in which form steadily eclipses substance. To make consumption *easy*, the pace gets faster and faster and the units of information get smaller and smaller. To those unfamiliar with these practices, a soundbite is a slice of an utterance edited out of context, while a factoid is a free-floating particle of information that has been chopped out of context. When news content is constructed by editing together these slices and particles into stories, a premium is placed on how news producers frame the bits and pieces into something meaningful.

Along with its ubiquitous availability and the scarcity of alternative viewpoints, the power of television news lies in this capacity to frame stories. But these factors do not explain the *authority* and *credibility* invested in it; it is the perceived balance and objectivity of television news that are critical to its acceptance by viewers. An objective viewpoint is an oxymoron—a viewpoint by definition implies choice, which indicates motive, not objectivity. Objectivity and balance can be more usefully understood not as *values*, then, but as the *names* given to journalistic practices which are routinely performed—some of them, indeed, so routinely as to be almost unnoticeable. While we question the description of these practices as "objective" and "neutral," *naming has its power.*

Framing refers to the way an issue is posed or set up. How a story is set up is already a frame in itself. For instance, the Republican marketing technicians who brought us Ronald Reagan practiced a version of framing called "spin control"—a method of trying to steer public discourse on any given issue. Frames range from the explicit to the implicit. For instance, when the subject on television news is the relationship between the U.S. and the Soviet Union, then capitalism (which is associated with democracy) is ideologically foregrounded and held superior to communism (associated with totalitarianism). But on the domestic scene, capitalism disappears as an explicit frame. Here, capitalism becomes a presumed but invisible background to the story being told.

A fundamental premise motivating this study is that television news constitutes a potential site for political intervention and ideological contestation. This is the flip side of our finding that television news has up till now upheld and reproduced a way of seeing the world that supports the interests of capitalist institutions and elites. The news media do this by representing the dominant interests as the universal interest. Indeed, the "objective standpoint" that the media take is situated in an assumed consensus about the universality of capitalist interests. Where we differ from the networks is in describing this as routinized conflict rather than as consensus—we contest the premise that capitalist interests are in the general social interest.

The test case for any analysis about the ideological character of network news is when there is a breakdown of the "consensus" for all to see—when there is a strike. What choice of viewpoints is then offered us? The "universalized viewpoint" of the media affords no overt signs of class or class conflict. Insofar as different classes exist independently of the mass media, however, this is a distinction that cannot be dissolved, only reformulated. The question then becomes, how do journalistic practices of balance and objectivity reformulate class relations and class conflicts? And where better to address this than in television news coverage of a labor strike? The routines of reporting, the strategies that operate to systematically prefer some views over others, are most transparently seen when there is a challenge to the assumptions of reporting—in this case, the assumption of capital-labor consensus in the universality of the state.

When we began this project in 1980, sociologists typically responded to arguments about ideological domination or capitalist hegemony in a defensive way—for example, "Oh yeah, well where is your proof?" If, on the one hand, this project began as an attempt to make sense of the ideological character of television news, it was also motivated by a desire to present an alternative to the dogmatic methodology that has dominated the discipline of sociology. Positivism had regressed from the elegant logic of Karl Popper into a banal formula which claimed exclusive access, but bore little resemblance, to the "empirical world." We believe that questions of ideological domination must be taken up empirically, so we have accepted the empiricist challenge, and charted in microscopic detail, frame by frame, how the evening news can "prefer" or "privilege" a way of seeing.

Our research has, however, made us suspicious of equating hegemony with the presence of a single "dominant ideology"—indeed, we find that television news is less likely to enforce a dominant ideology on its viewers than it is to block out alternative ideological perspectives. We also argue that as a practical matter, hegemony in the contemporary United States does not require a single, uniform interpretation of texts. Too often, theories of hegemony are read as "conspiracy" theories. Our point here is simple, hegemonic ideology in the United States today does *not* require conspiracy. Hegemonic ideology is today usually a derivative of the routinized, structural logic of treating news as a commodity.

AN UPDATE

We would be remiss if we did not mention the recent Pittston strike. A decade after the 1977–78 BCOA–UMWA strike, similar issues were played out again, both in the coalfields and in network media coverage of the conflict. Despite the fact that Pittston was demanding even more extensive labor concessions than those we discuss in this book; refused to bargain, much less in good faith; and were in repeated violation of federal labor law, the miners' struggle dragged on month after month without the slightest network news attention. Though the dispute between the Pittston and the UMWA might have begun as a story on network television news in November 1987, it did not register on television screens until the second quarter of 1989, when an extensive publicity and media campaign on behalf of the union finally paid off. Aside from one piece of coverage on CBS's prime time *48 Hours,* coverage usually meant 20 seconds of film in a 30-second report, not enough time to detail the dispute and the negotiating positions. A few instances of violence between striking miners and scabs got a few sentences. Still, just a little media attention pressured Pittston back to the bargaining table. Months later, the question of whether the Secretary of Labor in the Bush administration would appoint a "super mediator" to resolve the dispute, got a little more attention. And then came the announcement one day in early 1990: There was a strike, and now maybe there isn't (see Seager, 1989).

Introduction

Although relations between capital and labor form a fundamental axis of capitalist society, the U.S. news media rarely report on this relationship. Network television news generally neglects labor-management relations as a news category. In fact, network television news consistently avoids both production and class relations. If such relations had become defunct in advanced capitalist society, then perhaps this omission would be understandable. But class and production relations do persist, and struggles between capital and labor remain a paramount force shaping modern politics.

Nowadays, network television news predominates as a medium of mass political socialization in the United States (Dahlgren, 1980). Fifty-one percent of the respondents in a 1976 Roper poll named television as "the most believable news medium," while only 22 percent cited newspapers. A decade later, a *Weekly Reader* survey of 340,000 children shows that a new generation trusts television news far more than print news. Television news has become a popular model of fairness and neutrality; its idiom and manner have become universally recognized signs of dispassionate inquiry. Those who control the network news apparatus would have us believe their product is beyond ideology—that they represent the interests of us all, as if ideology was nothing more than taking "sides." The success of their "nonpartisan" message would seem obvious. Opinion polls confirm that people prefer and trust the kind of news that most completely excludes class and production relations from view. Of what consequence is it that the primary medium of political socialization cuts out the subject of class relations in order to sustain the illusion of neutrality?

In this book, we see news as inherently political and ideological.

1

News is a social product literally structured by, and filled with, ideologies. Television news formulas that aim at preserving "the appearance of neutrality" should not be confused with a "nonideological" informational source. Journalistic ideals of neutrality and impartiality are impossible insofar as there exists no materially neutral sociocultural standpoint from which "facts" may be gathered, ordered, and presented. However, when these ideals are socially defined as real by news producers—and, apparently, by news consumers as well—they have practical and ideological consequences. Whether or not the networks achieve their goal of "fairness," the aim of neutrality is routinely "operationalized" in the encoding procedures performed by television news. Instead of dismissing reporters' professional codes as being unfulfilled, we investigate the ideological possibilities established by the television news code of narrative neutrality—that is, claiming to tell stories without taking sides.

Our agenda is twofold: to investigate the question of ideological hegemony in network television news, and to analyze an instance of how network television represented industrial conflicts in the United States in the late 1970s. To this end, we have intensively disassembled *CBS News* coverage of a dispute between the Bituminous Coal Operators Association (BCOA) and the United Mine Workers of America (UMWA) in 1977–78. Strikes offer a paradigmatic instance of capital-labor conflict in capitalist society, and their representation in network television news offers an example of how class relations are presented and interpreted by the mass media. To news producers, strikes represent a breakdown of a societal consensus. Strike coverage therefore offers an ideal opportunity for analyzing how news producers articulate that consensus.

Ours is a study of television news outputs. Social scientists are notorious for asking but one question about U.S. mass-media—"what *effects* does it have?" Though we would like to know how audience perceptions and values are affected by television news, these questions remain premature until we have examined how those news texts mean. The forms and processes of signification—as much as what is signified— are crucial to grasping television news' sociocultural and political impacts. Our critical analysis joins this level of analysis to an ideology critique based on historically contextualizing the news texts.

We conceptualize television news as a specific form of discourse, as a form of socially structured meaning with its own codes and interpretive rules. The dictionary defines discourse as "conversation" and as the act of expressing meaning in speech, writing, and photography. Another meaning of discourse is "a formal and lengthy discussion of a subject." But at a basic theoretical level we must further specify that discourse refers to socially produced meaning, as well as to the context of producing meaning. Marx pointed to the social materiality of meaning, to the dialectical interplay between ideas and practice: "Language is practical consciousness that exists also for other men, and for that reason alone it really exists for me personally as well . . . Consciousness is, therefore, from the very beginning a social product" (Marx & Engels, 1970, p. 51). From Marx, we understand discourse as both act and product.

Whenever we engage in discourse, we utilize a system of discourse rules which are bracketed or put aside as unspoken background assumptions. Once these have been performatively learned, we don't normally notice these assumptions until a rule is violated. Discourse in daily life rests on our shared implicit understanding of the assumptions which organize our discourse—this tacit understanding is called *meta-communication* (Bateson, 1972). Television news is a specialized discourse with its own normative background assumptions. Broadcasters do not dwell on these, but convey them in a tone of voice or the way an image is framed and presented. One tacit understanding is the premise that news is *public* discourse—this represents the moral ideal of a democratic society that news ought to permit the "rational" presentation of conditions and arguments that will allow viewers to assess the validity claims of one argument versus another (cf. Habermas, 1975).

Broadcast news also advertises itself as an open field of discourse which is constraint-free. But there can be freedom from constraint only when

> all participants [get] a symmetrical distribution of chances to select and employ speech acts, when there is an effective equality of chances to assume dialogue roles. In particular, all participants must have the same chance to initiate and perpetuate discourse, to put forward, call into question, and give reasons for or against statements, explanations, interpretations, and justifications. (Habermas, 1975, p. xvii)

Our study shows that this was not the case on CBS. Neutrality-oriented news did not produce an open field of discourse, nor were there equal opportunities to present either evidence or argument.

HEGEMONY

Hegemony refers to processes of securing and shaping consent so the power of the dominant classes appears both legitimate and natural.

4   Mapping Hegemony: Television News Coverage of Industrial Conflict

The definition of a hegemonic viewpoint is (a) that it defines within its terms the mental horizon, the universe, of possible meanings, of a whole sector of relations in a society or culture; and (b) it carries with it the stamp of legitimacy—it appears coterminous with what is "natural," "inevitable," "taken for granted" about the social order. (Hall, 1980, p. 137)

The concept of hegemony defines "a whole body of practices and expectations . . . our shaping perceptions for ourselves and the world . . . It thus constitutes a sense of reality for most people in society" (Williams, 1977, p. 110). This "sense of reality" is variable, and not singular historical and not fixed. Marx argued that "human consciousness is conditioned in dialectical interplay between subject and object, in which man actively shapes the world he lives in at the same time as it shapes him . . . Even our perception of the material world is conditioned by society" (Giddens, 1971, p. 21). The definitions of reality which prevail at any given historical moment may be conditioned by the "logic" of dominant institutions as well as the interests of dominant class fractions. This is not, however, the result of some mechanical imposition of ideas but derives from processes of "framing all competing definitions of reality within their range" (Hall, 1977, p. 333). In the *Prison Notebooks*, Gramsci (1971, p. 323) located this process in the practices and language of daily life. Elaborate philosophical systems were not necessary, he argued, to reproduce or justify the dominance of a ruling class. Rather, everyday language replicated and transmitted a

"spontaneous philosophy" which is proper to everybody. This philosophy is contained in: 1) language itself, which is a totality of determined notions and concepts and not just words grammatically devoid of content; 2) "common sense" and "good sense"; 3) popular religion and, therefore, also in the entire system of beliefs, superstitions, opinions, ways of seeing things and acting, which are collectively bundled together under the name of "folklore".

Hegemonic ideology refers to a dominant way of seeing/making sense of the world around us. Such ways of seeing are predicated on taken-for-granted rules of discourse and cultural codes. Hegemonic ideology does *not* produce domination, although—depending on how vigorously it is contested—it helps reproduce domination by steering inquiry away from the structural hegemony of interests (economic, social, political) which prevail at any given moment. One modern rule of political sociology is that dominant interests seek to secure the consent of the governed through legitimate means. Hall (1977) and Gitlin (1980, p. 10) have emphasized the dialectical character of hegemony—hegemonic ideologies are partially resisted and contested and, at the same time, pliable, fluid, and able to encapsulate that which opposes them. Gramsci also argued that subordinate classes participate and collaborate in the ideological consent which masks their own inequality and domination. As a result, hegemony represents an uneven historical formation. "Traces" of ideologies from a previous era may be preserved, while elements of emerging worldviews become incorporated. The contradictions of market and class interests likewise impart an uneven character to hegemonic ideology. One premise of studying television news texts is that because they are structured by such contradictions, they can be made to reveal them.

Locating the role of news media in this "moving equilibrium" of the hegemonic process has proven difficult because (a) ideology so thoroughly "saturates everyday discourse [and, by extension, the discourse of news] in the form of common sense" (Hebdige, 1979, p. 12) that few of us pause to recognize it even when it touches us; (b) those who operate news producing institutions explicitly deny their part in ideology production, calling themselves a transparent conduit for carrying messages; (c) hegemony is elusive. Try to grab it and name it, and the process squirms away, leaving behind a reified nugget of a "dominant ideology."

Television news provides a social text that can be made to illuminate how ideological consent is both contested and secured. We intend to track how television news assembles and relays hegemonic ideologies and influences consent to forms of inequality and domination in advanced capitalist society (cf. Tuchman, 1976; Kellner, 1979; Gitlin, 1980). Exhaustive textual analysis of news reports allows us to map what it means to speak of hegemony in network television news. This mapping process combines thick description with theoretical excavation and produces maps full of contradictions—what others have called a "contested terrain." These contradictions do not deter us; rather we embrace them because confronting them enables us to clarify "how news forms contribute to broadcast images of cultural, political and economic hegemony" (Altheide, 1985, p. 351). We intend to literally disassemble the taken-for-granted rules and codes of discourse which form the backbone of hegemonic narratives.

Throughout this study we have intentionally distanced ourselves from any view that casts hegemony in the mass media as a product of conspiracy or intentional bias. Our research shows quite the opposite— hegemony is the product of the routine, daily institutional practices of treating news as a commodity. We argue that a social theory of commodity relations best explains the ideological character of news in advanced capitalist society. Television news' reputed fairness and neutrality is a product of the drive to maximize its commodity status. News producers' formulas of fairness and neutrality unintentionally accomplish what the formulas were designed to prevent: They become material, tool, and framework in generating a new historical form of hegemonic discourse. Television news producers believe ideological accounts can be cleansed when passed through the grid of commodity logic, yet they merely bury the ideological character of their discourse so that it is less penetrable. We argue that the networks have labored mightily to purge themselves of overt attitudinal biases; instead, they now permit the routinized, structural logic of treating news as a commodity to define the character of hegemony.

TELEVISION AND THE BIG PICTURE CIRCA 1977

As Marx was wont to remind us, ideology does not simply float around. The issues of hegemony and ideology are always grounded in historically specific social formations. By 1977, the system of corporate capitalism in the United States had stumbled at the end of a 30-year growth swing following World War II. The Labor-Capital Accords—the arrangements between business and labor that permitted U.S. capitalist hegemony to reign supreme in the world system—were crumbling. The Federal government grew constantly during this period, partly to defend the American empire, partly to pay for all the inadequacies of the capitalist system—paying for the environment; keeping alive those excluded from labor markets; keeping up necessary infrastructure; subsidizing research and development; and so on. The growth of the state to regulate class conflicts between business and labor had worked for awhile, but by the 1970s it was paying an unanticipated dividend—fiscal crisis. By 1977, the Federal government was no longer the means of solving and displacing crises, now it was the source of crises. Bouts of stagflation now sandwiched steady inflation. Meanwhile, rates of profit and productivity in the corporate economy were declining and organized labor drifted without purpose or direction.

During the postwar era, television emerged as the dominant media form and network news became the pivotal player in the construction of public discourse. How did the eye of television represent relationships between business, labor, the State and the audience—the public—at that critical juncture where the U.S. came to the end of its postwar economic dominance and the nation entered into a bitter struggle to rearrange our political-economic system?

1

Network News and Ideology

TELEVISION NEWS AND PUBLIC DEBATE IN CLASS SOCIETY

The television news media constitute a primary source of information for people as a whole in the United States, where the supposedly informed consent of mass publics forms a critical means of legitimizing state measures while providing reassurance of their democratic basis. The nature of information available to these mass publics does, accordingly, influence the character of consent that justifies the current organization of the state.

To insure their own legitimacy, network news organizations offer themselves as servants to the general citizenry, committed to "the public's right to know"—aka "the public interest" or "the public trust." Behind this public pledge to defend and preserve the heritage of democracy, network news has become a corporate business. CBS's Dan Rather acknowledges that "Our dilemma is this: are we a business or a public trust?" News broadcasts are shaped by the structure of markets and processes of capital accumulation. To be sure, these broadcasts are also influenced by ideals about a public sphere that might serve as a means of enlightened control against potential abuses of State power and authority. But under conditions of increasing concentration of media ownership, broadcast news has become thoroughly a consumer product made to be sold—the balance continues to tilt toward cost-effectiveness over the public interest. The bottom line is that networks produce news as a commodity and in order to sell their news product, they flatter their audiences with an ever more hollow cultural ideal of news as enlightening citizens.

Every society has legitimation requirements that must be met. From 1946 to the present—the television era—the principle of a representative government responding to the collective public will has evolved into a form of mass-mediated plebiscite in which legitimacy is measured in public opinion. Television network news promotes itself as a means by which popular opinion is channeled into an extralegal countervailing force against domination or abuse of authority by the Government. In this mass-media version of the public sphere, public opinion undergoes continuous (weekly) reproduction as a commodity assembled via the coordinated mechanisms of public relations work and public opinion research. Corporate marketing practices compose this "public" by collating the separately held opinions of dispersed individual respondents. Public opinion polls measure this abstract collectivity, the serialized mass audience addressed by broadcast news. Separating speaker from speaker, and speaker from listener, and listener from listener, network news intervenes to situate and interpret the meaningful relationship between public discourses. This method of mediating public opinion inevitably inflates network news' own institutional importance in determining the composition of public opinion. It also reduces the agenda of democratic public debate to tabulating abstracted opinion measures about how many respondents will support—or not support—either of two elite party positions. Broadcast news treats public debate as a circular dance of opinions. News broadcasters apply formulas of neutrality and balance to political dialogue by pairing ostensibly competing interests in frameworks of formal equivalency, and then marching through a ritual of mechanical turntaking.

Network news professionals prefer to distinguish their "objective" news product from the "show-biz" variant called "infotainment." They shrug off the mass entertainment side as "one-of-those-unhappy-facts-of-life" that stem from the picture-hungry nature of television and the "insatiable desires" of consumers to be entertained. In point of fact, the television news media structures the public sphere of discourse as spectacle because news has been made a commodity. Paraphrasing Guy Debord (1977), we may say that all public discourse becomes presented "as an immense accumulation of spectacles. Everything that was directly lived has moved into a representation . . . The images detached from every aspect of life fuse in a common stream . . ." The fact that television news builds so heavily on video editors' arrangement of photographic images amplifies the networks intervention into the assembly of public discourse. Techniques of photographic reproduction remove the depiction of conflicting discourses from their organic context (Berger, 1972; Berger & Mohr, 1982).

The meaning of an image is changed according to what one sees immediately beside it or what comes immediately after it. Such authority as it retains, is distributed over the whole context in which it appears. (p. 20)

As a media form, television disconnects meaningful images and voices from context, which are then recontextualized through the use of formats and formulas. Making news a commodity (i.e., the creation of "news value"/exchange value) reinforces the structural tendency to abstract events and discourses from context. Armed with "value-free" format rules, the networks claim to simulate a "world out there" and rechannel it into our living rooms, but the news product they transmit is processed discourse—broken up and reconstituted.

The broadcast news media have so expanded in economic scale that they can no longer claim to be disinterested observers. Anchormen and network reporters have become celebrities who possess elite status. And, corporate ownership generates support for its own substantial economic interests and the general conditions that make these possible. The broadcast news media find it difficult to openly reflect on questions about how their own corporate interests might shape the news. This is because between network news divisions, economic success means competing for "public trust": rating points accrue from wooing audiences. And, network news divisions cultivate this legitimacy by promoting themselves in terms of technocratic virtues such as being "impartial," "fair," "reliable," "accurate," "balanced," "fast." In network television news, legitimacy represents a crucial form of currency which translates into other forms of currency—rating points and advertising revenues (i.e., accumulation). Put simply, network news divisions have an interest in self-promotion, and an interest in denying how their own corporate organization may shape news—to do otherwise would damage the legitimacy of their currency.

A privately owned press formed a necessary institutional support to a democratic public sphere in the late 18th and early 19th century in the U.S. Social spaces which promoted exchanges of rational discourse were crucial in the bourgeoisie's struggle to secure "democratic control of state activities" (Habermas, 1974, p. 50). But corporate concentration of media ownership in the 20th century has permitted commodity logic to negate democratic public debate by channeling discursive exchanges through the form of its mass-media apparatus. Television has reshaped the social spaces in which discursive exchanges occur, and thereby fundamentally reshaped the processes of public debate. Here, as we all know, appearance has come to predominate over substance. Here, debate has been narrowed to a ritualized television *event*, with the terms of debate formulated from above by political and media elites.

In late capitalism, a public sphere of discussion consists of two spheres. One sphere continues to function as the bourgeois public sphere, addressing a relatively elite, literate audience. In this sphere corporate leaders, professionals, and technocrats take the lead in conducting discursive exchanges about practical and political agendas. The other sphere, however, is not a proletarian public sphere, but a television public sphere, organized according to an altogether different principle—here processes of discursive exchange are made to fit the logic of equivalence exchange!

News media occupy a contradictory position in advanced capitalist society. Traditions of a free and independent press have been a key ingredient in the development of liberal, democratic societies. Broadcast journalists zealously trumpet their independence from particular interests so as to legitimate themselves in the eyes of consumers, their mass publics. Reporters adhere to professional norms of integrity and tend to resist interference from media owners. In their day-to-day routines, the broadcast news media operate autonomously from both State interests and specific capitalist interests.

Commodity news producers recognize that they cannot survive in the markeplace without public legitimacy, which in turn is dependent on appearing dispassionately neutral. Trained professional journalists sell their reportorial labor as a commodity in exchange for making (organizing) the events and activities of society into a commodity called "the daily news." Organized as a commodity relation, both reporting as an activity and news as a category became reconstituted by the logic of Capital (Marx, 1967).[1] The structural framework imposed by Capital conditions how news is defined, produced, and consumed. Attempts to maximize audience size (and therefore market size) require news producers to conceal and deny class relations as a relevant category within which to situate explanations of events. Since the use of class categories divides and reduces audience size, a predominant strategy of producing news to maximize market share relies on a rhetoric of impartiality and neutrality in reporting.

Claims of objectivity and neutrality—voiced by professional journalists and news organizations alike—in making news must be rejected,

---

[1]News people seek to capture "news value." Though the rules which justify a hierarchical ranking of news value are rarely articulated, they form a tacitly understood language. Paraphrasing Marcuse, news value is informational use value mediated through the structural relation of the commodity form and exchange values (Marcuse, 1960, p. 298).

since all news is socially constructed (Tuchman, 1978; Epstein, 1973). Still, when something is socially defined as real, it is real in its consequences and it remains to be shown how these ideals/practices actually materialize in the news product. Market interests and professional norms motivate reporting procedures designed to achieve balance and impartiality, and these practices ideologically omit class relations as an analytic category. In historical context, we recognize the network ideologies of objectivity and pluralism as attempts to transcend the contradictory relations of class in order to maximize market shares of the news as commodity. Of course, the news media's denial of "class" has not abolished the reality of class contradictions in civil society or state, though we suspect it has altered collective understandings of how social, economic, and political life are organized.

Television journalism's mechanistic adherence to neutrality practices has not nurtured a plurality of viewpoints, but rather restricted those who depend on it for information to a decidedly unitary perspective—witness the mimetic quality of the news product offered by each professionally trained and oriented network news division. Further, the pursuit of balance—the quest for ideological neutrality—is not realized by this unitary method, because the technical and practical means of carrying out demands for objective balance result in partial, unbalanced, accounts. Contradictory relations are too complex to be handled by means of these tools. Techniques of formal balance and judicious restraint do not produce objective knowledge, but a style of abbreviation which reinforces a top-down model of leadership and technocratic ideology of trust in specialist expertise.

We must not, however, ignore the ideological power of the ethos of objective balanced reporting. Network news organizations regularly advertise themselves in terms of "integrity," "independence," "objectivity," "accuracy." The premise underlying virtually every broadcast "hard" news story is that it is a communication free of bias. Whenever criticism of the news media arises, it centers on whether or not newspeople are meeting this mandate to be objective. Right-wing coalitions like Fairness in Media see CBS News as having a "liberal bias." Liberal slant, along with reporters' skepticism, cynicism, and willingness to turn anything into a "story" translates for these right wingers into an "immoral, disruptive, and unpatriotic" set of practices.

In recent years, questions of "media bias" have been taken up by academics concerned with whether or not a "liberal elite" dominates broadcast journalism. Like the networks they study, these academics fixate on politics narrowly defined—that is, on party politics—and an ideological universe defined by a facile conservative-liberal dichotomy. Bridging the concerns of conservative political forces and academic research have been corporate advertising campaigns like those of United Technologies and Mobil Oil attacking the news media as unfair toward business. These campaigns justify their claims by appealing to studies demonstrating "liberal press bias."[2]

When offered a forced dichotomy, a majority of professional journalists would probably describe their own political views as "liberal." Yet, liberalism has historically been one voice of capitalist elites and the "liberal elite" making media decisions has reinforced the staunch anticommunism of dominant political elites since World War II (cf. Gibson, 1980). Defining foreign "otherness" in contrast to our domestic situation invalidates, a priori, agendas such as public ownership and worker self-management. Despite the adversarial mantle its takes up, television news legitimates State institutions and corporate enterprises (Guzzardi, 1985). News "confirms the legitimacy of the state by hiding the state's intimate involvement with, and support of, corporate capitalism" (Tuchman, 1978, p. 210). Network news equates "free enterprise" with a "democratic" way of life. It validates capitalist institutions by concealing their actual operation and by concealing the entanglement of these institutions in the operation of the State.

A "code of narrative objectivity" where class relations are involved is not innocent. "By network news reasoning, the ideology of the state is no ideology at all. It is precisely this blindness which constitutes ideological reasoning" (Gibson, 1980, p. 99). The very "neutrality practices" employed by professional broadcasters produce and reproduce the form of partiality (Connell, 1980). Though "neutrality practices" once offered a reform aimed at preventing dominant interests from gaining unfair advantage, these same practices today reproduce capitalist hegemony: representing dominant interests as if they are universal interests.

DEMOCRACY, CAPITALISM, AND OBJECTIVITY

The "penny press" of the 1830s and 1840s accelerated the treatment of news as a marketable product. It also represented a movement toward

---

[2]These studies purported to show a bias against businessmen on television and a liberal tilt among journalists. These findings, vigorously amplified in corporate ads, were based on sophomoric methodological approaches (Winston, 1983). The well-publicized studies done by Rothman and Lichter relied on methodology which "departs from scientific practice" (Gans, 1985). Shown sets of oversimplified statements, journalists were asked to agree/disagree and on the basis of these forced-choice responses were then tagged with an ideological label of "liberal." Similarly, the Christian Right perceives network reporters as "secular humanists"—"soft on" homosexuality, divorce, and abortion.

nonpartisan ideologies and objectivity in reporting. Initially, adapting news to a market had a democratizing impact in the sense that entrepreneurial journalists sought to widen their audience for papers. But, despite the air of egalitarianism that clung to the penny press, it was probably less effective than the preceding multivocal partisan press had been in promoting a democratic sphere of vigorous public debate. True, penny papers lowered their prices to compete against 6-cent papers for mass circulation; adopted laissez-faire advertising policies; and introduced financial and ideological independence from political parties (Schudson, 1978). The search for more readers led journalists to cater to a growing urban populace. And, as the logic of the economic sphere penetrated into the cultural sphere, the press became both more sensationalist and disavowed partisan political interests. Competition to sell news meant emphasising the timeliness of what was reported; neutrality as the absence of political perspective; and a calculated interest in what consumers would buy. Over the rest of the 19th century, editors' quest for power and profits led them to cater to raffish tastes rather than the goals of enlightenment and understanding (Altschull, 1985).

Though the penny press propagated a mythology about the news media's responsibility for maintaining a public sphere in which the untrammeled interchange of information enlightens citizens and acts as a check on their institutions, its own development frequently contradicted that goal. The idea of a public sphere during the Enlightenment was instrumental in promoting the rising bourgeoisie, by attacking corrupt and reactionary forces of absolutist states (Hohendahl, 1974). Newspapers in the 18th and early 19th centuries served an openly partisan purpose of safeguarding the interests of their own public constituencies (Schudson, 1978).

The public sphere mediated between civil society and the state, providing a social space in which public discussion and debate could take place independent of the State. The public sphere defined the "position and function of discourse by which the bourgeoisie could give public expression to private interest and so affect public policy" (Brenkman, 1979, p. 101). This bourgeois public sphere provided a means of conducting a democratic politics around a system of market relations: Each entrepreneur could engage in public articulation of reasoned opinion by giving public voice to his private interests.

This model of the public sphere anchored the legitimacy of the liberal democratic state—premised on the "assumption that the participants' needs and interests, as they were formed privately, separately, individually, were the legitimate basis for publicly articulated opinion" (Brenkman, 1979, p. 102). This supposedly balanced private, market , and property interests with universal, societal interests, and initially, the bourgeois public sphere supported diversity (Gouldner, 1976). However, the ethical-political principles that made a public sphere of debate possible—freedom of discussion and the sovereignty of the public will—never fully coincided with the political-economic reality of inequality of wealth, power, resources, and life-chances structured by capitalist relations of private property and wage labor. As soon as the bourgeoisie secured state power, this model of the public sphere proved inherently unstable.

> The social basis of the public sphere meant . . . the bourgeois or liberal idea of free speech and discursive will formation was always at some distance from reality: the discrepancy increased with the development of the capitalist economy. (Held, 1980, p. 262)

The consolidation of capitalist social relations changed the character of the public sphere. The universal franchise and increasing literacy expanded the public sphere to include a broader portion of the populace, thereby transforming the public sphere both quantitatively and qualitatively: Working class persons soon constituted the potential bulk of the public sphere. The Jacksonian era of the 1830s, when this change occurred in the American press, marked a transition from a political culture of gentry rule to a new "democratic market society." The origins of a modern American system of "nonideological" politics may be traced to this period (Schudson, 1978, pp. 51–52). In the new market society dominated by an ascendent capitalist class, universalizing capitalist interests found expression in new reportorial maxims of objectivity and neutrality. Since working people were now among the principal consumers of newspapers, reporters focused more on issues of concern to them, and reports were styled in a more populist fashion. In this way, markets for news could be maximized.

> The penny papers' appeal drew on and reanimated the core political beliefs and rhetoric of the artisans and mechanics who made up perhaps 40% of New York City's working population during the 1830s. Craft workers shared a coherent political vision ["artisan republicanism"] . . . that existed before and independent of the new commercial press. For them, equal rights to property, power, and knowledge were the just basis for the public good, the highest ideal of state. (Schiller, 1987, p. 410)

Preceding the penny press by five years, a cheap labor press gave voice to this political critique. The cheap commercial press, in turn, appropriated and transformed this political critique.

> The labor press tried to speak to and for the artisan . . . it was a species of what was called "class journalism." In contrast, the penny press carved out an enduring institutional role by purporting to "shine for all."

Opportunistically but systematically, the penny press insinuated itself into . . . the tissue of social and cultural life, as an independent defender of public virtue. One staple means of animating this new role was crime news, which relied on the technique of journalistic exposure of public and private corruption. An early variant of journalistic objectivity, homologous to emerging positive science and photographic realism, bolstered the cheap papers' claims to independent status. (Schiller, 1987, p. 410)

By the 20th century, emphasis on objective methods of reporting stemmed, as well, from a growing distrust of subjectivity and the rise of public relations. The ethic of possessive individualism along with the socially privatizing impact of market relations eroded faith in traditional belief systems and encouraged relativism. During the first decades of the 20th century, growth of both the State and corporate capital spawned the emergence of "public relations." Leading journalists saw that institutional leaders could thus "feed" the press "facts" which served special interests. If unchecked, this would threaten the credibility and legitimacy of an "independent" press serving the public interest. One journalistic response was to invoke a method of objectivity: "scientific" methods of empirical testing and observation were codified into professional codes of journalistic ethics. Journalists thus claimed to mediate disputes among special interests, while insulated from them by procedures which distilled the "facts" from partisan accounts (Schudson, 1978).

While journalistic ideals of balance and impartiality were declared to be serving the masses, they developed as an expression of a more limited and homogeneous "public" composed of property owners. How could capitalist interests sustain their hegemony over public agendas if they were outnumbered in the public sphere by nonproperty owners? As a class, they sought to redefine the relationship between "public" and "private" issues so that matters touching on capital accumulation were made "private." Further, they tried to block the articulation of counterhegemonic ideologies.

Meanwhile, the problem faced by market-oriented journalists was how to address a "public" composed of both capitalists and workers, with structurally opposed interests. Adopting the mantle of neutrality seemed to provide a way of accomodating this contradiction—first, by omitting touchy questions about capital accumulation, and second, by passing the discourses of both interested sides through its own disinterested—"neutral"—categories and formats. Still, the news media persisted in touting themselves as the conduit to information and discourse, permitting a citizenry the opportunity

to form opinions on issues and to convey their political will to their leaders and, thus, constitute a public sphere. "Truth" would emerge in Mill's "marketplace" of ideas. (Dahlgren, 1980, p. 201)

Paradoxically, turning news into a commodity negated the possibility of such a "marketplace of ideas." The commercialized press excluded practical and political agendas from a public sphere of debate, thus annulling the model of enlightened "public opinion as the advocate of general interest" (Held, 1980, p. 262; Hohendahl, 1974, p. 94). Though the commercial press voiced commitment to sovereignty of the public interest, its mechanical model of objectivity masked unequal class power over public agendas.

NEWS AS COMMODITY

Historically, growth in the size and complexity of productive forces brought forward a corresponding pressure to rationalize consumption as well as production. Corporate organization of mass media stimulated attempts to systematize the organization of viewers, listeners, and readers as *audiences* who were then sold to advertisers. This practice of producing audiences as a commodity for which advertisers pay to communicate messages to selected demographic segments affects not just the content of news, but also its form. In the commercial mass media, materials transmitted by broadcast news organizations serve the economic purpose of recruiting potential audiences and securing their attention with information and entertainment as enticements. "People are the merchandise, not the shows" (Smythe, 1977, p. 5; Brown, 1971, p. 16). CBS News expanded from 15 minutes to a half hour in 1963, motivated by a quest for higher ratings and expanded advertising revenues in their competition with NBC. And as competition for ratings intensified, managers of news divisions resorted to the marketing strategies of news consulting firms: "In terms of news . . . ratings are improved not when listeners [viewers] are told what they should know, but what they want to hear" (in Barnouw, 1978, p. 199).

The quantity and character of news in newspapers, magazines, and radio altered as the institution of mass advertising matured. From 1940 to 1980, the average number of pages in newspapers increased from 31 to 66, but with this increase, nonadvertisement pages decreased from 60 percent to 35 percent of the total space. "Hard news" is not popular with advertisers, and nonadvertisement pages in periodicals increasingly fall into a gray area, called "fluff" in the trade, to put readers in a "buying mood" (Bagdikian, 1983, pp. 138, 140). Serious news was deemed too distracting from the consumer emphasis. Television developed a similar relationship to mass advertisers, eschewing overly serious issues, as well as controversial matter liable to offend its sponsors.

Television news soon developed its own methods of treating issues to avoid jeopardizing the "buying mood" of viewers. Since the 1970s, the "audience success" of evening news programming has hinged on grabbing the attention of the "18–49 female demographics": Hence the inflationary spiral of "talking heads" and "pocketbook" stories (Diamond, 1978, p. 103).

The most frequent popular criticism of network news refers to the impossibility of depth coverage in 23 minutes. Newsmen like Walter Cronkite acknowledge the evening news provides little more than a reading of headlines. Of course, such restrictions on newscast length are a function of their commodity status, subject to the logic of markets and the calculus of profitability.

Produced by corporate capital, and channeled through its electronic communication apparatus, television news tends to restructure forms of association so that subjects become more and more connected to one another by virtue of their separate, private consumption of mass-mediated images and symbols. Commodity relations are serial relations: The mass media address an aggregate of individuals serially dispersed as viewers/listeners/readers, who are unable to directly respond (interact) with this one-way communication, but exercise feedback through the ratings.

When structured as a commodity subject to the dynamics of market competition, news acquires self-contradictory characteristics. For instance, repetition becomes a predominant feature. At the same time, like other commodities in advanced capitalist society, news is structured by a kind of immediate obsolescence. Reporting tends to concentrate on the new, the different, the immediate, passing over what may be background details, to deliver "the fact that advances the story, not the one that explains it" (Gitlin, 1981, p. 154). Producing news as a commodity requires a constant flow of new facts, while all that remains constant is the presence of structuring frameworks and formats. The patterned regularity of formats establishes a "socialization into discontinuity of experience, velocity and hunger for jolts of change" because the formats work by "contracting time and eclipsing context" (Gitlin, 1980, p. 237). In television network news, the ideologically significant omission of information is usually accompanied by the repeated inclusion of other ideological frames of reference. The use of formal frames, sequencing, patterns of camera work, and correspondents' speech patterns acquire the character of naturalized codes and assume a deep but usually unseen ideological impact. The formulas used to "guarantee" balance and neutrality contribute their own distinct conceptual frames of reference, while cutting out others. Not only the processes determining the selection of images, but also the network's mode of discourse (through which the reported discourses pass) are structurally mediated by the requirements of commodity news production.

We can see, then, that production conditions the mode of consumption as well as the object of consumption. Mass media practitioners fabricate not merely the "content" of the news, but also the form of consumption, and what is the same thing, the prevailing modes of interpretation. Within the capitalist organization of mass media technologies, the prevailing form of consumption has become privatized participation in a "public" process.

Caught between the conflicting agendas of ratings versus legitimacy, broadcast journalists find themselves hemmed in as well by the framework of television news. Competition for audience ratings has resulted in networks' adoption of formats (e.g., the "trustworthy" talking head) which encourage a tendency towards a "declining rate of intelligence" among audiences. Reporters substitute simplified and culturally resonant categories for analysis. This both conserves time and "supposed[ly] enhances understanding by audiences deemed to have little patience with abstraction or complexity" (Paletz & Entman, 1981, p. 202). This is amplified still further by the video-intensive media form itself, which elevates imagistic and symbolic aspects of story telling at the expense of the written word, reinforcing a "decrease in rationality from earlier print-media forms of ideology" (Kellner, 1979, p. 14).

In a world characterized by increasing complexity and rapidity of change, people turn to the mass media for clarification, to make sense of events, to "find out what's happened." On television news, which has the widest audience and is regarded by consumers as the most credible news medium, the news anchor orchestrates and cooordinates stories from both distant and familiar parts of the world, conveying "the news of the day." The variety and complexity, the remoteness and inaccessibility of events are uniformly accomodated and domesticated, their confusion clarified, their intricacy simplified for the benefit of consumers organized as audiences. If the news media overcome distance and banish isolation in a fragmented, discontinuous, and privatized world, they confirm it at the same time through the necessity of their activity for this purpose. This simultaneous unification and fragmentation is visible in the formulaic composition of the television screen on network news shows. Specifics are neatly fit into the formally defined spatial relations set up on the screen. A world map in the background signifies "totality," while the foreground composed of the anchorperson's head and a rectangular frame delivers the verbal and symbolic visual representation of any particular story. The style of abbreviation and decontextualization employed to fill this frame contributes to a fragmented succession of formally equivalent spaces, each space filled momentarily with this or that story.

By selecting or excluding, emphasizing or glossing, media professionals recreate the social world in visual and verbal terms for audiences who possess otherwise limited access and perceptions of events. The theater of broadcast news denies this selection function by proclaiming itself as encompassing the whole drama of "world news." News organizations like NBC, CBS, and ABC regularly advertise such claims—for example, "bringing the world to you" or "the mirror of the world"—to attract greater audience share. In spite of their mirror metaphors,

> the media specialize in orchestrating everyday consciousness—by virtue of their pervasiveness, their accessibility, their centralized symbolic capacity. They name the world's parts, they certify reality as reality—and when those certifications are doubted and opposed, as they surely are, it is those same certifications that limit the terms of effective opposition. To put it simply, the mass media have become the core systems for the distribution of ideology. (Gitlin, 1980, p. 2)

As the logic of capital and commodity relations has penetrated cultural life, the alienated character of production relations has manifested itself in the sphere of consumption and reproduction.

> Just as people as *workers* have no voice in what they make, how they make it, or how the product is distributed and used, so do people as *producers of meaning* have no voice in what the media make of what they say or do, or in the context within which the media frame their activity. (Gitlin, 1980, p. 3)

News organizations like CBS make much of their role in facilitating a democratic public sphere, but their methods of producing news tend to be antidemocratic because of the way they abstract discourses from their social context.

THE NEGOTIATION OF HEGEMONIC IDEOLOGY

Professional journalists in the United States have historically struggled to maintain autonomous criteria for selecting and composing news as a public service. Professionally, journalists choose to wrap themselves in the appearance of immunity from bias or external political influences and pressures. Yet, "because news has consequences . . . journalists are susceptible to pressure from groups and individuals (including sources and audiences) with power to hurt them, their organizations, and their firms . . ." (Gans, 1979, p. 81). Making news involves "the exercise of power over the interpretation of reality." Who, then, exercises power over the interpretation of reality? Broadcast journalists not only must distance themselves from every special interest, they must also disavow their power to interpret by invoking mirror metaphors that have them merely reflecting power relations as they exist "out there" in the world. This mythology persists because the networks have found audience ratings go up when they are perceived as reassembling "reality" according to a universal moral ethic shared by all. The attempt to insulate themselves from the continuously negotiated "tug of war" between interests has led the networks to overcompensate with formulas designed to avoid appearing "susceptible to pressure." Ironically, these formulas inflate network power over defining and interpreting reality.

Despite the concentrated ownership of mass media news organizations, there is little evidence that professional journalists directly serve dominant economic or ideological interests. There are exceptions—for example, George Will of ABC—but most journalists work to preserve their autonomy, both in appearance and practice. The question then remains: How do the news media, while remaining independent from organized political forces, and engaged in no conspiracy to hoodwink the public, nonetheless regularly reproduce interpretations of events which are consonant with the interests of dominant political and economic groups?[3] News production is undoubtedly a complexly negotiated and contested terrain, yet it displays patterned regularities which are hard to dismiss. How is it possible that broadcast news can be relatively autonomous and still be hegemonic?

Gramsci's concept of hegemony describes an active, ongoing process performed by dominant groups, and participated in by subordinate groups. The institutional forms which stand behind everyday actions are rarely questioned. Unthinking repetition of these actions legitimizes them, as well as the deeper institutional relations and framework which structure them. Hegemony refers to the interpenetration of everyday routines and a "way of seeing" the world which assists in reproducing the material and ideological conditions of domination. Hegemony does not refer to a dominant ideology per se, but to practices and relations which predominate in structuring definitions of social reality.

Gramsci described the hegemonic process as a dialectic of "consent

---

[3]Gans (1979, p. 79) found that reporters "rarely make selection decisions on overtly ideological grounds; rather they work within organizations which provide them with only a limited amount of leeway in selection decisions, which is further reduced by their allegiance to professionally shared values."

and coercion." As the reverse side of consensus in liberal capitalist societies, there exist sanctions against the violation of consensus. Penalties meted out to law breakers render the consensus more meaningful, help define it more clearly, and lend it moral force. When rule by coercion is necessary, it tends to be more effective where there is consent to the exercise of coercion (Gramsci, 1971, p. 247). State use of coercive force lacks both legitimacy and efficacy in the absence of such "public" shared consent. The consent itself, if utterly free and unforced, lacks moral value: Knowledge of possible sanctions by the patriarchal authority of the state validates and strengthens consensual action. "Even the coercive side of the state works best when perceived as legitimately coercing—i.e., with the consent of the majority. The state enforces its authority through both types of domination; indeed, the two types are present within each apparatus of the state" (Hall, Critcher, Jefferson, Clarke, & Roberts, 1978, p. 203).

The consensual nature of hegemony allows room for dissent and dispute over particular features of the dominant ideology. Liberal hegemonic ideology is far from static since there is both an ongoing contestation of the consensus and internal contradiction within the value system itself (e.g., civil rights versus property rights; private versus public interests; first amendment rights versus the imperatives of national security). Broadcast journalists like those at CBS do not shy away from such value conflicts; in fact, they rejoice at ironies because a good irony invariably makes a good peg for a story. But they are chronically unwilling or unable to trace these ironic tensions to their source in the immanent contradictions of institutions.

Hegemony is a relational concept. It does not name a fixed set of ideological content, but refers to a set of processes shaped by a continuously negotiated dialectic of domination and resistance. We found CBS News' strike coverage set up hegemonic frames that a static, rigid view of capitalist ideology would never anticipate. The mass media rework genuine articulations of their middle-class and working-class audiences—fears, anger, anxieties—but refract and reconstitute their meanings in ways which divert them from exposing and attacking the roots of domination. In its mass-mediated forms, hegemony consists of multiple ideological regions which may be uneven, unstable, and internally contradictory (Kellner, 1979).[4]

In the cultural form of news, neutrality became a means of denying the existence of class, and a strategy for warding off criticism about

---

[4]The most severe challenges to hegemonic interests occur when television news reports on *scandals*—for example, Watergate or the Iran-Contra Connection (cf. Molotch & Lester, 1975).

journalists' work (Tuchman, 1972). Expanding markets by means of recruiting mass audiences eventually made the pose of a neutral observer a structural necessity. To achieve the largest possible audience it was necessary to gloss over class differences and espouse an agenda of ideological neutrality. Far from promoting enlightened, democratic public debate, network practices of relative autonomy and impartiality have become "necessary conditions" for reproducing dominant ideological frames and meanings (Hartley, 1982; Connell, 1980; Hall, 1977).

Commodified news does realize a limited degree of neutrality, but it is a culturally situated neutrality that replicates the logic of the market within which it is produced. Rather than espouse the interests of this or that section of the capitalist class, as newspapers tended to do in the earlier epoch of a "free press," the broadcast news media accept and promote the values of the "free market" [capitalist] system as a whole. The neutrality thus achieved is secured at the cost of explanatory context and understanding. It also requires that class relations vanish from accounts. The owners and operators of capital—the dominant class—have disappeared from "the world" as portrayed on the screen. This is accompanied by a taken-for-granted allegiance to the nation-state (network news shows use red, white, and blue in their logos, or weld their names to images of the flag or the Statue of Liberty).[5]

Consistent with network television's commitment to their viewing public/audience, the 1977-78 coal strike was framed in terms of consumption issues rather than production. Neutrality was accomplished by balancing accounts of striking miners versus those of the consuming public/national welfare.

---

[5]This must be distinguished from network newspeople's readiness to come down on incumbent political authorities. There are multiple factors responsible for this animus toward political authority, while upholding the sacred honor of the nation-state. First, there is a longstanding populist tradition of distrust toward politicians which broadcasters play on in their pursuit of audiences. Second, broadcasters believe their civic mandate is to be ever vigilant in exposing scandal and corruption. Finally, because reporters assigned to the "Washington Beat" cannot afford to appear naive about "the game of politics," they assume the voice of knowlegeable, savvy insiders who know how the game of "hardball" is played.

2

Studying Network Coverage of Strikes

We propose to examine television news texts and the potential field of meanings these establish by assembling a map of deep cultural presuppositions that premise what is seen and heard. Our research strategy has been to offer an in-depth analysis of a single U.S. network television news portrayal of a national capital-labor conflict.

We focus on a strike because strikes are the archetypical American industrial conflict (and because, frankly, network news reports little else about labor or corporate industrial relations). We selected *CBS Evening News* broadcast coverage of the UMWA-BCOA strike of 1977–78. *CBS News* then led the network audience race with a nightly average of 25 million viewers. CBS had a reputation in the industry as the standard-setter for television journalism. The networks, in any case, do not differ substantially in their content (Gans, 1979, p. 3). "The selection of news has become so standardized that rival newscasts often present similar items in identical sequence" (Barnouw, 1978, p. 129), a point confirmed in examining coal strike coverage. Standardized network news is a result of structuring news as a commodity because the networks rely on formulas of presentation designed to enhance their standing in the currency of audience ratings.

Why choose the coal strike? The 1977–78 coal strike was the second "record-breaking" national strike in a "basic" American industry in as many years, following the United Rubber Workers 146-day strike against the four major tire corporations in 1976. It was also the major strike during Jimmy Carter's Presidency. As a historical drama, this coal strike marked a crossroads in relations between American labor and capital in the industrial sectors: rank and file workers pressing to democratize their union and their workplaces, while employers pushed for greater

23

labor discipline and the return of benefits conceded to labor in previous rounds of collective bargaining. Because energy supplies were at stake, the media treated the coal strike both as a service sector strike and as an industrial strike. Finally, because the President of the United States became involved in trying to resolve the production stoppage, coverage of the BCOA–UMWA dispute allows us to probe how relations between capital, labor, and the state are presented on television.

RESEARCH ON TELEVISION NEWS AND LABOR

Virtually no research has addressed the question of how U.S. network television covers industrial-labor relations. In contrast, a growing body of research has examined this matter in the British context. The Glasgow University Media Group systematically disassembled television news reports in order to "unpack the coding of television news" and specify a "rule-governed structure of presentation" and the routinized journalistic procedures that stand behind it. They found British television framed strikes as labor-instigated and disruptive and did not report industrial news unless it was "bad news"—bad news, that is, for Capital (Glasgow University Media Group, 1976).

The absence of U.S. research concerning network television coverage of labor-management issues and strikes ought not be surprising, considering the relative paucity of network coverage of strikes and labor disputes. Academics and network news gatekeepers alike seem to presume the "end of ideology" thesis—that is, that class conflict is defunct (see Bell, 1960). American academics have studied network news' handling of elections, Congress, the Presidency, foreign affairs, and minorities (blacks and women and gays), but they ignore how working conditions, trade unions, and strikes are portrayed in network newscasts. Perhaps this is because network television news has so assiduously averted its cameras, and our eyes, from examining relations of production.

Hoyt (1984) questioned journalists about why labor journalism had declined. His respondents focused on newspapers, where the quality and quantity of labor journalism has historically been more substantial than on network news. In corporately organized newsrooms, business coverage expanded and labor coverage declined since the 1950s.[1]

---

[1]There is a rough correspondence between the decline of labor coverage and the transformation of the labor movement with the "capital-labor accords" of the late 1940s and early 1950s.

Newspapers cut back on labor reporters, and many "just stopped covering organized labor." As editors gave labor coverage less primacy and financial resources for hiring labor journalists dwindled, the prestige associated with the labor "beat" also declined. "Today the labor writer is a tired guy without much history or background, who doesn't go to the factories." "Reporters don't understand the language, texture, or history of labor relations. They just don't seem to know what to ask" (in Hoyt, 1984, p. 71).

Strictly speaking, there are no television labor reporters. Television news "has only a handful of substantive beats, in science, health, ecology, and the economy" (Gans, 1979, p. 132), but not in labor. On network television, generalist reporters cover strikes, and few network reporters seem to accumulate specialist knowledge on the subject. Opportunities for promotion up the network television news hierarchy go to those who cover national politics. The picture of a "tired guy" without much status does not apply to television news where the route toward upward mobility draws reporters away from the labor beat. But because of how beats are carved up, and the generalist status that entails, television reporters show even less familiarity with the "language, texture or history of labor relations."

The resurrection of "business" news in recent years is the flip side of a decline in labor coverage. Today, when labor issues receive attention, they appear in "business" news sections and segments where they are reported because the primary question is, "how do these matters impinge on business and profits?" U.S. television news builds on an overarching assumption of "responsible capitalism." Within this framework, strikes represent momentary incidents (aberrations) to be resolved, rather than outgrowths of structural conflicts of interest. For this reason, and because of its Marxian "ideological" connotations, U.S. television reporters shun the concept of "working class" (Gans, 1979, pp. 24-25). The decision to omit the "working class" is by extension a choice to dispense with class relations and class conflict altogether. In the context of "responsible capitalism" strikes "are frequently judged negatively, especially if they inconvenience 'the public,' contribute to inflation, or involve violence" (Gans, 1979, p. 46).

The International Association of Machinists sponsored a study that asked rank-and-file members to monitor the content of network news in February 1980 (1500 monitors) and April–May 1981 (2000 monitors). The International Association of Machinists (IAM) summary of rank and file perceptions concluded:

1. strikes were the most frequently reported aspect of union news.
2. strike coverage emphasizes violence. Because network news is

selected to maximize visual entertainment impact, violent confrontations receive preferred coverage over "informative reports of . . . non-hostile negotiations, meetings, speeches, or community service" which lack "drama and thrill."

3. the networks "almost never articulate the reasons why workers are on strike"; coverage of strikes and negotiations do not explain "the benefits to the community when workers' needs are met."

4. language used to describe contract negotiations casts labor in a negative light: "phrases such as 'worker demands' are used, but never 'management demands,' even though most corporations and employers have a laundry list of such items" (Rollings, 1983, pp. 138-44; IAM, 1981, p. 3).

Observers have long noted conservative and anti-labor tendencies on network television. In its early years, television news preferred items "unfavorable" to labor, and television news in the 1950s and 1960s was apparently more likely to carry management presentations of issues than labor's side of disputes (Skornia, 1968, p. 53). In 1961, Liebling described a systematic presentation of organized Labor in the national news media:

It is still stubborn, selfish, unreasonable, overpaid, grasping, domineering, un-American, irreverent, blind to its own interests and living in a unreal world. It is also inefficient, undemocratic and gangster ridden . . . (p. 107)

Many of these negative connotations associated with the union movement stem from a period when labor news fell under the police beat (Raskin, 1979). Some such meanings continue to flavor television news reports but now take the form of implied background presuppositions— the standard inference in most television reporting on industrial disputes is that they are about more pay and nothing else.

Our observations of the 1976–1986 period show that when the networks do air stories about industrial relations there no longer exists an imbalance in time and attention given to labor and management. In strictly quantitative terms workers' images and voices are more likely to be on the screen than those of owners and managers. And, over the same time period, management has more regularly employed public relations techniques which diminish management's public visibility and reporters' access to managerial representatives.

From late November 1977 till April 1978, the period spanning the coal strike, CBS, NBC, and ABC combined made reference to but five other labor disputes in the United States. On the same evening, all three networks reported on a New York mass transit workers' strike; one network reported a strike by government workers in Rhode Island; two reports referred to a firefighters' strike in Illinois; CBS did a report on the Amalgamated Meat Cutters versus the Iowa Beef Producers; a "news brief" mentioned a UAW press statement; and, though no union was involved, each network covered the "farmers' protest."[2] A comparison with aggregate data on work stoppages for the same calendar period shows how selective network news is in reporting strikes (Monthly Labor Review, June 1978).

Month & Year	No. of stoppages	Workers involved	Days idle	Days idle % of est. working time
1977 December	559	266,000	4,425,000	.25
1978 January	394	318,000	4,689,000	.26
1978 February	449	329,000	4,221,000	.26
1978 March	527	367,000	4,290,000	.22

Network coverage of strikes tends to be less detailed and specific than local television news coverage (obviously, if a Pittsburgh station ignores events in the steel industry it may lose the local working-class audience that depends on conditions in the steel industry). Because network news aims at national, and more diversified, audiences, its reports are more homogenized. Network television coverage tends to be reserved for (a) violent strikes, (b) immediately consumer-related strikes (e.g., transit workers, nurses, airline pilots), (c) government workers and the provision of "vital" services (e.g., firefighters), (d) national unions, and (e) Presidential involvement or intervention.

AUDIENCES AND TEXTS

Maggard (1983/84) and Seltzer (1978) found the business press carried more in-depth analyses of the internal relations of the UMWA and BCOA, the condition of coal markets, and the prospects of the strike's success or failure. Business elites demand such information because they require a comprehensive grasp of industrial and political conditions in order to make rational investment calculations. In contrast, larger circulation newspapers and broadcast news aim at mass audiences who

---

[2]In the two months preceding the coal strike, there was limited coverage of strikes in the aerospace industry, with particular reference to an IAM strike against Lockheed Corporation. The three networks together aired a total of 16 reports on a Longshoremen's strike, and one reference apiece to Minnesota Iron Miners, the dispute at Greyhound Bus Lines, and teachers.

have a less direct financial stake in the events. National audience surveys from October 9 to November 19, 1977 showed 67.3 percent of the men and 76.9 percent of the women watching the CBS Evening News had no formal education beyond the high school level. 57 percent of the males and 63.1 percent of the females earned less than $15,000 per annum.

Television news reports are structured by a concept of the audience they address. How are viewers implicitly positioned and addressed? How is the audience designated in the news? What characteristics and values are viewers projected as having? Whereas the business press explicitly treats readers as a fairly homogeneous body with common interests (e.g., "the financial community"), mass viewing audiences are treated as individuals, related to each other only in their shared, but dispersed, status as citizens and consumers. Events are portrayed to them in a highly reified manner, representing, we would suggest, the alienation of modern publics from spheres of decision making. News broadcasts are directed at people who, for the most part, have no influence over "what happens" in "the world of affairs." Network news organizations portray events for audiences who, if they figure at all in these events, are the objects of decisions and developments in higher circles of power. There is, hence, a tendency toward naturalizing the social world. Figures of authority may be questioned only in personal terms: The relations of authority between them are beyond judgment or self-reflection. This division between the business press and the mass media corresponds to a two-tier cultural system wherein the media reproduces the social division of labor, and hence reproduces basic class divisions. The reproduction process derives from the structural organization of news and audiences as markets, and the day-to-day routines and constraints that develop from that system of organization. The practical requirements generated by this organization solidify into a commonsense accepted by news producers, which justifies acting as if there is a natural difference in function between television news and the prestige newspapers. Catering to a different audience, television news aims at naming a few key "facts," highlighting personalities, and conveying the mood of a time and a place.

Mass media news is constructed against "the structured ignorance of the audience," taking for granted the limited access of people to information (Hall, 1972, p. 77). Most of the 62 reports CBS broadcast on the coal strike assume a relative lack of interest in the events themselves, and deal mainly with the possible consequences to audiences. This method of framing news stories contributes to, and reinforces, the presumed indifference to "industrial relations" stories. Audiences are treated as consumers in the sphere of industrial relations, with no direct political interest in the issues of production relations. Broadcasters assume audiences are chiefly interested in privately consuming goods: Therefore, threats to the stability of their privatized consumption receive priority as "news" angles in covering industrial relations. Though it is perhaps unwitting, broadcast news thus reinforces the tradeoff of privatism for a depoliticized public sphere (cf. Habermas, 1970). This is certainly compounded by how news reports are sandwiched amid advertisements that counsel viewers about consumption as a privileged way of life.

Every news product "is a structure of meanings in linguistic and visual form" (Hall, 1975, p. 18). Our interest in news texts as structures of meaning leads us to scrutinize news outputs as the production of discourse. In order to understand how news texts mean, we have tried to dissassemble the formal linguistic codes and interpretive rules which underpin this discourse. We have no illusions, however, that mass-mediated signification processes produce singular, monolithic meaning. News reports are polysemic, and their mass-mediated character inherently gives rise to some range of unanticipated meanings. Meanings of news are imparted not simply by reporters, editors, and camerapeople, but are produced as well by viewers' active negotiation and interpretation. Though network news texts are constructed to delimit the range of meanings, interpretation invariably generates multiple, ambiguous, and contradictory meanings. This is amplified by the privatized mode of reception which predominates in the United States. At the interface between public, socially shared language and personal experiences lies a realm of private meanings and idiosyncratic interpretations. Despite the plurality of meanings of television news items, one set of meanings tends to get "preferred and offered to the viewers, over the others, as the most appropriate. This 'preferring' is the site of considerable ideological labor" performed by both encoders (newspeople) and decoders (consumers) (Hall, Connel, & Curti, 1976, p. 53).

METHODS FOR ANALYZING NEWS TEXTS

We examined videotapes of each *CBS Evening News* broadcast report on the coal strike between November 25, 1977 and March 30, 1978. The Vanderbilt Television News Archives recorded and indexed these tapes. We supplemented these data with written transcripts of the CBS reports.[3] We did not examine videotapes of NBC and ABC strike

---

[3]Four reports—February 25, March 4, March 11, March 25—were missing from the tapes. Though we could not analyze the video for those reports, we had the transcripts for them.

coverage, but made intensive use of the Vanderbilt Index listing their coal strike broadcasts. The Vanderbilt Index includes information about the location and length of news reports, name of reporter, and a brief gloss of the report's subject matter. Because our analytic task was to map out the conditions of meaningful possibility established by the form and content of the news discourse, we defined our database as all coverage of a single strike on one network. This does not make it necessarily comprehensive or typical. But studying every frame of coverage for a single strike does have several methodological advantages. Conventional content analysis disconnects content from both the *form* of its cultural production and the *context* of the reported events themselves. Content analysis usually abstracts slices of news data from the frameworks in which they appear and relies on a priori categorization procedures. Restricting the data set to include every report on the coal strike allows us to bypass both the problematic generation of categories and criteria for assessing the content, and the sampling problems associated with content analysis (Winston, 1983). It also forces us to confront the contradictoriness of the news reports. A contextual analysis places external accounts alongside the television news accounts, permitting an assessment of the news texts in terms of the historical events they represent.

Our approach does mean that we lose the opportunity to assess variation. How much can be generalized from examining a single case determined as much by the vagueries of personalities and the confluence of historical accidents as by patterned institutional effects? Certainly, the 1977–78 coal strike was atypical in terms of television coverage, receiving more network attention than any other strike in the late 1970s. But precisely because the strike lasted 110 days, and occurred in what was perceived as a critical industry, we might argue this strike coverage reveals something of CBS's general philosophy of what information people should know about conflicts between unionized labor and corporate management.

Our sampling strategy owes less to the idea of a case study than to what Theodor Adorno called the "concrete particular." Adorno viewed every cultural object as a "concrete particular" that could be interpreted ("deciphered") by seeing it as a meaningful intersection between institutional structures and the actions of historically constituted subjects. The concrete particular—whether a song, an architectural style, a pro football game, or a news broadcast—has meaning only in relation to the social totality which structured and contextualized it. Inscribed in the concrete particular is an imprint of the totality, along with a trace history of the internal contradictions of the social whole. Every specific aspect of society contains "the possibility of unravelling the whole abundance of the totality from within itself." But this possibility could only be realized when the structure of the social totality was identified. (Buck-Morss, 1977, p. 26)

Following Marx, Lukacs, and Adorno, we identify that crucial structure as the commodity form. Like any other network "story" about industrial relations in the late 1970s, the coal strike story was a product of practices structured by a system of commodity relations. We do not mean by this that every "concrete particular" is equal (they obviously are not) but that dialectical analysis of any 'concrete particular' may reveal a broader understanding of the sociocultural relations which produced it.

Every method of interrogating news texts, indeed any cultural text, draws on a theory. Just as there is no pregiven world out there and no neutral ground from which to produce "news facts," so too there is no neutral ground from which to assess those cultural productions. No matter how empirical we may try to be, our "facts" are still tinged by the theoretical and methodological lenses we use. We have adopted a dialectical *way of seeing* to guide our interpretation and organize our use of other methods to analyze news texts: quantitative analysis, ideology critique, semiotic analysis, hermeneutics, symptomatic reading, and historical contextualization. We have also learned from the Glasgow University Media Group's application of conversational and linguistic analysis to news texts. These analyses enabled us to isolate the frames and framing devices used to explain the events concerning the strike, and examine how they vary over the course of the strike. Our decomposition and interrogation of these texts is explicitly intended to rearticulate the ideological tensions concealed by the homology between the commodity form and the news form. We seek to repoliticize the depoliticized by bringing back into the picture the crucial institutional relations which have been glossed in the broadcast reports.

Studying CBS coal strike coverage began with a detailed examination of the structured interconnections of the audiovisual texts. First, we used a videotape recorder to dissect and disassemble each CBS strike report, systematically charting each report scene by scene, frame by frame, sentence by sentence. We used a reverse "storyboarding" technique to record these exhaustive descriptive summaries, noting the composition, content and camera distance of each photographic scene in detail; the location and nature of edits and cuts linking scenes; length of scenes and interviews; number of interviews; correspondence between the visuals and the reporter's voiceover narrative; the location of word stress; and the verbal text itself. This provides us with an index far more detailed than the Vanderbilt index. The sheer empiricism of this reverse storyboarding enables us to say precisely, for example, how many scenes showed miners as opposed to managers, or to delineate the content and frequency of visual images, or to locate sequencing patterns.

> We adopted the practice of giving as much of the evidence in its own terms as we could manage: so that the reader can see for herself how a particular interpretation has been arrived at, and also check the reading offered against the material and offer counter-interpretations where they seem appropriate. (Hall, 1975, p. 16)

Next, we historically reconstructed the strike and the relations between media participants. This provided a broad comparison of CBS's version of the coal strike with other more comprehensive accounts of the strike which left less to the understandings of "common knowledge." Our study thus rigorously demonstrates what we already knew—that *CBS News'* strike coverage constituted an incomplete and partial record of the events. The survey of literature on the strike enables a deeper explanation of the "facts" presented by CBS, while simultaneously giving historical basis to ideology critique. This comparison brings to attention the scope and limits of CBS's coverage, indicating the nature and patterns of its overall emphases and exclusions.

To analyze the news reports themselves, we chose a series of qualitative methods over the enumeration of categories. The key ideological "effects" of news texts are often felt precisely through their recurrence, their nearly daily usage as explanatory categories in accounts of events. Once we identified intertextual categories and framing patterns, counting has been useful. But we have preferred the more flexible and exhaustive approach of analyzing how these "categories" are themselves created, how linguistic usage, narrative strategy, and semiotic structure of edited visuals combine to produce arrays of meaning. Quantitative analysis, however sophisticated, fails to penetrate the forms of the "content" it analyzes, to illuminate the ways in which content is structured by its forms (oddly, content-analytic procedures ignore the most frequently repeated features of texts—format features). Analysis must remain focused on the ambiguity and contradictoriness of texts—and these are crucial features of news films and texts that seek to be "objective" and "neutral." Content analysis is unequipped to handle emphases which, while not occurring frequently, may be especially important in conjoining and highlighting crucial explanatory themes. Conventional content analysis is too rigid and one-sided: It masks complexity and ignores the difficulty of pinning down "the meaning" of texts.

The more "soft" and supple approach of qualitative analysis is often deprecated as "subjective" and "intuitive," and therefore "unscientific," as opposed to sturdy numerical content analysis. But, this criticism ignores the arbitrariness of content analytic categories. Once fixed and counted, they seem invested with scientific authority, whereas their origins are in fact as lowly as those of qualitative research in their "subjective" assumptions about what is significant in the texts (see Winston, 1983).

> Literary/linguistic types of analysis also employ evidence: they point, in detail, to the text on which an interpretation of latent meaning is based; they indicate more briefly the fuller supporting or contextual evidence which lies at hand; they take into account material which modifies or disproves the hypotheses which are emerging; and they should (they do not always) indicate in detail why one reading is the most plausible way of understanding it. Content analysis assumes repetition—the pile-up of material under one of the categories—to be the most useful indicator of significance. Literary/linguistic and stylistic analysis also employs recurrence as one critical dimension of significance . . . recurring patterns are taken as pointers to latent meanings from which inferences as to the source may be drawn. But the literary/linguistic analyst has another string to his bow: namely, strategies for noting and taking account of emphasis. Position, placing, treatment, tone, stylistic intensification, striking imagery, etc. are all ways of registering emphasis. The really significant item may not be the one which stands out as an exception from the general pattern—but which is *also* given, in its exceptional context, the greatest weight. (Hall, 1975, p. 15)

We use a variant of semiotic methodology to examine the conditions of textual meaning. This approach treats the news reports as cultural texts: "literary and visual constructs, employing symbolic means, shaped by rules, conventions and traditions intrinsic to the use of language in its widest sense" (Hall, 1975, p. 17). We seek to analytically disentangle the shared preconditions and understandings which make interpretation possible. A structural semiotics of this sort cannot stand alone, but must be joined to hermeneutic interpretation.

Semiotics need not be mysterious or esoteric.

> A sign is quite simply a thing—whether object, word, or picture—which has a particular meaning to a person or group of people . . . The Sign consists of the Signifier, the material object, and the Signified, which is its meaning. These are only divided for analytical purposes: in practice a sign is always thing-plus-meaning." (Williamson, 1978, p. 17)

Signifiers are material—for example, a printed word, a sound, a visual image, a photographic representation. The signified is a mental concept which bears no intrinsic relationship to the signifier (i.e., a rose by any other name would smell as sweet). The sign is the unity of signifier and signified, but neither signifier nor signified exist outside "the sign." And, "the sign" cannot signify apart from an active interpreter (Eco, 1979).

"Simply because the 'same' message goes out to twenty million people, it does not follow that twenty million people . . . get the same 'meaning' and the same understanding" (Hartley, 1982, p. 148). Viewers and their grammars are differentiated by gender, class, religion, ethnicity, race, income—by the conditions of their experience. We insist on distinguishing acts of textual disassembly from acts of decoding. Viewers decoded the *CBS news* reports, while analysts like us decompose the reports. No matter how detailed, we cannot pin down a single precise set of meanings in these reports; rather we use semiotic methods to suggest probabilities in decoding strategies.

The relationship between interpreter and sign hinges on access to an intersubjectively shared set of interpretive conventions and rules—a grammar or code. What we recognize as news, an institutionally specialized form of information, is a form of discourse organized by a code (GUMG, 1976; Hartley, 1982; Nichols, 1981). Viewers interpretively decipher the sequenced relation of signifiers and signifieds by drawing on their grasp of this code and their "anterior" knowledge (the accumulated knowledge brought to each successive interpretive task).

Semiotics as a method of inquiry is especially well-suited to the study of commercial television news, because the news in this medium is not an end in itself, but a means toward another end, ratings and profits. To achieve these ends within a framework of rigid time constraints, newspeople labor to "overcode" their discourse. Television news adopts the posture of using photographic evidence a la *Dragnet*—"just the facts ma'am." The apparently "natural" character of the images stems from the fact that photographic iconic signs "look like objects in the real world because they reproduce the conditions (that is, the codes) of perception in the viewer" (Eco cited in Hall, 1980, p. 132). Yet, the "natural sign" is an illusion—there is no message without a code.

Signification is not a mechanical process, but rather a context-specific act which requires human subjects to constitute meanings. Signs convey different levels of meaning, or orders of signification. To illustrate, take a photograph of a car. At a first level of signification, the photograph indicates a material object as referent. Here, the sign appears self-contained and meaning is denotative: the signifier stands for a physical object which has weight and shape. At a second level of signification, this denotative meaning coexists with an entire lexicon of cultural meanings that do not spring from the material referent itself, but from prevailing cultural meanings associated with it. In our society, a car, or the sign of a car, has acquired connotative meanings of wealth, speed, convenience, virility, freedom of space, autonomy of movement, and individuated social status.[4]

Television news is a form of discourse structured by multiple codes and agendas. We conceive of news discourse as the intersection between codes and levels of signification (see Hall, 1972). News discourse is produced or encoded, via the networks technical/production capacities and limits. It is mediated by a journalistic code, a film code, an elaborated speech code, and suffused by the shared cultural codes of the world it refers back to.[5] Hall examines hypothetical stances from which viewers may construct decodings of television discourses. In the "dominant-hegemonic position" viewers' decode in close correspondence to its encoding. These interpretive practices reproduce domains of preferred meanings which have

> the institutional/political/ideological order imprinted in them . . . the whole social order embedded in them as a set of meanings, practices and beliefs: the everyday knowledge of social structures, of "how things work for all practical purposes in this culture", the rank order of power and interest and the structure of legitimations . . . (Hall, 1980, p. 134)

A second position is characterized by a "negotiated" interpretive code. A negotiated interpretation may accept the "grand totalizations" used to

---

[4]Of course, there can be no pure form of denotation. It is impossible to totally disentangle the denotative level of meaning from the connotative. Like the distinction between signifier and signified, the line between denotative and connotative is a useful analytic fiction (Hall, 1980, p. 133).

[5]"There are two essential logics governing the rules for juxtapositioning—for cutting—newsfilm shots. The first is film logic . . . an extremely simple set of rules . . . in which the permitted juxtapositioning of any shot is determined by the content of the shot preceding it. Thus, classically, a general shot is followed by a closer shot of something within that general shot or vice versa . . . In the classic narrative film the logic within the frame of each specific shot determines the content of the next . . . There is nothing sophisticated about the way they use film, they seldom flash back; they never flash forward; they almost never move from shot to shot except by a straight cut . . . But routinely in newsfilm this logic is not the dominant one. In most newsfilm the shots do not directly relate to one another in the ways we are used to from the feature film. Rather they are used to illustrate the audio-text and the rules governing their juxtapositioning come not from the visual but from the audio-track—indeed largely from the commentary . . . they are filmed and cut according to an alien narrative logic—the journalistic" (GUMG, 1976, pp. 27-29).

situate events and actions, while contesting specific "truth claims" or framing devices that appear in this or that story. Audience members may contest the content of news reports that does not resonate with their experiences or interests (Brundson & Morley, 1978). However, viewers are more likely to actively negotiate the content of a news report than the formal coding rules which structure it.

Symptomatic reading pushes analysts to identify the connections between what is said and what is left unstated. That cars can connote individual autonomy and freedom is true; the conditions of this automobile-driven individual freedom are capitalist relations of production. As reward for their performance of labor, workers are "invited" to express their "freedom" (enshrined in the wage contract) in the private consumption of commodities such as cars. Material consumption, however, requires and reproduces the need for production, along with the prevailing social relations of production. In this way, an individual's commodified expression of her individuality and freedom confirms, and tends to reproduce, her subordination and lack of freedom in the sphere of production, as well as her severance from community relations.

Thus, embedded in the significations of the sign 'car' may be an ideological account of freedom and individuality. Only when we pursue the question of how free the individual is, and within what context, do we see a lapse in the meanings of these terms: They cannot extend beyond the bounds of capitalist relations of production (the individual's freedom is defined as that freedom available to a consumer under capitalism). It is therefore necessary to interpret not only what is "present" in the discourse (which includes overlapping denotative and connotative levels of signification), but what is "absent" as well, that cannot be articulated within the terms of the discourse. "Any oversights, inadequacies or concepts invisible to the theoretical discourse in question are seen to be built into its vision or problematic as part of its whole field of operation" (Sumner, 1979, p. 165).

We read each news text in the context of lapsed background which shapes the text, and the code for interpreting it. The decontextualized relations signified in a newsphoto or story are thus situated within a larger historical field, the same field within which the text itself is produced. The lapses and silences are the unspoken meanings on which the "truth" of the text rests, and the guarantee of this "truth" is that they should remain unspoken. By articulating the gaps and silences in the text with what is said, we arrive at a critique of the text. In this way, symptomatic reading offers another angle of ideology critique, as well as a means of dialectically grounding the meaning of hegemony.

3

The Coal Strike in Historical Context

CBS Evening News' broadcast its first report about the UMWA strike on November 25, informing viewers that talks had broken down, making a coal strike nearly inevitable. The report focused on enormous coal stockpiles and mentioned nonunion operations, thereby indicating the availability of supplies despite the strike. Stockpile size continued to be a primary theme in following reports. These reports included interviews with miners financially hurt by the labor stoppage, emphasizing that miners were the strike's immediate victims. Reports mentioned problems the UMWA faced in staging a strike, namely, internal union dissension and low funds. Cronkite began the December 5 report by tersely stating that a major reason for the strike was a dispute over the right-to-strike over local matters, but then left the issue dangling and unclarified. On December 6, capsule graphics listed miners' "basic demands" on the screen: full restoration of medical and retirement benefits; a limited right-to-strike; and more pay. No further discussion of the strike's causes took place for more than two months.

In the media, a faint collective memory persisted about coal strikes in the late 1940s—pitting John L. Lewis against Harry Truman—that precipitated "national emergencies." After the 1973–74 oil embargo and energy crisis, U.S. news media remained acutely sensitive to any possible disruptions in the energy pipeline. Hence, CBS presented the strike as a social problem. Like a natural disaster, the coal strike was a matter for general concern framed by an anticipatory fear of bad news— here, fuel shortages in winter. Not only were many "factual" details deleted in processing the story, so also was any relevant historical, social, political, and economic context. Like most network news reporting, these reports presume certain kinds of social knowledge while deleting others. CBS seemed to presume strikes were well-known phenomena, requiring little explication. The general conditions that give rise to strikes were taken for granted; like other social problems, they seem too commonplace to be labored over. Meanwhile, the specific conditions which gave rise to this strike were considered part of an "arcane" body of knowledge too remote and specialized to be spelled out for a national audience.

Viewers received no means by which they could come to grips with the specific causes and circumstances of the coal strike. So much was assumed, or ignored—it is impossible to say which—that beyond registering the mere fact of the strike, and its unpleasantness, viewers could have been little wiser for CBS's efforts. Why was there a coal strike? Who were the disputants? Why were negotiating parties "far apart," and why were mines "apt to be closed for a long time"? To understand more fully what was going on, we must turn elsewhere.

Drawing on other sources, we offer an overview of the dynamic, and self-contradictory, relations that formed the historical context in which the coal strike took place. This chapter presents our report of the coal strike.[1] Alternative accounts of the coal strike have been drawn from academic research, the wire services, regional newspapers (*Charleston Gazette, Pittsburgh Post-Gazette* and *Louisville Courier-Journal*), the national business press (*Wall Street Journal, Business Week*, and the *New York Times* and *Washington Post*.[2] These contained more inclusive and detailed accounts of "facts" about the contract dispute.

The network's predominant frames resembled and echoed those in the written press, but in abbreviated and simplified form. Sometimes, CBS joined in unison with the other media, as in the inflationary reporting of fuel crisis (Maggard, 1983/84, 1983, p. 73; Ackermann, 1979). Yet, basic differences also appear. Where the national print media gave cursory attention to the strike's historical context, or how market conditions shaped operators' bargaining strategy, the CBS slate was blank. The business press reported a "connection between opera-

---

[1] Like all reports, ours is partial. Matters not fully mentioned here include: (a) struggles to organize the coal fields in the early 20th century, for example, "Bloody Harlan County," (b) the relationship between mechanization and market history, (c) John L. Lewis's near-dictatorial leadership of the UMWA, (d) the political economy of electric utilities, (e) technological organization of mining processes and social relations underground, and (f) environmental regulations and safety laws and their history of enforcement.

[2] Researchers have critically examined print media coverage of the coal strike (Seltzer, 1978; Maggard, 1983/84; Ackermann, 1979).

tors' inflexibility and market economics"; the *New York Times* reported the adversarial relations between the union and operators; CBS reported neither. The print media began by emphasizing the UMWA's state of disarray, while CBS's frames centered on a visual projection of Arnold Miller's persona pitted against unruly miners.[3]

Unlike the print media, CBS did not cover the "Miners Right to Strike Committee." This enabled CBS to steer clear of whether or not communist ideologues were involved in the right to strike movement, a subject which received considerable attention in the Appalachian press.[4] So, while CBS did not engage in "red baiting," neither did they include the MRTSC's rhetoric of class conflict. Like the other networks, CBS was more inclined to emphasize "what does this mean for consumers." And, unlike the written press which cast the strike impasse in terms of BCOA demands for "labor stability," CBS never used the term, preferring instead the miners' term, "right to strike." Significantly, however, CBS explained neither position. But their continual focus on the miners, whether sympathetic or not, excluded the other party who by structural necessity belonged to the story, the BCOA.

AN ALTERNATIVE ACCOUNT

Since 1950, the bargaining association for most of the soft coal industry has been the Bituminous Coal Operators Association. In 1977, over 80% of UMW members worked in mines owned by the 130 companies which comprised the BCOA. In the late 1940s a wildly competitive coal industry consisting of 4000 coal operators faced an uncertain future. Though John L. Lewis's UMW stood strong in 1946, Lewis was con-

---

[3]Paradoxically, "personalization" (as opposed to an institutional analysis) of the strike was accomplished even while the national news media exercised humane restraint (compared with the local media) in airing Miller's significant personal problems during the strike.

[4]A long history of "red baiting" in the coalfields, both from within the union and from coal operators, resurfaced during this strike. A recurrent theme in the coalfields blamed wildcat strikes on "outside agitators." Miller regularly labelled dissent against his leadership as "radical" or "red." Though a small handful of ideological communists were MRTSC members, coverage in the Appalachian press (e.g., a series of articles in the *Charleston Gazette*) tended to inflame the "red baiting" rhetoric of operators such as Ralph Bailey of Consol Coal and of Miller. As Franklin (11/25/77, p. 18) reported, these charges lacked "real justification."

cerned about the ebbing vitality and stability of the coal industry, and therefore encouraged larger operators to coordinate their policies. Lewis sought to align UMWA interests with those of the most stable operators. In 1950, Lewis negotiated a tradeoff of higher wages and benefits in exchange for cooperating with introducing technological innovations to mechanize the labor process in mining.

> While he attempted to guarantee labor peace (there were no contract strikes in the next two decades) and to encourage mechanization (the UMW went so far as to make loans through its bank to help the coal companies automate), the big companies finally agreed to royalty payments, to other bread-and-butter provisions, and to consolidate a "destructively" competitive industry. The consolidation involved the major producers dividing up market areas and acquiring or neutralizing their competition in those areas. (Yarrow, 1979, p. 172)

The 1950 negotations created the BCOA and abolished the differential between Southern and Northern wage agreements. The UMW helped bring in "labor-saving" machinery; agreed to help reduce output and price competition from smaller producers; and policed UMW members (Seltzer, 1980, p. 47-48). This agreement brought impressive gains in the quality of coalfield medical care, but also sowed the seeds for declining UMW power as layoffs eliminated nearly 200,000 mining jobs between 1950 and 1969. Introducing "continuous miners" (and later, longwall mining systems) in underground mines boosted productivity, but also vastly increased the amount and fineness of coal dust. Black lung disease, pneumoconiosis, "was a direct product of the lack of dust controls on underground machines, industry's disregard for the health implications of its new technology, the UMWA's inattention to occupational health protection, and Congressional and administration disinterest . . ." in establishing coal dust standards (Seltzer, 1980, p. 48).

Mechanization of mining during the 1950s and 1960s increased productivity and spurred centralization of ownership.[5] Rationalizing production permitted larger firms to negotiate long-term contracts with utilities, thereby rationalizing market conditions as well. In the mid-1960s, multinational oil corporations began taking over coal companies to diversify their interests in the energy industry. After Gulf Oil acquired Pittsburgh & Midway in 1963, Continental Oil took over Consolidated Coal Company in 1965, and a series of takeovers by multinational oil

---

[5] "Big companies reduced competition among themselves through a kind of industrial conference of Versailles in 1954 when the victors—the big companies—decided which smaller companies each was to get" (Seltzer, 1980, p. 48).

corporations followed between 1966 and 1968. By 1977 oil-owned coal mines controlled over one-third of U.S. coal reserves and accounted for one-third of actual production (Schmidt, 1979, p. 124). Large mines were owned by Continental Oil, Occidental Petroleum (Island Creek Coal), Ashland Oil and Hunt Oil (Arch Mineral), Standard Oil of Ohio (Old Ben Coal), Exxon (Monterey Coal and Carter Coal), and Standard Oil of California (20% of Amax Group).[6] U.S. Steel and Bethlehem Steel, along with major utilities, owned "captive" mines which produced for their own furnaces and not the market (*BW*, 11/28/77, p. 76).

As corporate ownership displaced independent operators in the industry, strikes grew longer since corporately-backed subsidiaries could more readily withstand prolonged strikes than could independents (Seltzer, 1985). This made "old coal" independents more receptive to making cost concessions to the UMW where it did not place them at a competitive disadvantage in the marketplace (Perry, 1984). Prolonged strikes weakened less-capitalized suppliers, making them easier prey to takeovers by energy corporations (Seltzer, 1985).

Energy corporations began acquiring large mining operations when mine productivity was rising, but BCOA-UMW coal tonnage declined from 423.7 million tons in 1970 to 330.8 tons in 1977 (Seltzer, 1985). Though corporate ownership increased capital equipment per worker by one-third between 1966 and 1973, productivity sagged. BCOA members blamed diminishing productivity on absenteeism and wildcat strikes, UMW work rules governing scheduling and equipment handling, environmental costs, and federal safety regulations. Miners argued productivity declines were due to inadequate expenditures on equipment maintenance and on safety, coupled with the fact that richer seams of coal close to the surface had been mined, leaving thinner and less efficient seams (Yarrow, 1979). So long as prices stayed inflationary, corporate owners tolerated inefficiencies in production. But, while prices continued to rise in the mid 1970s, rate of return on investment declined from 12.1 percent in 1974 to 3.3 percent in 1977 (Navarro, 1983).

An expanding western surface mining industry posed a future threat to profits of BCOA deep-mining operators. Oil corporations including Arco, Texaco, Sun, Shell, and Mobil acquired unmined coal reserves and nonunion labor forces in the western coalfields. Western coal placed BCOA deep-mine operations at a competitive disadvantage because (a)

---

[6]Of the 40 largest corporate coal producers in 1976, 22 were owned by firms listed in the Fortune 500 (Vietor, 1980, p. 256-257). Peabody, the largest coal producer in 1976, had among its principal stockholders, Bechtel Corporation, Boeing, and Equitable Life Insurance.

surface mining tended to be quantitatively more productive (b) western coal reserves were on land leased from the federal government at low rates (c) strip mining operations were less likely to use union labor and therefore could "escape" the social wage costs of the BCOA bargaining agreement (Perry, 1984; Yarrow, 1979; Seltzer, 1985). Further, new air pollution regulations sent utilities searching for lower sulphur coal which lay in the west. Between 1970 and 1977 western coal increased from 6.6 percent to 22.8 percent of midwestern coal consumption (Navarro, 1983). BCOA-affiliated energy corporations therefore had an interest in increased productivity, escaping tonnage royalties (which financed health and pension funds) and "eroding" union power (Perry, 1984). Larger firms with multiple mines wanted to abolish the agreement that a signatory firm is automatically bound to make each new mine site a union operation.[7] Oil companies also pushed "converting health coverage to company-managed insurance and spearheaded the effort to decentralize collective bargaining" (Seltzer, 1985, p. 193).

Both oil corporation takeovers and expansion of a western mining industry weakened the UMWA's bargaining position. UMWA organizing efforts in western surface mines achieved little success. Some surface mines belonged to other unions, a few were organized by the UMW, but most resisted unionization by paying higher wages than union scale (Seltzer, 1985). More serious, however, was erosion of UMWA influence in the eastern coalfields (*BW*, 12/19/77). The struggle to organize strip mines throughout Kentucky, Ohio, and Tennessee was marked by prolonged, bitter, and sometimes deadly, conflict.

CBS reporters did observe that UMW members covered by the BCOA contract now mined less than half the nation's coal: Between 1970 and 1977 coal mined under UMW-BCOA contract declined from 70 percent to 48 percent. The national press heralded the UMWA's ebbing power, no longer able to generate a national emergency by striking, since non-union and western coal could fill part of the void (Ackermann, 1979).[8] However, transportation costs made western coal unattractive to eastern markets which remained dependent on BCOA coal and eastern nonunion strip mines (Simon, 1983).

---

[7]Subsequent to the 1978 contract, Consol challenged this by demanding NLRB elections at its new mines.

[8]Some miners felt this statistic alone was misleading. Late in the strike, Harry Patrick observed that the 50 percent mined by the UMW included high grade coal and a major proportion of metallurgical coal, and he added "50 percent control over anything is a lot of control" (UPI, 3/24/78).

RANK-&-FILE AGENDAS FOR CHANGE

The era of UMW-BCOA accommodation closed in the mid- to late-1960s. An older generation of miners who worked under UMW presidents John L. Lewis and Tony Boyle, and accommodated themselves to an authoritarian union and contract violations by coal companies, retired in the 1970s, many disabled by the occupational disease of coal mining—black lung. After severe layoffs in the 50s and 60s, a boom in coal markets opened up new jobs—employment nearly doubled since 1969—and large numbers of young men were hired. In less than a decade, the average age of mine workers dropped from 49 (in 1968) to 31 (in 1977). By 1977, half the UMW miners were under age 30 (Green, 1978; *BW*, 11/7/77). Many young miners had served in the Vietnam war, and this may have inculcated different values among them, making them less amenable to harsh authority such as coal miners faced. Because many were young and unmarried, they felt less need to work regularly, since a few days' work per week could bring in money enough for their needs (Bensman, 1978). They tended to be less intimidated either by union officials or company foremen, and less afraid to protest unsafe production speedup plans. Their disdain for authority and their irregular work habits were made possible by an increased demand for miners.

Coal mining employment rose from 144,000 workers in 1970 to 240,000 in 1978 (Seltzer, 1985). Increased demand for miners again made the wildcat strike a powerful weapon for the rank and file. During the 1950s till the mid-1960s miners stayed relatively quiescent, hemmed in by high unemployment and a union hierarchy which ignored health and safety questions in the interest of maintaining an alliance with the BCOA. Tony Boyle continued Lewis's preference for negotiating contracts minus strikes: There were no UMWA-authorized strikes between 1952 and 1971. Boyle's commitment to not rocking the operators' boat made him callous and indifferent to miners' health and safety concerns. Wildcat work stoppages became a method of compensating for weak and corrupt union leadership. Increased employment spurred miners to pursue long-neglected matters of health and safety and work conditions, and rank-and-file work stoppages escalated in the mid-1960s. Unauthorized work stoppages increased from 111 in 1964 to 500 in 1970 (Dix, Fuller, Linsky, & Robinson 1972; Green, 1978; Clark, 1981).

In 1969 an association of Disabled Miners and Widows formed to seek medical coverage after disability and retirement, a graduated pension linked to time served in the mines, and pensions for mine widows. They filed suit, Blankenship v. Boyle, against the UMW, BCOA, and the Funds on fraud charges (a suit they won in 1972). They also contested union policy by using picket lines to disrupt production. Above all, their "strike against the UMWA and the Fund legitimized the idea that union members could challenge UMWA leaders without being disloyal to the union itself" (Seltzer, 1985, pp. 90-93).

In 1969, West Virginia miners formed the Black Lung Association and demanded compensation for the occupational disease. A pivotal wildcat strike in support of a black lung law closed West Virginia's mines for three weeks and brought political pressure on a recalcitrant state legislature to pass legislation. Boyle opposed the strike and derided the black lung insurgents (Seltzer, 1980). His failure to support miners on health and safety issues crystallized rank-and-file pressure for a more open, more democratic union. The Lewis and Boyle regimes denied working miners the right to elect district officials or have a say in ratifying contracts. "Boyle persisted in applying the model of industrial partnership and union autocracy beyond its time" (Seltzer, 1985, p. 87).

A Pennsylvania miner, Jock Yablonski, a loyalist to Lewis and Boyle for years, ran a reformist candidacy against Boyle in the 1969 union election. Yablonski sought to capitalize on widespread anger among miners over a point of production issue—black lung disease. Encouraged by Congressman Ken Heckler and Ralph Nader, Yablonski raised a nascent rank-and-file agenda: End corruption and nepotism in the union; local autonomy; health and safety reforms (Clark, 1981). Though Yablonski charged Boyle was "in bed with the coal operators," Boyle defeated the insurgent slate in a controversial election marked by charges of voting fraud and intimidation. Shortly thereafter, gunmen acting on orders from Boyle murdered Yablonski and members of his family.

Over the next three years, a coalition of activist lawyers and a small core of rank-and-file miners called Miners For Democracy worked to oust Boyle. The MFD issued a list of rank-and-file demands prior to the 1971 UMW-BCOA contract talks: a four-shift day (one shift devoted to safety and maintenance); increased Fund royalties; a new grievance procedure; sick pay; a $10/day wage hike; a right to strike over safety disputes; federal oversight of regularly collected dust samples (samples collected by miners and not company officials); and rank-and-file contract ratification (Seltzer, 1985). The MFD scored victories in court battles: By 1971 Boyle and associates had been convicted for embezzlement and improper use of UMWA funds during the election. Boyle's role in the murder conspiracy came to light, and a court order overturned the 1969 election and scheduled a new election under Justice Department supervision. In 1972, the MFD nominated Arnold Miller of the Black Lung Association, and he defeated Boyle for the presidency.[9] The new UMW leadership encouraged more independence among union locals, gave miners the right to elect local union officers, and promoted greater expression of rank-and-file opinions. Miller's reform administration altered Boyle's legacy of corrupt, authoritarian control over the union apparatus, returning to miners the power to vote on contracts.

Once Miller took office, the previous MFD strategy of relying on activist lawyers rather than building an "organic base in the rank and file" proved an impediment to effective administration (Seltzer, 1985, p. 113). Neither Miller nor his staffers had a sufficient network of organizational or grassroots support. Their victory in hand, Miners for Democracy disbanded, while the Black Lung Association came under the control of the union hierarchy (Green, 1978). But Miller's control over the national union offices was not matched at the local level. Local union elections had just been introduced and Miller was unable to field candidates in various districts sympathetic to him. Local initiatives arose which were more far-reaching than anything Miller and his associates foresaw, and the union infrastructure was not yet sufficiently developed to cope with such rank-and-file democracy.

> The reformers were victimized by the rapidity of their own success. They had pulled off a palace coup . . . Much of their momentum had been sustained by courtroom victories and masterful press relations . . . The price of engineering a coup through the media and the courts was that there was no solid organizational base within the union. (Seltzer, 1977, p. 6)

The "molasses of bureaucracies old and new" paralyzed the reformers. "The transfer of power from Boyle to Miller had been bitter and chaotic" (Bethell in Seltzer, 1985, p. 129). Competition for staff positions (including holdovers from Boyle's regime), the inexperienced staff, and policy differences led to factions and political infighting. When Miller's appointees took office, they discovered the UMWA's administrative machinery had ceased functioning. Over time, Miller's lack of political acumen antagonized district officers and alienated the rank and file. His leadership and administrative skills came under attack from a hostile UMW Executive Board packed with political enemies.

In "bread and butter" terms, the 1974 contract was an improvement over the 1971 contract. But, pension provisions remained inequitable and the 1974 contract still lacked a right-to strike-clause. Rank-and-file disappointment also stemmed, in part, from expectations raised by their participation in shaping contract demands at the 1973 convention. And problems with the Health and Pension Funds' solvency grew under the 1974 contract. The 1974 UMW contract contained language bolstering the commitment to safety, but the grievance procedure failed to enforce it. It gave miners "the right to refuse to work" if they thought they were in "imminent danger." Miners soon discovered their real choice lay between running an unsafe piece of equipment or being discharged (Yarrow, 1979).[10]

WILDCAT STOPPAGES VERSUS BUREAUCRATIC ARBITRATION

After the 1974 contract, wildcat work stoppages mounted in intensity and number. In February 1975, 11,000 miners stayed off the job to protest UMWA delays in distributing copies of the new contract and the absence of a right-to-strike clause. At the 1976 UMWA convention the political climate demanded that every candidate for UMW president endorse a right-to-strike proposal (Clark, 1981).

UMWA-BCOA contracts had never contained an explicit no-strike clause. But in 1970, the Supreme Court ruled in Boy's Market v. Retail Clerks International that a signed contract that included a grievance procedure implied a "no-strike obligation." This ruling defined any strike during a contract as illegal, and coal operators soon made full use of the federal judiciary: Injunctions against strikes increased from 2 in 1970 to 111 in 1974 (Clark, 1981).

Miners saw neutrality stripped from the law. No matter how legitimate their grievance, no matter how blocked their grievance channels, the federal courts automatically issued injunctions against them. Injunctions transformed conflicts within the private sector into a contest between labor and the federal judiciary. (Seltzer, 1985, p. 89)

Operators remained unwilling to recognize the union's changing character, "locked into labor-relations attitudes formed fifty years earlier" (Seltzer, 1978, p. 5). Not surprisingly, the break with Boyle's proindustry program led some coal operators to "an all-out assault against the miners' union" to bring it to heel again (Nyden & Nyden, 1978). They refused either to spend more money required to make mines safer, or yield greater control over the labor process to mine workers. The BCOA introduced "labor stability" demands, unprecedented in recent years: "Nothing like it had been seen since the 1920s" (Seltzer, 1977). *Wall Street Journal* reporters (2/24/78) observed: "Col-

---

[10]There remained a lurking unhappiness with the 1974 contract. During the 1977–78 strike, rank-and-file miners emphasized they would not quickly ratify any contract until they had thoroughly examined it. While some miners remained convinced they had been "sold out" in 1974, many recognized that they simply had not read what they were signing.

lective bargaining itself may be unsuited to such basic changes in the culture of the coalfields as were contemplated by the industry . . ." As the strike wore on, *Business Week* (3/6/78) noted the "operators tried to change the culture of the coalfields through a labor contract—a goal that was, in retrospect, too ambitious from the start."

Wildcat strikes multiplied in response to health and safety issues, the breakdown of the grievance system, authoritarian foremen, favoritism in the mines, and federal court injunctions against the work stoppages (Yarrow, 1979; Green, 1978). Wildcats comprised one of the miners' more effective tactics of countering operators' actions and challenging the internal power structure of the UMW. The tradition among miners to honor a picket line took on both an institutional character and the dynamic of a social movement: An energetic band of miners could quickly close down large areas of the industry. "They struck over safety, compulsory shift rotation, gasoline rationing, seniority rights, Black lung legislation, cutbacks in health benefits; they struck over the right to strike, and they struck against the court orders enjoining them from striking" (Seltzer, 2/3/78, p. 6).

Conflicts between miners and operators over mine safety repeatedly formed the pivot of walkouts. Lost workdays resulting from "disabling injuries" were triple the average of all major industries in the United States. Though fatalities and disabling injuries declined substantially throughout the 20th century, in 1976, 141 miners lost their lives and 13,944 suffered disabling injuries in coal mine accidents. Following the 1974 contract, companies harassed union safety committee members with "threats and layoffs, and safety discrimination by which miners who complain about unsafe conditions are assigned undesirable work" (Shapiro, 2/3/78, p. 23).

Wildcat stoppages generated worker and community solidarity. They also produced disunion among miners. "Any political reflex can be abused and manipulated; honoring picket lines was" (Seltzer, 1985, p. 137). Abuses of the "stranger" picket line meant lost income to miners due to "someone else's gripe";[11] lost royalty income to the Funds; and constant internal conflict in the union. "Nickle and dime" strikes eroded miner incomes enough (by up to one-third in 1976) that miners themselves sought a remedy for wildcats.

One index of community solidarity was that picket lines extended outside strictly labor-management issues. One strike aimed at West

---

[11]Letters to the editor in coalfield papers carried complaints (unverified) about wildcat strikes over "foolish" or "stupid things": for example, no soap in the bathhouse; who would clean the portable toilets; or a man's boots stolen in the bathhouse.

Virginia Governor Arch Moore's gas-rationing policy restricting gas purchases to those who had less than a quarter of a tank. Since miners frequently drove long distances to and from work, this was actually a work-related matter (Clark, 1981). The Kanawha County texbook protest had less to do with operators than the internal political and cultural dynamics of the union. Wildcat strikes were a double-edged sword: They stoked up rank-and-file solidarity and emotional fire, but at the expense of building "a coherent, positive alternative to union procedures" (Marschall, 1978, p. 110).

The grievance procedure formed under the 1974 contract to settle contract disputes proved cumbersome and inadequate. Between 1974 and 1977 the coal operators and the union sought arbitration in 5710 cases. From September 1976 to September 1977, 2700 local arbitrators' rulings were appealed. The Arbitration Review Board, composed of members from the UMWA and BCOA, was overloaded: Grievance cases took months and years to be settled, and even then only a small fraction of the appeals was decided (*BW*, 11/28/77, p. 93). Though coal operators were repeatedly charged with violating the contract (Nyden & Nyden, 1978), most miners' complaints were thrown out, leading to charges the committee was unfair and partial to coal operators. Unauthorized work stoppages became a frustrated response to blocked formal grievance procedures (Seltzer, 1985).

But the politics of unauthorized work stoppages were more complicated still. Despite the operators' clear distress over wildcat stoppages that disrupted production and challenged their authority over the labor process, union officers charged coal companies with intentionally provoking local walkouts when demand for coal was slack. Coal operators countered miners' grievances by using "arbitration as a tactical weapon" to stall and bog down issues. Union officials perceived coal companies as fueling the wildcat crisis by repeatedly delaying disputes through the costly, time-consuming arbitration machinery instead of negotiating them immediately at local mine sites (Shapiro, 2/3/78, p. 23). [12]

Miners felt companies used the grievance procedure as a calculated method of obstructing health and safety enforcement and as a means of

---

[12]A 1970 study of work stoppages observed an inclination to "view the grievance procedure, not as a flexible tool through which bargaining over issues which arise on a day-to-day basis takes place, but as a formal, almost judicial procedure for settling conflicts . . . It may well be that emphasis on procedure rather than problem solving is so entrenched in the labor relations of this industry that no changes are possible. If this is so, the grievance procedure will continue to fail as a substitute for the wildcat strike" (Dix et al., 1970, pp. 15–16).

winning back what they had lost at the bargaining table. Companies held a decided advantage in the grievance procedure. First, "company grievance handlers are generally better trained than the UMW's and the companies traditionally make lucrative offers to lure away the union's more effective grievance handlers" (Shapiro, 2/3/78, p. 23). Second, the companies could "legally" box in union locals. When firms intentionally violated the contract, one of two consequences would follow: (a) instigate an "illegal" walkout, in which case the companies would obtain court injunctions resulting in fines against the union and arrests of local officials, or (b) force the miners to follow the grievance steps, which permitted the contract violation to stand as a de facto operating practice while the complaint made its way through the time-consuming process.[13]

During the summer of 1976, nearly 150,000 miners stayed off the job to protest federal court injunctions against wildcat strikers in West Virginia.[14] As wildcat strikes escalated through the 1970s, companies

---

[13]An explanation of miners' view of the situation is excerpted from an unsigned, handwritten statement: "To continue to follow the procedure takes a lot of time—too much time—and even though the grievance is carried forward in the process, it becomes necessary to strike simply to stop the violation of the contract. If, for example, a miner bids on a job but the company awards the job to a miner with less skill and seniority for doing that job, then the miner files a grievance with his/her immediate supervisor. If the decision is not changed, then the grievance is appealed, but in the meantime the less senior miner is doing the new job. Weeks might pass before the senior miner is awarded a favorable decision or perhaps the arbitrator will rule in favor of the company. Every miner in that mine knows the company has violated the contract and perhaps gotten away with it. If, however, they walk out of the mine, then their strike action does a couple of things: First, it stops the situation of the less senior miner doing the job . . . Second, it is the only action miners can take directly to express their sentiment that the company violated the contract by awarding the job to the less senior miner. Even if both the strike and the grievance are lost, the miners have stood up and fought against the company's attack on their seniority system, an important foundation of trade unionism."

[14]This strike started "when Local 1759 at Cabin Creek demanded that an important mine communications job be filled by a UMW member. The company refused the demand, but an arbitrator later settled the matter in the union's favor. The company, however, refused to comply with the umpire's award, citing a technicality. The union tried to have the award enforced by Judge Dennis Knapp of the federal district court, but the judge turned their appeal down saying he "hadn't the time to hear the case." The case went back to the umpire, who this time, in a vague award, ruled in favor of the company. Local 1759 struck, and within two days was slapped with a back-to-work order by the same Judge Knapp they had asked to enforce the arbitration award. The local

responded by seeking court orders to restrain workers. In 1976, strikers defied federal judges as well as Arnold Miller and won—the judges backed down and Miller reportedly pledged to seek a "right to strike" plank in the 1977–78 contract (Green 1978). Again in the summer of 1977, massive wildcat strikes involved up to 90,000 UMW members who protested cutbacks in health benefits and the retirement fund, and then turned in "revolt" against Miller's misrepresentations regarding his handling of the cutbacks (Marschall, 1977). Notably, operators did not seek injunctions against this strike, probably because its timing could be expected to drain miners' resources for the upcoming contract strike and help tighten up a slack coal market.

The rank and file saw their "right-to-strike" proposal as a solution to both controlling work stoppages and stalling tactics. The proposal would give each union local the right to vote a work stoppage when a local dispute could not be settled via the grievance procedure. A strike would require a majority vote of the local membership. This "democratic authorization procedure" would apply only to that local's mines, preventing a union local from posting roving pickets at other mines. Miners saw the idea as a safeguard against abuses of the picket line, while also ending the abuse of grievance procedures (Franklin, 11/28/77, p. 21; 12/1/77, p. 17). The 1976 UMWA convention endorsed this proposal in matters pertaining to safety, health, working conditions and job security (Clark, 1981; Seltzer, 1985).[15]

Wildcat strikes cost the industry millions of tons in production, and a lost-time rate 10 times the average for all industries (*BW*, 11/28/77). In 1976, strikes and unexcused absences totalled 17.9 percent of all days that BCOA mines were open for work, and amounted to one-quarter of all the industrial disputes in the U.S. (*BW*, 12/19/77). From 1973 to 1976 an escalating number of wildcat strikes resulted in an increased number of man-days and tonnage lost. In 1976, 2,787 wildcats cost BCOA members 1,950,300 man-days lost and 20,477,300 tons of potential coal

---

again tried to see the judge, but once again he was too busy. When the miners refused to end the strike, Judge Knapp fined the local $50,000 for the walkout and $25,000 for each day the strike continued" (Clark, 1981, pp. 71-72).

[15]The right to strike proposal advanced an alternative grievance procedure: "For an issue to be considered, it would have to be 'of such magnitude as to affect all, or a large number of the members working' at an affected mine.' No vote could be scheduled until local officers met and gave their approval. A seventy-two hour cooling-off period would then be necessary before a strike vote could be held . . . a meeting could be scheduled at which a secret vote would be taken. Any strike required the approval of a majority of all miners working at a particular mine" (Clark, 1981, p. 118).

production, while miners lost wages of $109,897,000 (Clark, 1981). In addition, disruptions created by wildcats "destabilized the relationship between BCOA suppliers and some customers" because of the latter's concern about "reliability of coal deliveries" (Seltzer, 1985, p. 139). Unless the BCOA could keep production levels up, which meant keeping the miners in, the potentially enormous profits that the market promised could not be realized.

In sum, a principal factor precipitating the 1977–78 strike stemmed from the collapse of grievance and arbitration procedures, and the intense clash of interests regarding wildcat strikes.

The rank and file's distaste for the arbitration procedures, supposed to be the grievance "safety valve" in a no-strike contract, grew quickly when many coal companies started choosing to send every miner's complaint through a time-consuming, multi-tiered hearings system, rather than settling differences "man to man at the mine," as Miller has put it.

The arbitrators' binding rulings were applicable only in the union district in which the grievance originated, so multiple and even more time-consuming arbitrations of similar or identical grievances became commonplace. Angry miners began to strike in violation of the contract.

In the summers of 1975 and 1976, when wildcat strikes spread to hundreds of mines, the companies resorted to the Federal courts, obtaining back-to-work orders with heavy fines for many union locals and jail terms for a few persistent violators. The courts became "company courts" in the minds of many miners.

The miners' suspicion and anger persisted even after a United State Supreme Court decision in July 1976 abruptly legitimized many of the miners' wildcat walkouts, by ruling that "sympathy strikes" and picketing by workers not directly aggrieved were outside the UMW contract's mandate to follow arbitration procedures instead of striking.

After that decision, the coal industry obtained a sweeping ruling from an arbitrator that sidestepped the Supreme Court and empowered the companies to dismiss any miner who pickets anywhere, or exhorts picketing, over a dispute that could be arbitrated. (Franklin, 11/27/77, p. 26)

CRISIS OF THE HEALTH AND PENSION BENEFITS

Compounding the union's troubles, the Health and Retirement Funds, managed by independent trustees,[16] had become insolvent—or as CBS put it, they had "run dry." These funds, based on a royalty system tied

---

[16]The three trustees were union representative Harry Huge; BCOA representative C.W. Davis; and neutral member Paul Dean.

to coal production in BCOA mines, financed a jointly administered, comprehensive health care system for miners and their families—the Fund served 820,000 working and retired miners and their family members. When it was created, however, John L. Lewis did not negotiate a royalty tied to profits, but to tonnage (anticipating increased productivity due to mechanized technologies). Because it was tonnage based, rising coal prices did not build the Fund's coffers. The 1974 UMWA-BCOA contract amended the formula for calculating the royalties, to include both tonnage and working hours. The 1950 Pension and Benefit Trusts were still calculated on a tonnage basis while the 1974 Benefit and Pension Trusts were based on tonnage and hourly rates.

In 1974, the Funds were reorganized into four programs. Soon, the Pension and Benefits Fund which served pre-1976 retirees was bankrupt. Union leaders and the BCOA blamed the problem on wildcat strikes. More accurately, a series of factors brought matters to a head in July 1977: (a) rocketing health care costs, (b) a harsh winter of 1976–77, (c) unanticipated stagnation in coal markets, (d) negotiators "underestimated" eligible beneficiaries in 1974, (e) administrative costs rose 90 percent between 1974 to 1977, and (f) lost royalty income because of wildcat work stoppages (BCOA firms paid into the fund production royalties of $1.54 per hour and $0.80 per ton of coal). Harry Huge, chief trustee of the Funds, overhauled the Funds after 1974 by pursuing a course of administrative efficiency at the expense of the programs's fundamental mission. In a nightmare of administrative rationality run amuck, a new computerized system served the demands of "health providers instead of health consumers" (Seltzer, 1985, pp. 143–145; Franklin, 11/27/77, p. 26).

Under the 1974 contract a two-tiered pension system gave post-1975 retirees payments of $425 as opposed to $225 for miners who retired before 1974 (Peeks, 3/8/78; Hughey, 1/30/78). A significant issue to miners' during the strike was this inequity in the monthly payments paid to retirees. Coal operators naturally did not want to include older retirees at the new benefits level, while working miners felt an obligation to their fathers who had suffered to build the union, and were now being discriminated against.

Just four days after the UMWA presidential election, in June 1977, the Health and Retirement Fund trustees ordered a steep reduction in medical benefits due to a growing fiscal deficit. The new plan called for a system of copayments, where miners and family members paid "the first $250 in hospital bills each year and 40 percent of all doctor bills up to $250 each year" (see Clark, 1981, p. 116). To avoid the cuts, the UMWA requested the BCOA to let the trustees divert funds from the Pension fund (which then had $300 million in reserve). The BCOA refused, claiming diminution of the funds was due to losses in production stemming from wildcat strikes. Though wildcat strikes resulted in lost royalty income, the amount was but 5 percent of the Funds' projected income of roughly $2 billion from 1974 to 1977 (Getschow, *WJS*, 12/1/77). Union members protested the BCOA refusal, calling it a punitive measure against the miners, as well as a measure taken to whittle away the union's resources in case of a contract strike (*UMW Journal*, 7/1–15/77; Green, 1978). And howls of protest were aimed at Miller over the announcement's timing. Both Lee Roy Patterson and Harry Patrick had warned during the election campaign that cutbacks were coming, and there was evidence Huge delayed announcing the cuts until after the election (Seltzer, 1985).

Probably the most hotly contested change demanded by the BCOA concerned health care. Operators wanted to replace the unique, union-controlled medical system that provided free health care with privately administered insurance systems where miners would pay the first $700 of costs. This would dismantle a system of free community clinics that provided not only curative, but preventative therapy to patients, in the nation's most advanced "socialized" health care program (Green, 1978). The "health card" anchored a way of life. Miners considered it sacrosanct. Clark (1981 p. 120) quotes a miner as saying the "health card" is the "only reason I'm working in the mines." Now, the union faced the possible loss of its most important recruiting advantage. Coal companies were motivated not only to reduce health care costs, they also hoped to gain a powerful means of disciplining workers, by making clear that management, and not the union, provided for, and thereby controlled, health benefits. By recommodifying health care and eliminating it as an element of the social wage, operators could induce a structurally more decisive form of discipline by compelling mine workers to provide for all personal needs via the individual wage (Rhodenbaugh, 1978, p. 26).

The final 1978 contract settlement contained a version of this provision. Though the deductible was cut to $200, its social consequences were quickly manifest. The change to company-by-company plans and private insurance carriers dramatically reduced health-care quality when it became available on a fee-for-service basis. Community clinics in the coalfields closed because they no longer received lump-sum payments to assure staff salaries (NYT, 6/26/78). Preventive medicine went out the window.[17] Miners now had to pay a deductible on each visit and perform extra paper work. In some instances hospitals and clinics began insisting

---

[17]Here was an ideal opportunity to compare a relatively "socialized" approach to health care with a thoroughly market-based approach. But the networks never examined the issue.

miners "pay the entire bill immediately instead of taking the deductible and then waiting to get the rest from the insurance companies" (Douthat, 6/25/78, p. B-5). Miners and their families became less willing to see doctors unless they were very ill, and paying the entire bill on each visit was simply prohibitive for most miners' families. Ironically, health care costs increased because of the additional paperwork and the fact that preventive medicine had held down costs (*NYT*, 10/9/78).

THE BCOA'S POLITICAL-ECONOMIC AGENDA

Prior to 1974 and the Arab oil embargo, profits from coal mining were steady and "unexciting" (*BW*, 11/7/77). The average price per ton remained between $4.39 and $5.08 from 1948 to 1969 (Nyden & Nyden, 1978). In 1973, coal operators seldom earned more than 20 cents a ton after taxes on coal sold for $8.53/ton. Due to the oil embargo, and an increase in worldwide steel demand which led to demand for high-grade metallurgical coal, prices skyrocketed. Between 1973 and 1974 the average price nearly doubled to $15.75/ton (Simon, 1983, p. 23). By 1977, the average ton sold for over $20. West Virginia coal prices shot up from $7.93 in 1970 to $32.50 in 1976. However, some firms were locked into long-term, fixed-price contracts with utilities which constrained their profits. The price of coal mined per miner rose from $10,973 in 1957 to $61,460 in 1976. Company labor costs over the same period steadily dropped, due to mechanization of the mining process. In 1969, 49 cents out of every dollar from coal sales went for miners' wages and benefits, compared to 36 cents in 1977 (*UMW Journal*, November 1977; Nyden & Nyden, 1978). Though coal company profits rose roughly 100 percent from 1970 to 1974, mineworkers' wages increased only 7 percent over the same period (Green, 1978, p. 15).

Under President Carter's Energy Plan, coal production was expected to increase to more than 1 billion tons by 1985 from 665 million tons in 1977. The coal industry anticipated a lucrative future of guaranteed demands and coal prices, spurred by the oil embargo, increasing to compete with oil prices. But along with the Energy Plan, Congress also passed environmental regulations (the Surface Mining Control and Reclamation Act of 1977 and the Clean Air Act of 1977) imposing stricter constraints on the mining and burning of coal. The coal industry lobbied against conservation and environmental regulations as an impediment to productivity and profits, and contested enforcement of Federal rules in the courts (Vietor, 1980).

Increased profits their aim, most coal firms took a narrow view of the relationship between mine safety and productivity. To them, complying with safety regulations cost money and reduced productivity.[18] For instance, the UMW secured a 1974 contract provision which required "helpers for the roof bolter and continuous miner as a safety measure." Because such helpers were not fully employed in the production process, they had an adverse effect on productivity (Yarrow, 1979). Still, there was counterevidence that improved mine safety and equipment maintenance increased productivity.

Rather than address the problems causing wildcat strikes, however, the BCOA developed a series of "labor stability" demands aimed at achieving stability by force. BCOA members also professed interest in greater cooperation and communication between themselves and labor (Simon, 1983). The BCOA sought the absolute right to discharge anyone for strike activity, for encouraging a strike, or even honoring a picket line. They proposed imposing cash penalties up to $200 on chronic absentees and strikers. Those participating in wildcat strikes would be required to pay penalties of $22 a day into the Health Fund: On this condition health benefits would be available. The power of union safety committees would be curtailed. Operators would be allowed to institute production incentive schemes. These measures would probably aggravate accident rates in the mines, already 10 times higher than in other U.S. industries, and three to four times higher than European coal mines (UMW Journal, November 1977).

Demand for steel dropped sharply from 1976 levels and reduced demand for metallurgical coal defined "captive" steel operators stance in the 1977–78 negotiations. "When demand for steel is strong, continuity of supply" becomes the primary bargaining consideration, but when demand for steel is down, "cost takes precedence" (Perry, 1984, p. 47). Big suppliers like Consolidated Coal had already agreed to cut back deliveries as utilities accumulated unprecedented stockpiles. One market index showed coal stocks down 33 percent in 1977, and demand was generally slack (Vartan, 11/27/77). A long strike would tighten demand, diminish utility stockpiles, raise profits, and—it was predicted—take the wind out of the miners' sails, making them agreeable to anything which meant employment and food on the table. BCOA members were prepared to swap modestly increased wages for a disciplined work force.

---

[18]Ralph E. Bailey, Chairman of Consol Coal, fought imposition of more stringent safety rules, arguing, "Our studies show that only 15 percent of the accidents in mines are attributable to the elements covered by the act." Instead, Bailey chose victim blaming as an explanation—miners' lack of motivation, carelessness and error—for accidents.

Wall Street securities analysts perceived the balance of forces, and judged the BCOA's best strategy would be to prolong the strike as long as possible before the government intervened. One analyst, after speaking with industry representatives, concluded they "probably wouldn't mind a six-month strike, and with some justification" (UPI, 11/10/77). Some observers considered the labor stoppage of December 6, 1977 more a lockout than a strike.

> For thirty years bargaining has focused on union demands: seniority rights, pay, pensions, layoff protection, time off, and medical care. But in recent months the spark points in contract talks have been management demands for givebacks or "takeaways"—the cancellation of labor's old gains. (Franklin, 3/26/78)

The BCOA was itself affected by internal conflicts and power struggles, reflecting the varying interests of its members. A handful of corporate giants dominated the BCOA because internal governance was based on tonnage. Most large firms were subsidiaries of steel and oil companies. Further splits existed between producers of steam coal and metallurgical coal. Different market conditions for steam and metallurgical coal created contrary incentives during the bargaining process (Hughey, 2/3/78). Where independent coal operators viewed labor as merely an aspect of the production process and had no specialists in labor relations, big steel companies operating "captive mines" were interested in cheap (efficient) coal, which made them hardliners. Oil companies sought a return on investment, and their negotiators considered themselves "modernist" managers. By January the "crisply efficient, monolithic image" of the BCOA was "frazzling at the edges" (Franklin, 1/9/78, p. A19). Corporate differences of interest erupted in fierce behind-the-scenes battles which were manifested in a "bewildering change of leaders in negotiations . . . this multiplicity of chiefs symbolized the disagreements within the BCOA" (*BW*, 3/6/78, p. 95).[19]

---

[19]There were numerous indications that BCOA members agreed to stay quiet about their internal disagreements during the strike. Press accounts rarely specified the nature of their disagreements: "the BCOA has maintained a relatively low profile. When it issues press releases, they are usually brief and in the name of an anonymous spokesman" (Brown, 3/11/78, p. 2).

In late December, Roderick Hills, CEO of Peabody Coal (the largest producer of coal in the United States) "organized a secret meeting with the UMWA and Horvitz to end-run the official BCOA negotiators," but failed (Seltzer, 1985, p. 155). In mid- January, there was again internal criticism of Joseph Brennan, BCOA President, and his hard-line bargaining strategy. Hills' efforts to revise the BCOA approach led to an abrupt reorganization of the BCOA bargaining team

From December through February the BCOA negotiating strategy was dominated by hardliners Joseph Brennan, president of the BCOA, Bruce Johnston of U.S. Steel, and Bobby Brown of Consol Coal. Consol Coal, the second-largest coal producer in the United States, historically dominated the industry-wide bargaining structure. The company had earned a reputation for belligerence in labor relations, and Brown was noted for his "never give workers an inch" approach. U.S. Steel and other steel firms which ran "captive" mines were aggrieved over two issues. Though their mines were better equipped for safety, and had better safety records than most others, they nonetheless felt the sting of wildcats when other operators were struck over safety matters (Moody and Woodward, 1978). Bolstered by a glut of stockpiled metallurgical coal, the steel corporations intently pursued strict disciplinary measures against wildcatters. Also, U.S. Steel had long opposed a contract provision requiring BCOA companies to pay tonnage royalties to the UMW Health and Retirement funds on nonunion coal they bought.[20] Johnston's insistence on deleting this provision delayed the first tentative settlement for several days, thereby weakening the BCOA's leverage (*BW*, 3/6/78, p. 95). After miners rejected the first two proposals, the strike's differential effect on coal operators became apparent. Steel company stockpiles cushioned them, and markets for steel and metallurgical coal remained weak, so they were still willing to take a tough stance. But other major operators—Pittston, Peabody, Westmoreland, Island Creek—showed significant losses in their first quarter earnings reports of 1978 (NYT, 2/16/78; *BW*, 4/3/78) and steam coal producers now saw a profit in making a few concessions in order to resume production. After rank-and-file rejection of the February 6 contract

---

(*BW*, 2/6/78). This committee consisted of Edward Leisenring (chair of BCOA; head of Westmoreland Coal), Roderick Hills (president of Peabody Coal); Nicholas Camicia (president of Pittston Coal); Bruce Johnston (vice-president of U.S. Steel); and Bobby Brown (president of Consol Coal) (Franklin, 1/25/78, p. B18). But Hills' effort to work a deal with Harry Huge collapsed, and Hills was succeeded by Johnston as lead negotiator. In February, Brown's "visceral antiunion hatred so stalled negotiations" that he and Johnston were replaced by Camicia. After the strike, Brown's ouster led to Consol Coal's temporary withdrawal from the BCOA. Consol later rejoined the BCOA under changes which empowered Consol, U.S. Steel, and Peabody to negotiate for the BCOA in 1981, (Seltzer, 1985, pp. 191–193).

[20]On October 5, 1977, U.S. Steel agreed to pay $9.7 million in back royalties to the UMW funds. The agreement came after U.S. Steel lost a suit filed under antitrust laws, which charged the "royalty requirement amounted to a secondary boycott against independent producers" (AP, 10/6/77).

proposal, splits within the coal operators' ranks grew: "We're almost as badly divided as the UMW," said one industry official (NYT, 2/16/78). Nicholas Camicia, chief executive of Pittston Coal, was named to lead the BCOA negotiating team in a move which reduced the influence of Johnston and Brown (NYT, 2/22/78). Following rejection of the second proposal on March 5, support for 'hardliner' policies declined further,[21] and "good ol' boys" Camicia and Stonie Barker Jr., president of Island Creek Coal, sought a private "exploratory" meeting with the union which planted the seed for a settlement four days later (NYT, 3/16/78; Seltzer, 1985; Perry, 1984). Surely, this was "news" as much as dissension within the union. CBS, like the other networks, however, did not report it.

NEGOTIATIONS

Contract negotiations in 1974 had been conducted in the euphoria of an anticipated coal boom. In 1977 the combination of less-than-anticipated industry expansion, an aggressively nonunion stripmining sector, and chronic wildcat strikes (see *BW*, 12/19/77) cast a pall over negotiations. As one miner put it, the BCOA held "all the stones" this time around and was in a favorable position to sit things out. The market was soft, and would improve with waiting. By early in December, utility industry stockpiles averaged 100 days (UPI, 12/4/77). Union funds were at an all-time low and health benefits and strike benefits could not last long. Internally, the UMW was weak and divided, and the BCOA hoped to use this dissension to its advantage. By taking a hard stance, they were confident a weak union leadership would eventually capitulate to their chief demands. *Business Week* (11/7/77, p. 30) commented: "In a long list of objectives . . . the industry has demanded unprecedented disciplinary powers over coal miners . . . call(ing) for contract changes that would take away many of the UMW's economic gains . . ." And, with some prescience, they continued: "The industry's hard line, however, may be based on a misreading of the difference between the UMW's weak leadership and a rank and file that can turn militant very quickly."

The first bargaining session took place on October 6, two months prior to the expiry of the 1974 contract. The BCOA was unequivocal from the start: "This year is a threshold year for labor relations in coal . . . This agreement must help restore stability and improved

---

[21]On March 13, the NY Times reported the reorganized industry bargaining group did not contain a single representative of captive-steel operators.

production in coal." Brennan announced prior to opening talks that the BCOA would insist on "the right to operate our mines during a contract term without the constant debilitating imprint of the wildcat" (*WSJ*, 10/3/77). Posing the union's options as cooperation or extinction, the BCOA asked the rhetorical question of "whether or not a proud labor union will meet in good-faith bargaining with an industry and together forge a contract that will permit us to grow together, or whether we will fail, and therefore, see the decline and possible extinction of the United Mine Workers of America" (BCOA, 1977, p. 12). Miller's initial position reflected the political will of his constituency: The operators must agree to rescind cuts in benefits and restore health services under the royalty-financed Funds. In late October, Miller discontinued discussions with the BCOA until this issue was placed on the agenda (*WSJ*, 10/28/77). BCOA negotiators would not discuss this matter unless it was tied to concessions on the "labor stability" issue. Again in late November after 17 meetings, Miller stopped negotiations after a war of words with Joseph Brennan. The primary issues remained the same: (a) restoration of the medical care system, and (b) the failed grievance system. Miller voiced public support for a right-to-strike clause. The BCOA bitterly opposed this, insisting instead on a series of penalties against miners (NYT, 11/26/77; 11/27/77).

The operators knew Miller's weaknesses as a negotiator, and exploited them well. Yet, they erred in their estimation of Miller's acceptance by UMW members. Miller won the June 1977 elections when two other contenders, Lee Roy Patterson and Harry Patrick divided the opposition vote. Miller had 55,275 votes to 49,042 for Patterson and 34,523 for Patrick (Clark, 1981). The vote split along geographic and age lines. Though an estimated 64 percent of working UMW members voted against Miller, retired miners's votes kept him in office (Seltzer, 1978). Retired miners, however, do not vote on contracts, so the Miller mandate assumed by some operators did not represent the union's working majority. Perhaps more critical, Miller ran third in the contest for younger miners' (those most willing to voice dissent) votes, who preferred Patrick (Clark, 1981).

Between 1976 and 1977 Miller's administration was decimated by resignations. Predictably, after years of political repression under Boyle, acute political differences emerged during Miller's first term in office, and surfaced at the 1976 union convention. After declaring he would run for reelection as UMW President, Miller grew paranoid about the loyalty of aides and allies. Miller banished key aides, Ed Burke and Bernie Aronson, in October 1976 for "being disloyal." This led to a split with Patrick and the subsequent departure of associates who spearheaded the 1974 negotiations. Tom Bethell (UMW research director) and

Rich Bank (UMW attorney) resigned, along with other talented members of the research and legal departments. Unlike 1974, when the UMWA came to the bargaining table armed with carefully documented position papers, in 1977 Miller and his "team" came unprepared (Clark, 1981).[22] Most importantly, in the 1977 contract negotiations, Miller was between a rock and a hard place: Miners wanted a right-to-strike clause and operators were equally insistent about punishing unauthorized strikes. As union president, Miller was legally obligated to enforce a contract unpopular with his members. Caught in this squeeze, Miller's behavior grew more erratic and he was frequently absent from negotiations (Clark, 1981).[23] "In many respects, Huge replaced Miller as the UMWA's chief negotiator" (Seltzer, 1985, p. 152).[24]

Ironically, Miller's weakness became a stumbling block to the BCOA. Their frustration with Miller surfaced quickly, describing him as "unpredictable" and "slow to grasp technical issues" (Franklin, 12/2/77, p. B7). Early in the strike and again after three months, the coal operators sought to have the UMW bargaining team restructured minus Miller. After the rank and file rejected contract proposals, Miller's alienation from miners prompted an industry source to comment: "We think it is futile to bargain with Arnold Miller. Whatever the deal, we can't have anything tainted by his name" (in *BW*, 3/20/78, p. 33).

How seriously Miller actually pushed a right-to-strike proposal remains open to debate. Seltzer (1985) argues Miller never really disagreed with the BCOA's labor stability program. Perhaps Miller's public show of insistence was but a negotiating maneuver vis-á-vis the BCOA and a

---

[22]President Carter perceived the mismatch of forces, and recognized that if rank and file miners received nothing in return for "labor stability" there would be trouble ahead. Therefore, FMCS director Wayne Horvitz took steps to enlist additional staff support for the UMWA bargaining team on the premise that "a well-organized union was a prerequisite for successful negotiations" (Seltzer, 1985, p. 152; Clark, 1981, p. 123).

[23]The strains caught up with Miller. Medication he was taking for high blood pressure made him groggy and woozy. Almost immediately after the strike, Miller suffered a stroke. During the strike, there were widespread accounts about Miller missing bargaining sessions while he drove around the Washington D.C. beltway to escape the tension. On one occasion during the strike, Miller made a public display of wearing a pistol in his belt, after alleging threats against his life.

[24]Initially, the official UMW bargaining lineup included vice-president Sam Church; District 17 secretary-treasurer Joe Duffie; district president Lou Antal; and International Executive Board members Wilbur Killion and Walter Suba (UPI, 10/4/77).

political maneuver vis-á-vis his constituency. Whether the right-to-strike issue commanded the same degree of concern among miners as the possible loss of health benefits was uncertain (Hughey, 11/23/77; UPI, 12/8/77). Some of Miller's public statements implied he was not against the labor stability proposals. His indecision continued throughout December as he waffled back and forth between agreeing to labor stability proposals and pressing for a right-to-strike clause.

On December 8, Miller claimed the "real issue" centered on how to rescue the bankrupt UMW health and retirement funds. Meanwhile, Brennan implied that "a dispute over the mine operators' insistence on a 'stable' work force was controlling the pace of the slow-moving talks." Calling the UMW "not the only game in town," Brennan threatened the union with extinction unless it engaged in concess ion bargaining on the BCOA's workforce stability measures (Franklin, 12/9/77, p. B9). The BCOA pushed an "incentive pay" system which would dock the pay of individual miners who engaged in an unauthorized walkout under a "no-strike" contract. Between December 12 and 14, negotiatiors met intensively on the "labor stability" issue and a method of "progressive discipline" to curb unauthorized absenteeism (NYT, 12/12/77, p. 28). Franklin (12/13/77) reported tentative agreement to a union proposal for the summary dismissal of any miner engaged in a wildcat stoppage who pickets at a mine other than his own. UMW negotiators considered dropping their demand for a "limited right-to-strike" clause in exchange for BCOA moderation of its "wagedocking penalties." Under this approach, the BCOA would redirect its penalties for unexcused absences into the health and pension funds (Franklin, 12/14/77, p. B14).[25] Reports of UMW negotiators' acquiescence to disciplinary penalties filtered back to the coalfields. UMW members' visceral reactions convinced Miller's associates that the rank and file would not ratify a contract containing penalties. Hence, UMW negotiators "backed away" from any such tentative agreement on December 30, triggering an angry walkout by the BCOA negotiators (Franklin, 12/31/7, p. 5).

In mid-January, BCOA President Joseph Brennan received a "slap in the face" for his bargaining strategy. BCOA moderates felt an inflexible hardline had been pushed too long and was now costing the BCOA negotiating leverage (*BW*, 3/6/78, p. 95). Roderick Hills urged revision of how to present the "payback" demands to the union, thus precipitating an "abrupt takeover of the industry bargaining strategy by five

---

[25]Franklin reported this would reduce fines to $22 per day from the companies' original proposal "that would have penalized absent miners 40% of their pay in a 10-day payroll period for each day of absence, with the employers retaining the difference" (12/14/77, p. B14).

industry leaders" (Franklin, 1/25/78, p. B18). Discussions with Harry Huge produced a 16-point offer "containing wage increases of $1.53 an hour over three years, including straight wage hikes to replace cost-of-living allowances, and 'guaranteed' health care benefits which would cost $1.37 an hour over three years" (*BW*, 2/6/78, p. 45). Huge pushed the offer to no avail. UMW bargainers rejected the offer and "countered with an old proposal" which had been previously discarded. Talks then collapsed as "irritated" BCOA negotiators refused to continue.

External political pressures mounted on both sides for a quick solution to the strike. Governors in the east central states began calling for federal intervention. Meanwhile, miners' restiveness grew and the longer they stayed out the more they wanted to get back in the contract. Further, the market for steam coal had stabilized, making a quick settlement more attractive to steam coal producers than metallurgical coal producers (Hughey, 2/3/78). On February 6 a tentative pact was announced. As miners "got wind" of the proposal's contents, they reacted in angry unison, against it "almost right down the line" (AP, 2/10/78, p. 1). They emphatically opposed penalties against absenteeism and wildcats. They saw the proposal as punishing miner solidarity by imposing monetary costs against individual miners. Miners viewed the issue as one of authority and an assault on their autonomy. Local officials and rank-and-file miners found nothing positive in the proposal, denouncing the new health plan and the inequitable treatment of pensioners.

By a 30-6 vote the UMW bargaining council rejected this settlement proposal on February 11 (Hughey, 2/11/78; Moody, 2/13/78). None of the "largely attainable" demands drawn up by the rank and file at their 1976 convention had been met, except for the wage package (*MDP*, 2/17/78). The rejected contract proposal offered a wage increase of $2.35 per hour over three years (a 37% increase from the 1974 pact of $7.80 per hour) but it did not extend the cost-of-living-adjustment formula from the 1974 contract. The proposal contained numerous BCOA's "takeaway" provisions: (a) replacing the health fund by private insurance plans, (b) instituting medical co-payments, (c) penalties against wildcat strikers and absentees (companies would gain the right to fire striking miners as well as those who honored picket lines), (d) bonus-for-production incentive plans, (e) no pension equality, (f) no safety concessions, (g) no right-to-strike, (h) an end to royalties on non-signatory coal, (i) the right to change shift starting times, and (j) a 7-day week (*CG*, 2/9/78; Seltzer, 1985; *BW*, 3/6/78; BCOA, 1978). To get their "payback" scheme, operators agreed to reimburse miners where flagrant operator actions initiated the dispute.

Miners across the coalfields demonstrated their ire at Miller for his capitulation. Images of their anger stood out as a convenient, self-evident story for television reporters, who opted not to report why miners were so upset. Typical of media coverage, *CBS News* stated on February 12: "The rank-and-file rebellion against a tentative agreement was successful . . ." The broadcast media emphasized a "lack of unity within the union" and demands for Miller's resignation. Instead of dwelling on takeaways, reporters concentrated on sketches of an anarchic union, "rebellious miners," and "troubled leadership" of Arnold Miller. Yet calls for Miller's ouster had been commonplace since the previous summer, when many working miners felt betrayed by Miller on cutbacks in health and pension benefits (NYT, 9/7/77, p. 18). Petitions to recall Miller after the first contract rejection focussed on precisely those charges (Rasmussen, 2/17/78).

After the UMW bargaining council rejected the proposed agreement, Miller requested negotiations be resumed. In turn, the BCOA argued a tentative agreement had been reached, but the bargaining council had been intimidated by unruly rank-and-file protesters. Leisenring's letter to Secretary Marshall on February 14 contended the UMW Bargaining Council had voted without carefully examining the contract proposal, which therefore should be reconsidered "line by line, so that it could be fully understood by all Bargaining Council members and another vote taken" (BCOA, 1978, p. 7).

WHITE HOUSE INTERVENTION

Proclaiming a gathering national energy crisis, "the White House moved directly" (sic) into "the bitter and complex dispute" (February 13). President Carter and his advisors anticipated a 60 day strike, and so prepared to steer a noninterventionist stance, accompanied by public rhetoric about letting the "free collective bargaining process work." But after miners rejected the first settlement proposal, Carter ordered Secretary of Labor Ray Marshall to get involved in the negotiations. Carter also began threatening unspecified "drastic actions" (presumably Taft-Hartley or Federal seizure) if negotiations to end the strike did not resume. But Carter preferred not to take this step because he feared a back-to-work injunction might further "inflame" the miners, prolonging the strike and risking a regional class war in Appalachia (NYT, 2/19/78).

President Carter's clumsy entrance into the fray alienated the BCOA. After meeting with Marshall on February 14, the BCOA committee felt they shared a common "recognition that the problems lay in getting an agreement approved by the Bargaining Council" (BCOA, 1978, p. 7). Hence, when Carter summoned both the UMWA and the BCOA to the White House the next day without prior notification, they were outraged. The BCOA initially refused the invitation, arguing that "since continuation of the strike was a result of a failure of an internal Union apparatus, the President should first summon the UMWA International Officers and the Bargaining Council" (BCOA, 1978, p. 7). With their finger on the pulse of the White House, CBS reported that the White House interpreted this as

> a direct challenge to the authority of the President. No one will quite confirm that President Carter was angry, but his aides were instructed to draft a statement that might fairly be characterized as blistering. Meantime, Mr. Carter had received word that some coal companies and other business leaders were not happy with the rejection of the President's request, and that the operators were having second thoughts. (Pierpoint, CBS, February 15).

Alas, television news is unequipped to further enlighten us about such conflicts within capitalist economic and political elites. Marshall met again with the BCOA, and they agreed to meet with Carter about resuming negotiations if three anti-Miller district presidents (Jack Perry, Kenneth Dawes, Tommy Gaston) were added to the UMW Bargaining Council. With Marshall presiding, two days of intensive bargaining produced a modest BCOA compromise which the UMW bargaining council promptly rejected by 37-0 vote because, though it dropped the 'payback' clause, it retained all the other penalty proposals (UPI, February 19).[26]

Four days later on February 21, "under intense White House pressure," the UMWA bargaining council accepted by a 25-13 vote a tentative agreement with Pittsburg & Midway, a Gulf Oil subsidiary which was not a BCOA member (Seltzer, 1985). The Federal Mediation and Conciliation Service engineered the agreement as a strategy to circumvent the impasse in the coal talks. William Hobgood of the FMCS had negotiated an agreement between a less-hardline company and less-hardline miners of Western Kentucky, Missouri, and Kansas, where the P&M mines were located. The mediation service canvassed potential agreements with independent coal companies for a "pattern-setter," rejecting a contract under discussion with Ziegler Company as "too liberal for the BCOA to ever accept" (Yarrow, 1978, p. 230). The P&M agreement was then urged on the BCOA, or any member firms willing to leave the BCOA to arrive at a

---

[26]In the flow of excitement, which they had themselves helped generate, CBS jumped to conclusions to inform their viewers of this latebreaking news item: "CBS News has just learned that there may have been a major break in the coal negotiations . . . in a secret, middle-of-the-night meeting . . ." (Cronkite, February 17).

separate contract. Miners expressed consternation at such a strategy, since it weakened the UMW's leverage in national bargaining. The dominant BCOA firms (including Peabody, Consol, U.S. Steel, Pittston, Westmoreland, and Island Creek which controlled 85 percent of BCOA board votes) were no happier about it. "Hard-liners" from U.S. Steel and and Consol Coal saw the P&M offer as decentralizing the BCOA, thus threatening their influence over industry-labor relations. Other oil-owned subsidiaries preferred "company-by-company agreements or 'pattern bargaining' in which a couple of companies cut a template for the rest" (Seltzer, 1985, p. 156) but they too felt "undercut" by Pittsburg & Midway. Close observers recognized the BCOA had lost its momentum and leverage. No matter the outcome, the P&M proposal meant the BCOA would "have to settle for a weaker agreement than it could have had" by bending earlier (*BW*, 3/6/78, p. 95).

Carter continued to threaten "stronger measures" (Taft-Hartley or Federal seizure or arbitration) as he orchestrated a campaign in the mass media and Congress to secure an end to the work stoppage. After the BCOA initially balked and "refused to accept the pact as model" (NYT, 2/22/78), they bowed to intense White House pressure (NYT, 2/21/78; 2/24/78).[27] Threatening to the last minute to invoke Taft-Hartley, Carter announced in a televised press conference on February 24 that the BCOA and UMWA had agreed to a modified version of the P&M proposal, in order 'to preserve the national interest." Carter's "strong" and "decisive" move temporarily blunted criticism of "his handling" of the strike (NYT, 2/25/78). Carter's speech was triumphant in tone, describing the agreement as a virtual fait accompli, even as he sought to appease and placate the coal miners by addressing them about the honor and respect he felt for those who risk their lives to mine the coal. But the miners would not be sweet-talked.

This proposal contained a wage hike to $2.40/hour over three years, and offered to extend the COLA in the second and third years. But union rank and file renewed their strenuous protests against the agreement because it would still dissolve the health and pension plans John L. Lewis fought years to win. Retirees called it a "rag" and a "yellow dog contract" because it maintained the disparity in pension benefits for pre-1974 retirees. It still gave operators authority to fire miners for striking or picketing (dropping sanctions against those who stayed home). New employees could be dismissed without explanation, with no provision of defense from the union. "These and many other

---

[27]To get the BCOA's participation, Carter promised the coal operators that he would appoint a coal commission to study the problems of productivity and stability in the coal industry (NYT, 2/25/78).

provisions would effectively dismember the UMWA—in the name of 'labor stability'" (Bethell, 1978, p. 13).

Miners' genuine grievances received occasional, cursory attention, while rumors grew daily of widespread blackouts due to diminishing stockpiles. Media coverage of "defiant," "dissident," and "stubborn" miners made the Administration's next move seem necessary and natural. In light of such coverage, an AP-NBC News public opinion poll showed 2/3 of the nation's citizens favoring use of Taft-Hartley (NYT, 2/24/78). Political pressure on Carter mounted to order miners back to work for an 80 day "cooling-off" period. Some "drastic action" might indeed have been justified if there was a genuine fuel crisis at hand. But was there a crisis?

ENERGY "SHORTAGES"

In the week preceding the first tentative settlement and rank-and-file opposition to it, reports began to circulate about fuel supply shortages at utilities. Stories about looming power shortages, extensive layoffs, and economic catastrophe took center stage in the days following rejection of that proposal. On CBS, these included interviews with utility officials who testify to "dwindling stockpiles," or with businessmen and mayors who predict grave unemployment problems. The President of Crane Plastics Company, interviewed on February 7, warned: "The plug will . . . be pulled on all business, all commerce, all industry and everyone will go into unemployment. And that's just three weeks away." William Sorrells, Indiana Energy Director, says on February 10: "We definitely have a very urgent, serious crisis situation." On February 17, Indiana Governor Otis Bowen reportedly said that unless the strike was settled in 7–10 days, Indiana would be "in a state of chaos."

These stories contained a kernel of truth. Some power users were voluntarily conserving power, and Ohio and Indiana were considering, or in the process of imposing, mandatory cutbacks.[28] After a month of regularly circulating press reports about fuel shortages, a February 27

---

[28]In Indiana, the Indiana Public Service Commission on February 13 ordered cutbacks for some industrial users where utilities stockpiles fell below a 40-day supply. In Ohio, utilities scrambled to purchase coal and electrical power from other utilities to avoid triggering a mandatory 50 percent curtailment if supplies dipped below 30 days. West Virginia, Virginia, and Maryland imposed a 10 percent cutback on Potomac Edison on February 22, and expanded this to 30 percent on Mar 2 for both Potomac Edison and Mon Power (both units of the Allegheny Power System) (*WSJ*, 2/23/78; Dodosh, 3/3/78).

Wall Street Journal article questioned the accuracy of coal stockpile figures. Gay Sands Miller cited charges against Duquesne Light Co. of fostering a "crisis atmosphere" to heighten political pressure for a settlement. She reported that Federal officials were reevaluating their own stockpile estimates, because "utilities are giving us different numbers than they give the States." Stockpiles lasted longer as coal use was cut because energy was being conserved, and utilities were shifting to noncoal sources. But utility industry stockpile estimates did not reflect either the switch to different fuel sources or the slower rate of dwindling. In addition, "deliveries of coal to utilities and factories were steadily increasing—not decreasing—as early as mid-February" and the volume of coal received by utilities rose slightly until the strike's end (Fineman, 11/6/78; Perry, 1984). Were energy utility officials disinterested spectators to this story? Why treat them as reliable technocratic sources of information rather than as politicking participants with a big stake in the outcome? Recalling the strike, George Getschow, a *Wall Street Journal* reporter, stated:

> The White House wanted the media to play up that false image, that a national emergency was imminent, and the press accepted their statements because of our tendency to seek out the sensational in a story. (cited in Seltzer, 1985)

On March 5, when rank and file rejection of a second contract proposal seemed certain, Energy Secretary James Schlesinger dramatically announced:

> In the near term, sometime toward the end of this month, we may be looking at as much as a . . . million people unemployed in the affected region of the Middle West. If the strike were to continue into the later part of April, we would be facing up to 3.5 million people unemployed because of the direct effects of the lack of power in the area, and that would have ripple effects throughout the country.

These "disaster" forecasts pronounced by Schlesinger were taken from a computer forecasting study using "best" case and "worst" case assumptions. The Energy Secretary selected the 3.5 million figure from the extreme "worst case" without identifying it as such (Seltzer, 1978). A GAO Congressional study released in December 1978 found the Carter administration "didn't present a fair assessment of the situation to the public," disseminating misleading information on both unemployment and supply figures (Fineman, 11/16/78).

The Bureau of Labor Statistics conducted weekly surveys during the

strike on the labor stoppage's economic impact. Their findings announced on February 25 ascertained the coal strike had relatively little
impact on employment and hours worked in other industries. Even at a
peak of 25,000 unemployed (from February 26–March 4), layoffs
amounted to a small proportion of 7.8 million factory workers in 11
strike-affected states (Ackermann, 1979; U.S. Dept of Labor, 1978).
Projected layoffs and reduction in hours were successively lowered in
each of the next five weeks (Monthly Labor Review, February 1979).
Another possible indicator of the severity of coal shortages was the spot
price of coal (which firmed slightly in late Feburary and early March,
suggesting utilities were buying some coal). The commercial mass media
missed these indices.

President Carter invoked executive privilege to keep secret a study by
the Presidential Council of Economic Advisors, which "assured the
President that no coal emergency existed" (*Newsweek*, 11/20/78). Meanwhile, under political pressure from Governors and utility directors,
Carter continued to assert the existence of a critical power shortage.
These exaggerations inflated local emergencies into the idea of a crisis,
which then assumed its own existence. "Drastic steps" did indeed have
to be taken, to quiet the numerous critics of 'White House'/Carter
ineptness in the face of a "national emergency." The Administration
sought a Taft-Hartley injunction on the basis of what it knew to be an
exaggerated case, and *CBS News*, like most of the national news media,
uncritically accepted President Carter's call for Taft-Hartley. Once
Schlesinger issued doomsday warnings publicly, there was pressure to
continue to portray the strike in the worst terms—in part to maintain
pressure for the two sides to negotiate (*Washington Post*, 4/1/78). The
fears which had been circulated now required appeasement.

Projection of a crisis did not occur apart from the media. It existed as
a media representation for most people, a phenomenon perceptible
through, and structured by the media. Uncritical acceptance of "reliable
sources," the lack of investigative reporting, and the newsworthiness of
a "crisis" itself combined to lead CBS to *find* crises. All CBS reports
detailing effects of a coal shortage looked exclusively at Indiana and
Ohio. Network television news portrayed the exception as the rule, and
elevated the East Central region's energy problem into a national one.

INVOKING TAFT-HARTLEY

Miner hostility to the second contract proposal focused on the same
issues that were problematic in the first proposal: penalty clauses;
pension benefits inequity; medical deductibles (UPI, 2/28/78). At local

1588 not one miner out of 223 attending a meeting on the contract had a single positive word for the contract (Poling, 3/3/78). The union's public relations agency devised an advertising campaign to push the contract, but it "alienated more votes than it got because miners thought if it had to be sold it wasn't any good" (Hughey, 3/6/78).

The Carter Administration considered the forms of intervention allowed by law: Federal seizure of the mines; a Taft-Hartley "back to work" court order; or both measures together. To openly prefer either resolution would be partisan, so CBS reported about unnamed "Administration sources" who disclosed the White House was "weighing the alternatives."[29]

Another political consideration Carter faced was the impact of a contract settlement on inflation. The Council on Wage and Price Stability and the Council of Economic Advisors called the contract inflationary in its effect on coal and electric prices. The media itself exhibited an inflated concern with the size of the wage package, and echoed questions about the Carter administration's resolve to enforce restraints (NYT, 3/5/78). Reports about "hefty" wage increases coupled with projections about subsequent hikes in the price of electricity to consumers continued to erode popular support for the miners (Maggard, 1983/84).

Once miners turned down the second proposal, there was little doubt what choice Carter would make. Public impatience with the miners justified choosing Taft-Hartley. Carter acted less in response to the strike's economic impact than to its potentially adverse political effects on his public image as a decisive leader. Federal seizure was ruled out, pragmatically, because of Congressional resistance to it (NYT, 3/7/78). Schlesinger's dire predictions of a national crisis, paved the way, the following day, for President Carter to declare a national emergency, invoke the Taft-Hartley Act, and move for a court-ordered that would order miners back to the mines for an 80 day "cooling-off" period.

A *New York Times* article said, "By selecting Taft-Hartley, the Administration was signalling that it regarded the miners as most to blame for the impasse" (3/12/78). Without examining Carter's justification for applying Taft-Hartley, the CBS focus turned principally to the miners' response—or rather, defiance—of it. In the explanatory vac-

---

[29]Carter's advisors did differ in opinion: Robert Strauss and James Schlesinger advocated a back-to-work injunction, while Secretary of Labor Marshall initially opposed such a move, and Stuart Eizenstadt pushed both Taft-Hartley and seizure. It should be noted however, that no President has come close to seizing capital since the Supreme Court overruled President Truman's seizure order against the major steel companies in 1952.

uum, the decision to *order* workers to return to work passed unaccounted for, and figures in the reports mainly for its consequences—would miner's "obey the law" or not?

Presidents had invoked the Taft-Hartley Act before (Truman used it three times between 1948 and 1950) only to have miners defy it. This time, striking miners' disregard of a temporary restraining order was widespread. So completely did miners ignore it that union pickets did not even show up at idle mines (Robbins, 3/14/78; Claiborne, 3/14/78). The BCOA said that only 60 to 100 miners out of the 160,000 employed by BCOA member companies showed up for work on March 13 (Franklin, 3/14/78). Despite the build-up in mass media—CBS concentrated on the fear of miner violence against miners who obeyed the law—reports of anticipated violence (an example of manufacturing future news), there was little violent confrontation between strikers and 'scabs,' or between strikers and Federal marshalls. In spite of Federal threats to withhold food stamps to miners who disobeyed the back-to-work order, strikers disregarded Taft-Hartley. More than fear of intimidation kept miners from going back to work; rank-and-file solidarity and determination to win a "fair" contract remained strong.

BCOA members were uneasy about the use of Taft-Hartley, concerned that

> the injunction would fail, which would push Carter toward seizure and perhaps a contract like the one in 1947 that gave miners a fair deal. Political considerations—not economic ones—might force Carter to federalize the mines. This prospect was worse than settling the strike with the union's rank and file. (Seltzer, 1985, p. 162)

Within days a third contract proposal emerged. On March 15 a third tentative contract agreement was announced, which the Bargaining Council approved by a narrow margin of 22 to 17 (Dewar, 3/16/78).

On March 17, after the third contract proposal had been sent to the rank and file for ratification, Cronkite soberly announced:

> Evidence is increasing that the severe economic disruption expected from coal shortages was exaggerated. Besides conserving power, utilities have bought some from other power companies, obtained more non-UMW coal, and lately been helped by mild weather. And last week the number of factory layoffs due to the coal strike actually declined. Today, federal Judge Aubrey Robinson, saying no national emergency has been proven, refused to extend last week's temporary Taft-Hartley order against the miners.

Here was proof the public had been misled. Yet, the report's casual nature, which came toward the middle of the evening's broadcast, belied its own importance. Like most of CBS reporting, this statement is most revealing where it is silent. Oddly, there is no mention of President Carter who sought the injunction; neither did Cronkite include mention of CBS's—in fact, of all the broadcast news media—own culpability in circulating, and thereby ratifying, such reports.

As the impasse stretched on, other labor unions began to step forward with material support for the miners. On March 7, the UAW donated two million dollars in strike relief, and the United Steelworkers and the Communications Workers of America each pledged more than a million dollars to aid the financial ly strapped UMW (UPI, 3/9/78; UPI, 3/23/78). Striking farmers also showed solidarity with the miners (Mason, 3/19/78). Following these pledges, there was some dispute as to whether the UMW hierarchy was withholding these relief funds from miners in order to "force" miners into accepting the contract proposal (UPI, 3/23/78).

Pact ratification remained uncertain during the following week. Miners vocally criticized the health care, pension, and production incentive provisions in the proposal, insisting that these still went "backwards." Pensioners and widows "vowed to picket mines" if the proposal was ratified (Spencer, 3/15/78, p. 1; Green, 3/19/78, p. 1B). Arguments against and for the proposal circulated during the next week, but many more miners simply seemed resigned to it (Robbins, 3/21/78; Clarity, 3/20/78, p. D10). As one miner put it, "nobody likes it but everybody done got hungry" (Hughey, 3/21/78). On March 25, with final returns from rank-and-file voters in, the vote was 58,802 to 44,457 to accept the latest contract (Franklin, 3/25/78). Disheartened by sometimes hostile and incompetent leadership, strained by nearly four months without pay or strike benefits, the miners gave up. Local union officers reported that many miners were not only hungry, but also faced imminent loss of their mobile homes. No doubt the news that there was no energy crisis to give them bargaining leverage also influenced their decision.

The new agreement granted a 6 percent increase in fringe benefits and a 31 percent increase in wages over the life of the contract. Miners had sought provisions that would have gone the other way: Benefits were mostly tax-free and not liable to inflation, while the wage increase moved them to a higher tax bracket and eroded real pay increases. Lost from the 1974 contract was the COLA pegged to the inflation rate (Simon, 1983).[30] The Council on Wage and Price Stability estimated the 38 percent overall increase in miners' income amounted to .08 percent on the overall price index over the three year contract (Seltzer, 1978, p. 21). "When inflation, taxes, and medical deductibles were

---

[30]The contract got rid of the inflation escalator in the first year, and put a $0.30 inflation cap on the second and third years (Seltzer, 1985, p. 163).

counted, real income might rise 5 percent to 9 percent if markets firmed up enough to provide full-time employment" (Seltzer, 1985, p. 163). Health and insurance pensions would no longer be administered by independent trustees, but by private insurance carriers.

The 1978 contract was not an unmitigated loss to the UMWA, but the BCOA won dissolution of the medical care scheme and the pension fund; the right to introduce production incentive plans; the right to discipline mine safety committees. Though the "labor stability" clause fining wildcat strikers was dropped, operators gained power to discipline wildcat strikers under an arbitration ruling, which was appended to the contract. The Arbitration Review Board, in an October 1977 memorandum ('ARB 108'), upheld a coal company's right to discharge miners for setting up unauthorized pickets (ARB, October 1977).

Rank-and-file determination did block the BCOA's demands for penalty clauses fining wildcat strikers. Their determination also produced a better contract than they would have gotten in December: more pay, lower "deductibles" for health insurance (down from $700 to $200 a year); the number of annual hours worked necessary to qualify for pensions reduced from 1,450 to 1,000; miners gained eye care coverage; and pre-1976 retirees would receive a $25/month hike in the first year, instead of over three years.

The television news media ignored most of these details, though CBS did finally list some of the key provisions of a contract proposal on March 14. And, despite professing concern about the consequences of events, neither CBS nor the other networks displayed an interest in the contract's consquences on miners and their welfare—for example, how would production incentive bonuses impact health and safety?[31]

Are such details ever part of a television news story? Does network television news report in this detail on any subject other than "The Presidency" and, sometimes, NASA? So why make a big deal out of it? The primary reason such detail is never offered is that television news is

---

[31]"Some plans would be linked to fixed goals, allowing a certain number of disabling injuries before the bonus was threatened. The pressure on miners and management to set a high cutoff number was evident. The numbers game also creates incentives for both sides not to report injuries. Even more ominous were the health implications of the bonus plans. No penalties were triggered if dust levels increased. Because health impacts are hard to measure on a day-to-day basis, they are not considered at all . . . Miners will be encouraged—and will encourage each other—to mine without proper ventilation and water sprays. Twenty years from the day they pocket a couple of extra fifties, they'll get their real bonus in the form of . . . pneumoconiosis, bronchitis, and emphysema" (Seltzer, 1985, p. 164).

a commodity constructed under the rules of commodity logic and market conditions. The question for us is not simply "how much and what can be omitted and still produce an accurate and fair news account?" We must also ask "how is it consequential that such details are rarely, if ever, part of television news stories?" CBS coverage of the coal strike was hardly unique in its method of abstracting from the details of the historical process. This kind of reporting fosters confusion and a loss of social memory—particularly an accelerating public amnesia about the importance of production relations.

The 1977–78 coal strike was one of the first major *takeaway* strikes in the United States, management seeking to recoup social wage concessions made over years of collective bargaining (Green, 1978). What management called labor instability was from miners' view "pressure for equity" (Seltzer, 1985, p. 150). This fundamental historical contradiction was not, however, spoken on television.

4

Reading Social Texts/
Mapping Ideology

What does it mean to map the ideological paths of hegemonic encodings? Let's begin by walking through one report. On December 5, 1977 Walter Cronkite delivered the news of the imminent UMWA strike call. Cronkite's "heightened 'news voice'" (Morse, 1986, p. 62) and intonation gave drama to the terse declarative statement before shifting to passive voice:

> At midnight tonight the contract covering one hundred and thirty thousand miners at eighteen hundred mines will expire and the work will stop. As it happens, a major reason miners are walking out is that coal companies would not agree to build a right to strike over local issues into the next contract. More on the story from Barry Serafin in West Virginia.

Both sentences reach the same linguistic result: Actors and outcomes are separated from one another as the actors disappear and their actions turn into things. Television news discourse follows this path of parsimony, turning a world of verb relations into a world of nouns. "The noun is a contraction of a significant kind" (Kress & Hodge, 1979, pp. 21-27) that partially deletes the actors and their relations. Subjects and predicates exchange places so that interactions appear to take place between frozen objects: "the contract . . . will expire and the work will stop."

Cronkite turned to passive construction to preface his explanatory account of the strike. "As it happens" suggests an authorless accident, an occurrence by chance. Rhetorically, however, it marks what follows as an ordered sequence. Where active verbs traced the actions of abstract objects in the first sentence, the second sentence located two collective actors within a mechanically fixed framework. But these actors are not named with equal clarity or force. The action appeared to stem from the initiative taken by the miners. The more abstract "coal companies" stand in the background and respond negatively, defensively, to the miners' demand.

Should we interpret Cronkite as describing a chance sequence or a causal chain of events and actions? " . . . A major reason miners are walking out is that coal companies would not agree to build a right to strike over local issues into the next contract." Were miners demanding a new privilege? "Coal companies would not agree to [it]," suggests they were, though the concluding words, " . . . into the next contract," leave it ambiguous. Did this right previously exist?

During the 1970s when public trust in government, business and unions had sunk to record lows, Walter Cronkite regularly topped the popular opinion polls of "who do you trust?" Cronkite's familiar vocal cadence and timbre, evening after evening, year after year, became firmly associated in popular consciousness as the 'newsman'—sturdy, patriotic, fair, knowledgeable and honest. As usual, Cronkite read the words he spoke.[1]

The subject matter was squeezed into a standardized news format designed to balance requirements of brevity, accuracy, and impartiality. "Though TV news narrative affects an oral style, it is written—and it is usually far pithier, more clearly structured, and more conclusively stated than in true conversational style" (Morse, 1986, p. 62). Though each concise unit of information in Cronkite's utterance, taken in isolation, satisfies in a minimalist way the truth-claims criteria of narrative neutrality,[2] simple ideology critique demands a comparison of this version with a fuller historical record.

This exercise in abbreviated objectivity glossed the negotiating positions of the aggrieved parties in a way which probably generated many forms of misunderstanding. At the very least, CBS's version demanded

---

[1]Morse (1986) analyzed the "reading behavior" of television news anchors, sampling newscasts from all the networks for 1968, 1974, and 1979. She uncovered a fascinating shift. "In 1968, newscasters were accomplished at glancing up to look at the lens while reading from notes on the desk. By 1974, glancing down at the desk was used primarily to make or emphasize a point . . . the newscaster was pretending to read notes when he was primarily using cues or a teleprompter."

[2]If we break down the sentence into a set of pared-down truth claims, it looks something like this: (a) "a major reason"—yes, it was; (b) "miners are walking out"—yes, they were; and (c) "is that coal companies would not agree to build"—correct, they would not.

that viewers *attribute* motives and agenda to both the union and the coal companies. Judging by the information *not* in this report (or in previous reports), this attribution process depended on the prior ideological dispositions held by audience members. Because the "right-to-strike" demand was not explained, the full weight of interpretation fell on its ideological sound or flavor. To save ourselves a lot of repetition, because this occurred in report after report, we emphasize that CBS *never* explained, defined, or illustrated the meaning of "a right-to-strike over local issues."

The coal strike was *not* a chance event, but rather had the weight of class history and political-economic interests and relations behind it. Now, look at the glaring absence concerning the coal operators' unprecedented demands for "labor stability" penalties against wildcat strikers. Remember, BCOA hardliners' negotiating strategy was to wait for the UMWA to capitulate. They had stockpiled immense amounts of product, and markets had been weak. Market prices might actually firm up, they reasoned, while they used their market advantage to insist on concessions from the unionized workers, including a restructuring of health care benefits. They saw the strike as a means of exhausting the union's resources and breaking its spirit. A focal point in the dispute, alluded to by Cronkite, was the widespread recurrence of wildcat strikes in the coal industry. Miners' insistence on, and operators' resistance to, stricter enforcement of health and safety matters spilled over into the structure and politics of the grievance and arbitration system used in the coal industry. Operators wanted to solve the wildcats with "labor stability" penalties, while the 1976 UMWA convent ion had endorsed a "right-to-strike" procedure based on voting by union locals.

The singular meaning conveyed by Cronkite, however, was that the *miners have gone on strike*. Everything else was interpretively negotiable to the viewer sitting at home. Cronkite's statement the next evening likewise emphasized this closure in a serious, somber tone weighted with regret at the occurrence: "The United Mine Workers, as they promised, have gone on strike". In each CBS announcement, what had been the coal operators' initiative appeared otherwise; each text was weighted to imply it was the miners' initiative.[3]

Reinforcing this narrative weighting, pictures of miners dotted the screen, while no coal operators appeared on camera. The operators' presence in the story was confined entirely to the abstract reference to "coal companies."

---

[3]Again, on December 6, the BCOA are accorded a veiled presence, " . . . and the negotiating parties far apart." But they are not named.

THE FRAMEBOX

As Cronkite spoke, situated next to him on the screen was a familiar hanging box containing an image coded to represent the news item. These seemingly innocent framing boxes are the result of considerable encoding labor and ideological activity and function as social site for the construction of *a news-sign*. The frame named the news story—"the coal strike." It created a visual shorthand marker—a tagline—for referencing a continuing story. The framebox's structure and location on the screen in relation to Cronkite's delivery is governed by several simple interpretive rules for joining together the verbal narrative with a visual summary image that takes the form of a sign. When viewers familiar with television news see the framebox present behind and beside the anchor's head, they recognize it as a message identifying what the story is about—its subject. Because we are so accustomed to seeing this format, we tend to bracket the rules governing its interpretation, and we forget or take for granted the ideological project in which we have participated. Recognition of the format itself permits the viewer to unproblematically read the boxed contents *as a sign* signifying the story "coal strike."[4]

On this occasion, the image inside the frame was an artist's sketch of a male head and shoulders wearing a miners' helmet in front of a filled coal trolley. CBS selected simple, stereotypical images to signal the meaning of "coal strike." Another framed logo, used nearly as often throughout CBS's strike coverage, consisted of a pickaxe on its side adjacent an internal frame bearing the words "COAL STRIKE." And as the strike wore on, the graphic representation of the miner wearing a helmet in front of the coal trolley became condensed still further to just a miner's helmet situated above the words "Coal Strike."

Even in their visual abbreviations, CBS cut out any other partners to the conflict. Minimally, the image consists of a miner (producer) and a coal trolley (product) spatially arranged in a foreground (miner and helmet) to background (coal trolley) relation to symbolize the coal strike. This constructed sign, along with Cronkite's reference to miners' right-to-strike demand and deletion of coal operators' labor stability demand, reinforced the appearance that the miners' union was responsible for this lapse in production.

Because the right-to-strike issue remained unclarified, its meaning hinged on how those words resonated with each listener. To those who perceived strikes as labor-instigated and disruptive, Labor's demand for a right-to-strike may have seemed an abuse piled on an abuse. However,

---

[4]We shall return to the operation of the framebox in Chapter 6.

the phrase "right-to-strike" might have resonated positively with sentiments held by prounion sympathizers, for whom it may have connoted
a necessary freedom. The network sought to present a class-neutral
message, but its televisual encodings still had to be interpreted by
audience members living in a class society where oppositional class
interests keep alive the possibility of contradictory decodings.

PICTURING THE STRIKE

Following network news conventions, Cronkite passed viewers to a
reporter in the field for "more on the story". How did the correspondent develop Cronkite's introductory frame? The scaffolding which
framed this report is the familiar, professional model designed to
efficiently promote the impression of narrative neutrality—balance and
fairness—and objectivity (cf. Epstein, 1974). The schematic framework
looked like this:

1. Reporter introduction
2. Statement of the news item
3. Background context
4. Interviews with miners
5. Interviews with mine operators
6. Interview with Arnold Miller
7. Reporter conclusion

Just as on November 28, Barry Serafin's report started with the
identical aerial visual of a coalmine. Serafin began with a voiceover
introduction: "In anticipation of the strike, scattered walkouts have
already begun." The aerial photography and the helicopter soundtrack
lent a feeling of drama and immediacy, though the report's on-the-spot
appearance may have been contrived.[5] Why use this aerial shot to open

---

[5]Serafin's voice was "supered" over already recorded sounds and images. The
aerial photograph of a coalmine visually locates the story as it did in the
November 28 broadcast when Serafin reported from "Logan County, West
Virginia"; this time he concluded the report from "near Charleston, West
Virginia." Why blur the referent of this scene? Normally, we would say the
shot's reuse indicates a reliance on stationing reporters and photographers in
centralized locations to facilitate access to dispersed geographical areas—"news
nets" (Tuchman, 1978, pp. 21-23). So too, the aerial photography is costly and
recurring referential demands make it inefficient not to reuse footage. In this

both stories? Aerial photography has, itself, become connected with disaster stories—a flood, devastation wrought by tornado, a riot. The aerial photo has become part of the rhetoric and grammar of "bad news" on television news. The aerial touch also deftly self-legitimates *CBS News* by indicating them as going to great lengths to get the story to you. In both reports the aerial photography was used to set the scene—this is "coal country". The picture simply illustrated the words: The aerial photos introduced both reports because of their metaphorical and connotative flexibility, and not for any positivist purposes of identifying an immediate, recordable "fact."

Serafin's report did not pursue Cronkite's "explanatory" cue and elaborate on why "the miners are walking out", or discuss the coal companies' refusal to the right-to-strike clause. Instead, he began by emphasizing the facticity of the "walkout" ("28 mines were reported shut down") and "40 percent absenteeism at this West Virginia coal mine" as viewers see eight miners filing out through a doorway in their work gear. From here, the report turns to the official strike declaration, the news item:

> Serafin: Bargainers for the Soft Coal Industry and the United Mine Workers met today in Washington with Federal mediators. At midday, Union president Arnold Miller declared a strike could not be averted.

> cut to Miller news conference clip: I believe the operators response today indicates there's been no change in their position since October 6th. And come 12 o'clock tonight the contract will expire, and no contract, no work.

Serafin then set up his version of a contextual analysis. A brief "historical" sequence assembled out of file footage (see Chapter 5) recalled that mineworkers' strikes have created crises before "but the Labor Department says this strike will present no national emergency." The present strike presents no cause for public concern since utilities and industries have been "stockpiling mountains of coal," and half the

---

instance, however, the aerial photograph is not included for simple descriptive purposes, but rather for overarching metaphoric purposes—"here's coal country." Hence, there is no real blurring of referents.

Reuse of photographic scenes in multiple reports recurred in CBS's strike coverage. These shots usually had little to do with the narrative of the reports, but were included as scene-setting "wallpaper." Only one instance of recycling an image deviated from this agenda, when on March 1, Rabel reused a scene (miners burning copies of a contract proposal) for narrative purposes.

nation's coal comes from nonunion western mines. The camera lingers over enormous heaps of coal, testifying to an abundance of supplies. The narrative movement from coal strikes' historic disruptiveness to the emphasis on stockpiles offers reassurance to consumers in the face of an acknowledged threat.

Serafin followed his discussion of coal stockpiling with a summary of problems confronting the UMW in this strike.

> Non-union coal and big stockpiles are not the UMW's only problems in staging a strike. The union has been plagued by wildcat strikes and internal dissension in recent years. It does not have enough money to provide strike benefits to its members; or health benefits, or even death benefits. And pension checks are expected to stop soon.

The UMW had indeed "been plagued by wildcat strikes and internal dissension." And yet, this text carries, nearly to the point of absurdity, the pattern of displacing and masking the role of coal operators and their agenda. If nothing else, the party that *felt* "plagued" (afflicted and cursed) by wildcat strikes was the BCOA, who responded by asking for a "labor stability" clause in the contract.

SYNCHRONIZING PICTURES AND WORDS

> In the relation between a photograph and words, the photograph begs for an interpretation, and the words usually supply it. The photograph, irrefutable as evidence but weak in meaning, is given a meaning by the words. And the words, which by themselves remain at the level of generalization are given specific authenticity by the irrefutability of the photograph. (Berger & Mohr, 1982, p. 92)

Let's backtrack for a moment and cover the same ground again. Thus far the report contained 20 visual scenes edited together to correspond with the verbal text. Each image has been sequenced on screen to visually identify and amplify what is being said. For example, keyed to Serafin's discourse about stockpiles were nine edited videotape scenes. When Serafin said "railroads which carry coal . . ." the screen showed train cars brimming with coal; "communities in coal states . . ." corresponded to an aerial shot of a small city along a river; and "mountains of coal . . ." showed a panoramic shot of surplus coal adjacent an industrial complex. The sites pictured—nearly identical to the pictorial frames used in the previous report by Martha Tichenor—are not plainly indicated. Each image has been abstracted from its context, and reassembled to match a spoken narrative.

Newstape is a ubiquitous form of "public" photography: the "public photograph . . . is torn from its context, and becomes a dead object which, exactly because it is dead, lends itself to any arbitrary use" (Berger, 1980, p. 56). Every picture "isolates the appearance of a disconnected instant," and this removal from context produces ambiguity (Berger & Mohr, 1982, p. 91). This is intrinsic to the project of photography—television news cannot recreate the context, so an attempt is made to minimize the "natural ambiguity of the photographic image" by giving the isolated pictorial moment a new context in television news formats. All this restates the obvious, for even its practitioners call television news the act of "narrating pictures." But it can never be an innocent act, since reframing images taken from a life-world invariably involves a process of selection. When selected, edited, sequenced, and narrated, public photos acquire an ideological character.

> By appearing literally to reproduce the event as it *really* happened news photos suppress their selective/interpretive/ideological function. They seek a warrant in that ever pre-given, neutral structure, which is beyond question, beyond interpretation: the "real world." (Hall, 1972, p. 188)

Though the kind of film footage contained in this report is often referred to as "actuality clips," these photos may also subjectivize reality because they depend on viewers' capacity for recognition and interpretation. How much opportunity for subjectivized readings "creeps" in depends, in part, on how tight the narrative reframing is.

Television news is widely regarded by consumers as more credible than other news media because videotape/film apparently captures "reality." What people usually mean by this is that documentary photography apparently records the "instantaneous" and the "immediate." The CBS pictures confirm, however, that video/film achieves its significance by the commentary that accompanies and explains it—the appearance of immediacy is itself the product of mediation. Barthes (1972) spoke of the "having-been-there" quality of photography as a crucial element in the realist and naturalist style that news reports cultivate. As this example indicates, the mere act of filming was not sufficient to achieve this; rather, artifice was required for news reports to appear "natural." Whether or not television news better grasps a reality "out there" is questionable, but the popular perception that it does cannot readily be dismissed. Networks actively cultivate this positivist ideology of photography in their ads.[6]

They sell themselves as objectively mirroring reality, to help "keep you informed about your world." This is the premise of their own legitimacy, and, their own economic well-being.

THE CHANNELING OF VOICES

Each interviewee represents another speaker than the reporter, with another potential point of view. Reporters and editors may clip and cut "soundbites" according to their own framing agendas, but an interviewee's expressive aura can never be fully reframed or controlled. The social and cultural character of miners pokes through in interviews where viewers confront the visually expressive images of miners themselves.

Serafin's discourse about the UMW's problems led-in to three selected miner interview clips. The screen abruptly gave way to an extreme closeup of an old man nominated as "Clue Richards." Interviewed through his car window, this retired miner epitomizes "mountaineer" crustiness. His accent and speech use are those of rural Appalachia. Gumming his words, he opined "the union's in bad shape. They'll take what they give em. When the deal goes down, wait'n'see, they'll take what they give em." Richards' comments offer an outspoken, colorful phrasing of the union's unhappy position.

Serafin pursued the issue of financial vulnerability with younger working miners. Visually, viewers see successive photographic closeups of miners. Chosen for their iconic resemblance, these black-and-white shots compose symbolic portraits. Each man wears a miner's helmet with lamp and decals on the hardhat. Their faces tell us they have just come from working in the mines. Covered with beard or grizzly beard growth, along with the dust, sweat, and grime of working, their faces also mark these men as "working class"—as "laboring men." The photos' texture capture and isolate a simple, quiet workingman's dignity much as the photos

---

[6]"Positivism and the camera and sociology grew up together. What sustained them all as practices was the belief that observable quantifiable facts, recorded by scientists and experts, would one day offer man such a total knowledge about nature and society that he would be able to order them both. Precision would replace metaphysics, planning would resolve social conflicts, truth would replace subjectivity . . ." (Berger & Mohr, 1982, p. 99)

of Walker Evans or Dorothea Lange. Serafin narrates, "Despite their financial problems, however, most miners are ready to support the strike, even if it means doing without at Christmas." Serafin's words emphasize the miners' determination in the face of adversity, along with their unity and loyalty to the union albeit a stubborn and, perhaps foolhardy, stand. As he finishes, the film cuts to a closeup of a miner nominated as "Billy Witherow." Serafin apparently asked whether the strike would put a damper on Christmas festivities. CBS reporters consider "doing without at Christmas" a penultimate sacrifice. Their fixation on Christmas is not unimportant. Metaphorically, the opposition between a festive and plentiful Christmas and a Christmas marked by privation is a "grabber." It provides a shiny consumer index for viewers to grasp the determin ation of the miners, while also assuring a news angle of 'pathos' by inserting a human interest angle that newspeople judge to be more watchable than strike negotiations.

Witherow responds, "There's other Christmases in other years, and that's what we've got to look forward to." Though Witherow speaks with the same West Virginia accent as the others, he is quietly articulate: "I've got to work a long time yet. My son's got to work. I gotta look forward to that rather than just to the present time." He is followed by "Johnny Mitchell, Coal Miner" (a black miner) who also affirms the miners' solidarity: "The union been broke this long, so I guess we'll just have to scuffle it out as best we can." Suddenly, for a brief moment, the light of rationality shines on the miners' actions, as Witherow injects an altogether different time frame in which to assess the miners' action and its meaning. With Billy Witherow, the relentless insistence of newscasters on immediacy without context is momentarily abandoned, and for an instant viewers see a miner who is aware of the trouble he undertakes, but who has weighed the possible consequences and judged it worth the risk. Newscasters' terms of reference, though, rarely accomodate this view. Witherow's remarks are on a trajectory that escape the framework of the story: In fact, they are part of a different story.

CBS portrayed the strike as an intentional action ("the miners are walking out"), but neither Serafin nor Cronkite probed their intentionality. CBS instead objectified the miners as cause for concern, alienating miners from both their own motivation and agency. The unfortunate miners face an austere Christmas, can expect little help from their union in terms of strike benefits, and hold a poor bargaining position against the mine operators. Nonetheless, they are going to strike: their attitude of stubbornness may be read as an implicit conclusion to the story told here. How much this portrayal is reinforced by pervasive media stereotypes of backward and obstinate "hillbillies" is uncertain, but it seems reasonable to suggest the story told here may itself be influenced by these myths.

NO SPOKESMAN WAS AVAILABLE

No viewer could have known at the time the significance of the ensuing sequence. The screen cut from the closeup shot of the black miner to a shot composed outside a mine with background scaffolding along a hillside. On a road leading away from the hillside, and toward us, several miners carry their gear. This visual covers Serafin's voiceover as he resumes his narration: "A spokesman for the mine operators was not available." As it turned out, this statement captured the critical element in the BCOA's media strategy, and subverted the network's formula for narrative neutrality. Until now in the report, CBS personnel carefully keyed each visual signifier to the narrated referents. *Only* this scene deviates from this matching process.[7] While Serafin makes the perfunctory statement about BCOA inaccessibility, the screen again pictures miners, not operators, walking away from a mine.

Serafin then turned to an interview with UMW president Arnold Miller prepared "a few days ago." Serafin frames the gist of Miller's statement, "that the operators have miscalculated if they have counted on the union's problems for leverage in the dispute." Miller's interview clip again contains fragments of information that could give a different twist to the story.

> Miller: What they're doin' is telling the membership of this union that "you're gonna take what we wanna give you, or else"—the or else isn't a very good alternative. But the membership will stand firm. I think they'll strike long as they have to.

Miller deplores the operators' uncompromising attitude, and expresses his resolve not to give into them. This offers viewers a different side of the story: Miller claims industry management refuses to cooperate. But what is it that operators are trying to shove down the union's throat, according to Miller? Serafin does not inquire about this matter—perhaps because he considers it a private dispute, and of little concern to the public. Audiences, according to this view, would only want to know how ongoing events affect them: Hence, this constant play of fears raised, only to be immediately appeased. Of all the interesting and revealing questions Serafin might have asked Miller, the only one he asks has to do with the anticipated duration of the strike, attempting, perhaps, to reflect his audience's concerns.

---

[7]Did CBS not even have a piece of file footage they could use to denotatively identify the mine operators?

THE MEDIA POLITICS OF DISCURSIVE SPACE

Serafin's conclusion did not take up the ideas expressed by the miner interview clips, but repeated an idea present in his earlier remarks: "For now, those who face the bleakest prospects because of the strike are the miners themselves." Here, Serafin attempted a present-tense closure of meaning, an effort to limit and redirect the possible interpretations in a particular way—that is, the strike is an unfortunate occurrence—perhaps the result of stubbornness on both sides, but, at any rate, not yet fully amenable to understanding—which will put the miners themselves in dire fiscal straits. In adherence with professional norms, the correspondent has reported the news item, *attempted* to counterpose opposing viewpoints, and then offered a conclusion which transcends the partisan positions—Barthes calls this approach "Neither-Norism."

This report conveyed a sense of concern for the welfare of miners. Yet, in spite of the sympathetic portraits, the report reproduced a familiar ideological framework regarding the relationship between laborers and industrialists. Though opportunities arose for discussing the BCOA and their role in the strike, those openings were passed by. And there is no historical context—no mention at all of the previous three years of constant conflict between companies and the union over safety in the mines and work assignments.

We've just witnessed how ideology *happens* in network news. Their polite treatment of miners as workers aside, CBS abstracted them out of their relationship to the coal owners, and then denied the workers the opportunity to define their own discursive argument—that is, to state their view of their relationship to their employers, and thus to explain what motivates them to act. Meanwhile, the coal operators deliberately chose to forego their opportunities at discursive agenda setting on national television.

> By network news standards "discursive speech" means that the speaker has between half a minute to just over a minute to express ideas in his voice rather than the correspondent's. Such time allows for one or two ideas to be expressed concerning the issues or events at hand, and for these ideas to receive some amplification and sense of context. Discursive speech is adult speech and only discursive speech is serious speech. It appears rational no matter what is actually said. (Gibson, 1980, p. 97)

In this vacuum, CBS imposed its own model of discursive logic which we call the "liberal newscode of narrative neutrality." The encoding practices which accompany this model are generated by treating news as a commodity. Narrative neutrality was accomplished by cutting out *class discourse* as such. There was far less chance of offending anybody by leaving the core conflicts unspoken. Paradoxically, the model does grave violence to the liberal ideal of a marketplace of ideas: The effort to preserve neutrality among competing class interests results in an emptying out of class discourses from our television-mediated discursive space. Equally ominous is the closure of public debate about production relations.

5

CBS's "Natural History" of the Coal Strike

A DESCRIPTIVE SUMMARY OF NARRATIVE CURVES AND FRAMES

CBS News broadcast 62 separate reports on the coal strike between November 25, 1977 and March 30, 1978. These reports ranged in length from 10 seconds to 8 minutes and 40 seconds. Overall, CBS spent 182 minutes and 50 seconds of broadcast time on the coal strike. This represented a substantial coverage commitment to a single strike, especially when compared to other coverage of Labor issues, almost nil during the same calendar period.

Using length of report as a preliminary measure of the network's perception of the strike's news value, two "prestrike" reports averaged 1 minute in length. The four reports following the official strike announcement averaged 2 minutes and 35 seconds. When the UMWA went on strike, reporters produced a series of background angles—for example, pictures of coal stockpiles, interview blurbs from "average" miners, and human interest stories. From December 30 to January 30, just eight reports averaged 34 seconds in length. But in early February the pace quickened and 30 reports followed in 34 days. Before February 6 the strike had not been the lead story; in the next 34 days it was the lead story 14 times. From February 9 to March 13, reports averaged 4 minutes and 26 seconds with 11 reports lasting longer than 5 minutes. Then, from March 13 till CBS's strike coverage ended on March 30, the frequency and length of reports subsided again—12 reports averaged 1 minute and 33 seconds. What accounts for these curves in the duration, frequency, and location of reportage? The coverage pattern conforms to the network's own assumptions about the "natural history" of strikes.

Prior to February 3, CBS aired only 17 reports totaling 25 minutes. These minimalist reports noted: (a) miners were "hurting", but utilities and industries were not; (b) "violence" had erupted in "coal country"; (c) "coal talks" repeatedly "broke down"; and (d) Columbus, Ohio had a fuel problem due to the strike. In contrast, spurred by story angles of White House intervention and the promise of "imminent" fuel shortages, CBS elevated the coal strike into a lead story and gave more time to it in five consecutive days in mid-February than during the first 62 days of the strike. Network assumptions about the centrality of Federal officials also shaped coverage patterns. Schlesinger's "forecast of doom" on March 5 prompted a report of nearly 9 minutes. During the week of March 5–12, President Carter invoked Taft-Hartley and miners resisted, and time allotted to the "story" soared: The seven-day average was 6 minutes and 26 seconds per report.

Between December 8 and February 5, four reports centered on the theme of violence; four tersely announced a "breaking off" of talks; three concerned the suffering of striking miners due to loss of wages and benefits during the holiday season. "Talks" between the UMWA and unnamed corporate coal operators, when in process, were not mentioned, nor were the circumstances precipitating their periodic discontinuation. On December 30, Roger Mudd announced, "Talks between the coal companies and the United Mine Workers broke off today, and that dimmed hopes of ending the 25-day strike anytime soon." On January 24, Cronkite stated, "Negotiations to end the seven-week coal strike broke down this morning just when it seemed they might be getting somewhere." Morton Dean began the January 29 report: "The coal talks have gone down the chute again." These reports lasted no longer than 20 seconds and offered no specific facts about the "talks" or the participants. After weeks of sporadic reminders about "talks" which "broke down," the strike was declared "a record."

Though negotiators were tight-lipped during this period, information about the negotiations was available. Discussions between the BCOA and UMWA centered on labor stability versus a right to strike, and on how health benefits would be structured. The December 30 'breakdown' occurred when BCOA representatives left in reaction to a UMW proposal "backing away" from a tentative agreement to "payback penalties" while also seeking complete restoration of the Funds. BCOA negotiators were unhappy because the UMW would not agree to link these benefits to a labor stability clause (Hughey, 12/31/77, p. 1; Franklin, 1/9/78, p. A16). Again on January 24, CBS did not report why negotiations stopped: BCOA negotiators walked out, upset about a secret meeting between a UMW aide and a smaller industry group (Clark, 1981). CBS defined the negotiations as unexciting and low in news value because there was no progress to report. This absence of movement in the negotiations, in and of itself, would have been newsworthy, had CBS reported the BCOA strategy.

Selections and pairings of interviewees varied with the network's perception of where the coal strike stood in its "natural history." The length and number of interview statements allocated to miners, utility managers, UMW president Arnold Miller, government officials, and politicians also varied. Of the seven film reports broadcast from November 28 through January 29, only two deviated from a formula of sandwiching two 8-second miner interview clips within the reporter's narrative. The exceptions occurred on December 4, when CBS featured the "other side" in the person of a utility director and on December 5 when Miller was heard formally announcing the strike. No coal operators or spokespersons, and no elected politicians appeared on camera for interviews. Between January 29 and February 9 the number of interviews increased. Energy Secretary Schlesinger, utility managers, elected officials, and businessmen were presented speaking about "energy shortages" in interview clips averaging 22 seconds. Segregated into separate reports were rank and file miners whose speech continued to be divided into soundbites averaging 9 seconds. Still no coal operators appeared.

In early February, CBS began thematically structuring reports to include "angry miners" on one side, and "growing crises" in fuel supply on the other. On one side, network reporters concentrated on the rift between "angry" miners and Arnold Miller. It made for great television, rank-and-file miners screaming for Arnold Miller's head. Both miners and Miller confronted one another through the reporters and the screen. Strands of internal union conflicts floated past on screen, without much guidance about how to make sense of them. CBS spoke of miners' "militancy about getting exactly what they want," the UMW's "disorderly" state and its poor leadership. Miner interviewees expressed their opposition in viscerally expressive terms rather than as a general worldview or in terms of concrete specifics. Reporters glossed miners' rationale or dissociated it from the interplay of context and motivation. Paradoxically, CBS's coverage focused visually on the miners' faces without addressing their motivations. Aside from their palpable anger toward Miller, there had still been no mention of a relationship between the UMWA and the BCOA.

The first contract proposal went to the UMW bargaining council for a ratification vote on February 6. When it became clear that this proposal would not produce a quick and easy ratification, CBS cranked their coverage intensity up a notch. On February 9, CBS noted that the union bargainers had rejected the contract proposal because of "the penalties the new contract would impose on wildcat strikers." This report also contained the first interview with anyone representing coal management's views, but positioned the views of an industry manager along with Arnold Miller opposite miners. From February 9–13, CBS pitted miner interviewees against Miller interview clips as the opposing sides defining the conflict. No further interviews with industry officials appeared.

Reporting of "crisis fever" began early in February and intensified when the union turned down the contract proposal. Already featured as a story angle on February 7, CBS positioned the "crisis" angle as the lead story on February 13, opening with Cronkite's warning that, "With the coal strike now threatening economic havoc to the nation's industrial heartland . . ." Again, the next evening, Cronkite stressed the "threat" as he introduced a 5 minute story: "With the threat from the coal strike growing daily, President Carter moved forcefully today to get the two sides negotiating again." Driven by the premise of impending crises to the public welfare, emphasis drifted to measures taken to protect coal shipments from "interference." Cronkite then introduced a second story prong: "And, as Barry Serafin's reporting the possible use of federal troops, Indiana moved to protect the precious commodity of coal with troops of its own."

The February 14 report was laced with references to "grave concern," "economic disruption," and "worsening effects." A CBS reporter declared, "It is an emergency situation, state officials say—life, property and the safety of residents are in danger." The climate of escalating fears about coal shortages intensified on February 15. Positioned as the lead story because Carter requested bargainers resume negotiations at the White House, the storyline turned to Indiana where "private truckers hired by the state's biggest utility were moving coal today under armed guard." Following this report about nails strewn in the road to prevent trucks from delivering coal, CBS created 'balance' by assessing the "depth of feeling" among miners. Five miner clips from a miners' rally total 62 seconds, expressing their determination to press the strike to get a fair contract, their refusal to comply with any Taft-Hartley orders that might come, and their scorn for threats of Federal takeover of mines. A meeting of Carter and Governors of strike-affected states at the White House on February 16 brought a 45-second statement from Carter, and warning voices from Governors Shapp (26 seconds) and Bowen (21 seconds) lamented the prospects of impending crises, job losses, and human suffering due to the strike. Awakened interest in potential bad news—"cutbacks," "curtailments," and "layoffs"—centered on the hyperbole of elected politicians.

During the period from February 13 to February 24—11 reports—a new set of actors dominated the story. This period began with President Carter becoming involved in trying to resolve the strike and culminated on February 24th with President Carter's speech announcing that (with much arm twisting and threats of Taft-Hartley) the union and the coal operators had agreed to a negotiated settlement. Though miners' squabbling among themselves continued to be featured, they became secondary speakers as CBS turned to elite male speakers. Mineworkers appeared in five of these eleven reports and Miller in four, while government administrators and/or elite politicians and governors from strike-impacted states appeared in eight of eleven reports. Reporters consulted government officials about the possibilities of an energy crisis and any government plans in the works to "meet the crisis." Likewise, elected politicians stepped forward to define the urgency of the situation. Secretary of Labor Ray Marshall also became a visible player. President Carter, government officials, and elected politicians took over as "primary definers" with 67 percent of the total nonreporter speech time from February 13 through 24.

CARTER TAKES CENTER STAGE

After the UMW bargaining council rejected the first proposal, President Carter stepped into the picture to prod the disputants toward a settlement. Carter's entry excited CBS as a news story. Like the rest of the news media, CBS followed Carter's statements of concern about the coal strike's impact on the nation's welfare. For CBS News, the question became, "would Carter do something now?"—would "drastic steps" and "stronger measures" be taken? Carter's threats to "take more serious steps" became the pivot of CBS's stories: Soon their questions centered on whether Carter would invoke Taft-Hartley injunctions and, if so, would miners comply with the law—would they defy the President? What was Carter doing to "minimize economic damage from the coal strike"? The partisan charges were aired: Was Carter "dilly-dallying around and indecisive"? Once President Carter became involved in negotiations, CBS paid some attention to covering the negotiations—something they avoided over the first 160 days of negotiations between the BCOA and the UMWA.

CBS, like the other networks, oriented its resources and energies toward covering Presidential politics. Framing the story around Carter's presence permitted CBS to use its familiar White House stakeout. At night and in trenchcoat, in front of the White House, CBS reporters introduced and concluded tape stories. The White House stakeout scene, implying presidential authority and decision-making power, relocated the impasse in the coal talks behind the familiar scenery of "Presidential politics." Carter and his presidency emerged as *the story*. CBS recast the coal strike in the shadow of their own "Presidency" mythology.

After President Carter entered the story on February 13th, CBS began to talk up a possible Taft-Hartley confrontation. Beginning on February 14th, reporters speculatively brought up "Taft-Hartley" in every report, and initiated a pattern of asking miners how they would respond. Soon a portion of miners' screen anger was rerouted toward Carter and "the government." It is nearly impossible, in retrospect, to disarticulate which came first, miner anger toward Carter or media "prompting" in that direction. In any case, CBS story frames consistently deflected attention away from Capital and onto the role of State/President. For example, Betty Ann Bowser reported on February 17 about layoffs in a Kokomo auto plant, saying many laid-off workers "blame their plight and the length of the coal strike on the President." A young bearded worker, chosen by Bowser as representative of laid-off workers' views, affirmed Bowser's assessment:

> Jerry Warren [Auto Worker]: Carter ain't doing nothing about it. When they were on strike for 30 days, he should have called them out to the White House and set them down and say, "hey, let's get a settlement right now." That's the way that I feel. He ain't going to get my vote no more.

The theory of the Presidency traded on by reporter and interviewee presumed an omnipotent Presidency with centralized responsibility for the operation of a capitalist economy, except in this theory it is not a capitalist economy, it is *the economy*. In spite of all the "free market" rhetoric, this basic expectation shines through—it is the President's job to keep "the economy" going smoothly.

During the week of February 17—24, CBS presented bits and pieces of the confrontation between the Carter Administration and BCOA negotiators. Reports, however, stressed a different tension—that created by "the worsening shortage of coal" and the sense of urgency among "top Administration officials." On February 20, the Federal Mediation and Conciliation Service announced the tentative P&M proposal. Serafin observed that the Administration invited "reporters and photographers . . . to be on hand. According to some sources, the Administration wanted to send a signal to the BCOA that it should get in step." Suddenly the BCOA's cover had been blown, but within minutes attention was again fixed on "cutbacks" in Indiana.

On February 24, Carter announced the second contract proposal in a nearly three-minute soundbite. This time, however, CBS was wary of prematurely declaring the strike over. Between February 25 and March 5, the date of the ratification vote, miners again became the primary focus in CBS coverage as reporters polled rank and file miners and union officers about the chances of contract ratification and how they felt about Taft-Hartley. February 25 did, however, include the first sound-bite from a BCOA negotiator, although his comments were aimed at Carter's interference and not the union.

Prior to President Carter invoking Taft-Hartley on March 6, CBS again lost sight of the BCOA, inflated fears of an impending fuel crisis and presumed the necessity of Federal intervention to protect the public welfare. The press questioned what Carter would do to end the strike, whether he could have ended it sooner, and how miners' actions threatened the public. A U.S. President using Taft-Hartley represented *big* news. The long-simmering conflict had finally come to a head and CBS finally mobilized its considerable reportorial resources. Reports on March 5 and 6 had reporters deployed and stationed across the geographic and institutional landscape.

Following March 14, when a third contract proposal was sent to the rank and file for a ratification vote, time allocated to the coal strike story again declined precipitously. Attention remained sparse until the miners actually voted and ratified the second contract proposal on March 23–24. Once the strike concluded, coverage vanished. Despite the earlier framing of the strike in terms of *consequences*, CBS pursued neither the outcomes of the strike or the new contract. The ratified contract meant the end of the story, period. Once the rupture in the social/economic order was patched over, the story vanished. The story was predicated on a rupture—"bad news"—or deviation from institutional order. Though television news broadcasters like to identify themselves as chroniclers of "our" history, they do not consider the space between ruptures as "history."

The Glasgow Media Group surveyed British television news and found industrial news was "news" only when it was bad news and crisis provoking. When production is interrupted, and the nexus of capitalist relations is disrupted, it represents a new development against the taken-for-granted background of industrial life. Thus, the archetypical industrial news story is "bad news." Capitalist relations of production and their continuous reproduction are unquestioned, and seen as a natural, hence unalterable context. In Goffman's terms, capitalist relations constitute a primary framework, operating to select and give meaning to events at such a basic level that the actors involved may or may not be aware of its existence (Goffman, 1974).

Though CBS reported the strike as potential "bad news," producers chose not to grant it status as a "real story" unless, or until, it became "really bad news", that is, until consumers felt the bite of energy disruptions. Using this yardstick, CBS elevated the strike in its hierarchy of news stories in mid February. By the network's definition of the situation, the strike would receive intermittent coverage unless miners' employed violence, or shortages created crises for the public.

ABC AND NBC

The tape logs for ABC's and NBC's strike coverage show obvious external similarities. ABC broadcast 49 reports on the coal strike totalling 136 minutes. Its coverage also began on November 25 with a blurb on the forthcoming strike, and likewise ended on March 30. Like CBS, ABC paid scant attention to the strike after its initial flurry (except for an obligatory "holiday season" report on December 27) until early February. From November 25 through February 6 a total of 14 reports averaged 1 minute and 44 seconds. From February 9 through March 13 ABC's reports became more frequent (29) and longer (averaging 3 minutes and 32 seconds). Prior to February 9, ABC had not made the coal strike its lead story, but between February 9 and March 14 it was the first or second story on 15 occasions. Like CBS, coverage declined after the 14th, but resurfaced on March 24 and 27.

NBC broadcast 59 reports on the coal strike totaling 178 minutes and 40 seconds. Prior to the strike, their reporting consisted of "news briefs" 20—30 seconds in length. NBC also concentrated reports in early December when the strike was called, followed by 10 reports averaging 46 seconds until February (except for their 5 minute version of the "coal miners at Christmas" story on December 20). NBC gave more attention to the strike negotiations in early February than did CBS or ABC, making it the lead story for the first time on February 2. NBC also put most of its coverage between February 9 and March 14 (29 reports averaged 4 minutes and 10 seconds), and the strike was the headline story on 13 occasions. NBC's lead story on March 24 was the final proposal ratification vote. Unlike CBS and ABC, which let the strike go out with a whimper, NBC made it the lead story on March 30, allotting it over 6 minutes.

Intensity of coverage on all the networks corresponded directly to Carter's involvement. Television news producers and reporters consider the President's actions and comments to be the primary news beat (Epstein, 1973). Carter's presence in the story instantly elevated its-importance, and permitted reporters to draw on their greater knowledge, familiarity, and sources in Washington DC.[1]

SUMMARY OF FRAMES

Paralleling the pattern in time allotted to the strike was a pattern in the frames employed over the course of the strike. When the strike began, news reports were structured by these dominant frames:

* its futility, in the context of huge stockpiles
* possible deleterious consequences for consumers
* probabilities of violence
* the harsh consequences of the strike on the miners themselves
* the miners as tradition-bound and suspicious

After its first week, the strike drifted out of mass-media consciousness until the end of January. With little violence to report and an absence of negotiating progress, reports merely reiterated that talks continued to "break down" for no apparent reason. As a news story, the strike was a *cold* item in January. The absent focus during this period corresponded to the preconceived narrative curve that network newspeople impose on strikes as events. When the UMW's bargaining council rejected a contract proposal on February 9, and murmurs of incipient coal shortages began to surface, the principal frames shifted to:

* the miners' militancy
* internal dissension in the UMWA, and its anarchic state
* the escalating fuel supply shortage and its consequent perils
* Arnold Miller's personal inadequacies as a leader
* Would Carter order Taft-Hartley or federal seizure?

As the strike stretched on, alarms about a growing fuel shortage intensified. Energy Secretary Schlesinger's appearance on national television

---

[1]CBS silently acknowledged its own (i.e., the mass media's) role in reproducing this exaggerated "spectacle" of the Presidency, in pictorial sequence which prefaced Carter's statement on February 14. While Serafin set the scene, interspersed between film shots of Carter and Ray Marshall at a news conference were three apparently superfluous shots of the overflow of reporters sitting crosslegged on the floor, writing notes on their pads, and a shot of other video technicians presumably capturing Carter on tape. Apart from Serafin's references to Carter and Marshall, the film scenes were not keyed to his words.

with his "forecast of doom" predicting between a million and three and one-half million job layoffs if the strike continued, impelled CBS to reiterate, in addition to their other frames, the Carter administration's "official" frames:

*the paramount importance of continuing production
*the threat to public well-being, or "the national interest," and the necessity for Federal/Presidential protection of the public welfare
*the sacred nature of "the law," that is, the focus on Taft-Hartley legislation: would miners obey or "defy" the law?

In the first phase CBS pitted the miners against utility companies; in the second phase it was miners versus Miller; the third phase had miners against President Carter; throughout, it was miners against the consuming public.

The way CBS set up the story all but guaranteed the frames of their later coverage. Like the BCOA and the Carter administration, CBS chose in effect to say this will only become big news if the miners can outlast this huge stockpile of coal. The network essentially set up two possibilities: Either the strike would be settled before the stockpiles were exhausted, or the miners would defy the odds, generate a coal crisis, and draw the government into the conflict. When the miners did so, the intensity of news production peaked.

PREVAILING FRAMES

Coal supplies Initially, the most important theme defining the strike was its effect on coal supplies. Here, labor is confronted by its social function: Since workers produce the goods which keep society running, it becomes imperative there be no pause in the process. This cast the State in the role of guardian of society, acting to minimize harm to society and get things moving again. The coal strike received unusual media attention because it could disrupt fuel supplies, bringing the winter into peoples' homes. Memories of the 1974 oil embargo's impact on energy prices and availability were still fresh to reinforce this angle. Coal strike coverage revealed television reporters' acute sensitivity to the interdependent division of labor in industrial society (organic solidarity), and "ripple effects" a strike may have on other industries. The emphasis on coal supplies initially ran in seemingly opposite directions: painting the strike in terms of both huge stockpiles and potential perils for consumers. The dual initial message in the early strike reports was "this shouldn't disrupt too many of you at home" and "things don't look too good for the miners." As the strike dragged on, the theme of coal supplies resurfaced as that of "coal shortages" and "energy crises."

Violence. Reports during the strike's first days consistently emphasize, by way of anticipation, its unpleasantness and the probability of violence. These stories predict efforts by union members to shut down nonunion mines. On December 8, union pickets burned a bridge leading to a large independent mine in Utah. The report featured film of a fire against the night sky, as the soundtrack recorded the crackling flames enveloping the bridge. Helmeted, leatherjacketed troopers escort a bus of nonstriking miners out of the mine past union pickets. The troopers glistening helmets and black jackets emphasized their power to guard against the threat of mayhem posed by striking miners. This image of power both symbolized that threat and the need for protection from it.

The report by Jack Ford of KSL-TV (a CBS local affiliate) concluded: "Authorities and union picketers expect the violence to increase as the strike continues." An act meant to spread labor stoppage, albeit forcibly, is simply dubbed "violence," glossing over the particular motivations which distinguish it from other acts of "violence" such as assault and murder.

When Ford questioned picketing miners, he asked *what* they will do to stop mines from operating, not *why* they want to stop them.[2] Because violence has "news value," Ford named and identified it by focusing on the method of force. Ford focused exclusively on the act's consequences, not to the picketing miners (who, he acknowledged, had temporarily

---

[2]Viewers don't usually get to see how a choice of narrative frames is made. An unanticipated contestation of "framing" takes place in this interview sequence. A group of picketing miners are lined up in front of the camera. While Ford asks whether they think any nonstriking miners will get through to the mine, the camera focuses on a young, expressionless gum-chewing miner. Suddenly, the camera moves left to a burly Chicano miner who has been asked the question. He is blunt, "No. We're not gonna let them go through." Having set up his point, Ford seizes on the predictable question: "What are you gonna do to stop them?" The miner responds, "We're gonna stop them. We're gonna get some clubs." This is the answer Ford wants, but as the miner speaks he nods his head to defer to another miner. The camera pans rapidly to our right to catch a second miner attempts to shift the frame of reference from "violence" to "solidarity": "We're going to reinforce our picket line as much as we can and try to keep them away from their job so we could all organize and keep ourselves together."

achieved their objective of cutting access to an "independent" mine), but to the men who cross the picket line and the coal operators. The goal of the latter group, continued production, was held up against the strikers, who attempt "violence" against those who seek the "right to work." Even the descriptive terms used to contextualize the "violence" are loaded: the violence was against "independent"/nonunion enterprises. These reports upheld the State's legitimate monopoly over the use of force to protect life and property against the indiscriminate violence of pickets: For example, on December 13, Cronkite matter-of-factly reported, "Police in Daviess County, Kentucky used tear gas to disperse a crowd of 400 pickets that police said were throwing bottles and rockets."

"Violence" is an especially prominent theme in the news, and forms a major parameter of what is considered "newsworthy" (Hall, 1973). It usually refers to a specific event, occurring over a circumscribed space of time, and perpetrated by specifiable persons. Just as these features rule out many possible stories as "news," so also they rule out many actions violent in their consequences from being defined as such in the news. A mine "disaster" involving the collapse of a mine roof, causing the death of miners, might by another set of criteria be viewed as an act of violence committed by company officials who willfully refuse to spend adequately on mine safety. Consider an alternative headline: "Dead laws and dead men: manslaughter in a coal mine" (Caudill, 1977). But since the principle of causality endorsed by network television news rests on linear relations resulting from single intentional acts, cave-ins, and methane explosions are not considered violence. A collapse itself, though dramatic, follows from a process of erosion or dilapidation that occurred over a relatively long period. The agents directly responsible are not immediately apparent, they may be institutional. But among newspeople, describing an act as violent carries the imputation of willful human agency aimed at immediately gaining an advantage.

"Violence" is a peg which guarantees coverage of a strike. Newscasters' formulaic descriptions of these events echo official pronouncements: "National guardsmen have been called in to keep the peace." The network equated "the peace" with permitting nonunion workers to take the place of striking workers. By mid February, when striking miners had outlasted the coal operators' and utility managers' stockpile strategies, the theme of violence resurfaced as "interference" with coal supplies. And again, after President Carter invoked a back-to-work order in March, CBS harped on anticipated miner violence and intimidation against those who might attempt to obey the law.

Regionalism. When compared to newspaper coverage of the strike (Seltzer, 1978) the cultural idiosyncrasies of miners were not played up as much in the televised narratives.[3] The written press (e.g., *Time, Newsweek, New York Times*) relied more heavily on cultural idiosyncrasy as an explanation of the miners' behavior. Unlike CBS's other frames, this frame was diffuse in nature; never really a focal point, but always adjectivally present in the visuals and miner interviews because the miners pictorially appeared on television, chewing tobacco and speaking in thick mountain accents. The difference of Appalachian mine workers emphasized by the print media, was to some extent only a matter of visually portraying "the facts" for TV newspeople. As anchor, Cronkite's "purely descriptive" inflection of the phrase "coal country" (e.g., December 13, December 23, March 1) presumed an uncontestable body of "common knowledge" that defined the region's distinctiveness in terms of "Hillbilly" culture (cf. Maggard, 1983 and Seltzer, 1978 on media treatment of Appalachia). The premise of cultural isolation and insulation "deemphasizes the class consciousness in the miners' militancy" while casting the miners in terms of "mountaineer" intractability (Green, 1978, p. 7).

Hardship for miners' families

At the start, a central motif in CBS's descriptive commentary emphasized the strike's harsh impact on the miners themselves. On December 5, Serafin concluded his report: "For now those who face the bleakest prospects because of the strike are the miners themselves." After the "burning bridge" film on December 8 until February 2, the only reports featuring film stories depicted the adverse effect of the strike on miners and their families. On December 23, CBS aired a predictable Christmas human interest angle on the strike. Cronkite set up the story with "there isn't much cheer at households in one part of the country, that's coal country." Despite the intrusive and patronizing character of this report, this report revealed the percarious nature of life based on being a wage laborer. In this report, Lorenzo Childress, a black miner, and his family appear as representative of "union families." We see the vulnerability of "union families whose breadwinners are out of work this holiday season" and a miner angry at the union for "causing" this to happen to his family. Keyed on-screen to Rabel's discourse were scenes of Childress's children and a closeup of his infant reaching for a ball.

---

[3]"Social commentators and reporters have routinely painted Appalachian people—and miners, in particular—as peculiar, sadistic, violence-prone halfwits. This picture has tangibly affected public perception and public policy. It all started with the Hatfield-McCoy feud that the national press featured as a kind of comedy among white savages" (Seltzer, 1985, p. 251).

Rabel: "Childress is concerned about the effect a long strike would have on his family. And he's angry over the union's timing of the walkout."

Childress [miner]: "I believe that if the contract runs out at a certain period of time, it shouldn't be right at Christmas time, or right at winter time, when you need a job more than ever."

Rabel: "The family does have a Christmas tree this season. But most of the presents underneath are brightly wrapped empty boxes placed there just for show."

[the black children singing]: "Yes, Jesus . . ." (it breaks off on the soundtrack, while Rabel continues with voiceover)

Rabel: "There is a deep religious feeling in the Childress family which they are counting on to help them through the strike. A feeling shared by many other union families here whose breadwinners are out of work this holiday season."

On January 2, Roger Mudd played on a similar twist: "The New Year traditionally means new hope for the future, but for thousands of striking coal miners, the New Year has not brought much happiness." This time, Barry Serafin delineated the "financial pinch" felt by miners' families—"Dickie Williams and his wife Nancy have three small children, house payments, furniture payments, utility bills, and no savings to cushion the lost paychecks." One cannot view these tapes without a sense of reporters' sincere sympathy for the desperate financial plight of the families they visit, what Ed Rabel called the "burden of hardship" (December 23). Here, the camera "speaks" with the kind of concern captured in the photographs of the poor during the Great Depression. Miners and their families were shown suffering, in poverty, without medical benefits and often unable to pay essential utility bills. Of greater interest, these reports consistently framed their situation in terms of what the union has done, without mentioning the role of the coal industry or operators. Suspect decisions by the "union" (spoken of as an entity quite apart from these people) may be responsible for worry, despair and suffering. Speaking in a humanitarian voice, CBS's commentary was accompanied by sharply edited soundbites of union miners *qua* family men apparently criticizing the union regarding the timing of the strike or its efficacy. These reports construct an image of miners and their families which the audience can sympathetically identify with against the implicit "them" of a union which makes unfeeling decisions.

Once again, owners were invisible and blameless in this story.[4]
The apparent contradiction between empathy for individual miners while legitimating capitalist economic relations stems as well from a series of frames which are not present in these reports. Moberg (1984) observed a similar pattern in press coverage of deindustrialization. Systematically omitting historical and institutional contexts means events are not depicted in relational terms. Because "'the market' is invoked as a holy talisman" which cannot be questioned or explored, events are implicitly accorded an inevitable quality. Hence, whether it is union busting or deindustrialization, reporters demonstrate empathy for the plight of workers who lose out, but that is just the way the world is.

Reporters show of empathy for workers tended to legitimate capitalist institutions by translating class subjects into individuated subjects. Consider the human interest angle in the report of January 31, 1978. After looking at a fuel shortage in Columbus, Cronkite redirected viewers to Ed Rabel's visit to retired miners in Jacksboro, Tennessee. An elderly man slips and slides as he attempts to navigate his way across an icy parking lot to a food stamp office. Rabel identifies him as a retired miner named Bishop Daugherty. Daugherty and another retiree, Tom Huddleston, are identified as men forced to swallow their pride in their independent ability to provide for themselves. Rabel narrated:

> UMW miner Bishop Daugherty retired after working for 33 years in the mines. He's a proud man and loyal to his union. But, on this day he says he has lost some of his pride because he is applying for food stamps, something he's never done before. He must do it he says, because the $225 per month pension check he and his wife depend on will not be arriving in February. The pension fund administered by his union and supported with coal company contributions, has run dry.

Accompanying scenes are laden with poignant affect. A tight, full-screen shot of Daugherty's hand holding a pencil (presumably as he fills out the application for assistance) is followed by tight closeups of his face as we bear witness to a proud man's humiliation. An interview clip with Tom Huddleston repeats the point: "I've worked for my livin'. And I'm the father of eight children. They never knew what welfare was. Me and my

---

[4]There are numerous points, however, where viewers might have furrowed their brows in puzzlement. On December 23, Ed Rabel visits a female miner and her unemployed husband who has emphysema. In this context one has to wonder how he acquired this disease—inhaling coal dust? Their dilemma stems from the fact "the strike brought a cut off of all medical benefits." Who cut them off?

wife supported our family." As he speaks, Huddleston pauses to choke back his emotions, and as he does Rabel's voice can be heard off-camera gently reassuring him. Throughout the report, Rabel's tone and the assembly of shots convey a profound sense of human pathos. These were hardworking men who now suffer physically and medically, as well as emotionally.

Yet, obliquely and indirectly, Rabel hinted the union may be responsible for their suffering. Notice the phrasing and structure of Rabel's comments above: for example, "He's a proud man and loyal to his union. *But* on this day he has lost some of his pride because . . ." The explanation for what compelled Daugherty to take this action follows in the sentence about the pension fund. To be sure, the pension fund **was jointly** administered, and drew on coal company contributions **made for each ton of coal mined, as stipulated in the contract** (the emphasized words indicate what Rabel's explanation left out). This partial and incomplete phrasing of "facts" conveys a sense that the union may have misadministered what the coal companies contributed (there is no indication of contractual obligation motivating these contributions). By failing to develop, even minimally, the historical and institutional relations which have shaped the pension fund, most viewers cannot possibly piece together why these men face humiliation.

Seconds later, Rabel's brief tour of a black lung clinic illustrated the tragic human consequences of the U.S. mining industry. For nearly 20 seconds, the camera showed men strapped to oxygen masks so they could breath. One wrenching scene showed three men seated in a row, each clutching a pillow to his abdomen, hunched over and coughing, gagging, and wheezing for breath. The sounds of their rasping agony are heard behind Rabel's comments.

> Rabel: "The strike has also meant the complete cutoff of medical benefits extremely important to the thousands of retired miners suffering from black lung disease. Many medical benefits had already been reduced drastically even before the strike began. Many coalfield clinics like this one have shut down."

Although the first mention of black lung disease in any CBS report on this strike, Rabel narrated these scenes from the black lung clinic about the cutoff of medical benefits as if the disease and its industrial etiology were common knowledge to most viewers.[5] The scene in the clinic was

---

[5]Rabel also referred in passing to the "drastic" cut in benefits prior to the strike without referring to, or explaining, the events of the previous summer (see Chapter 3).

like watching war victims who lie mangled in their hospital beds. Yet, nothing in this report mentioned how these "wounds" were suffered; nor were there inquiries about how mining has influenced these health conditions.

Sympathy for these men and their families did not undermine the legitimacy of capitalist social relations in the CBS reports. For their predominantly working-class and lower-middle class audiences, CBS showed sincere concern for the common man and his family without questioning capital or the state, but by raising an eyebrow about how well a working class institution—the union—cares for its own. As with all other aspects of the coal strike story, two critical matters were absent. The coal operators/capital were cut out of the narrative, and production was a non-issue.

ABSENT FRAMES

Every frame selected to tell about the strike precludes the inclusion of some other frame. Along with the wealth of empirical information which never got into the story, missing frames had a significant impact on how this strike story (and we believe most strike stories) got told. We identify five absent frames: 1) Management/Capital; 2) analysis of market and commodity relations; 3) conflicts over production relations, 4) whose side the State is on; 5) as a "takeaway" strike versus "democratic unionism."

Missing Capital. Coal operators did not figure in the story. From the first report until February 9 (66 days into the strike), there was one vague, passing reference to the BCOA and no interview with any BCOA representative. Placed in perspective, these same reports included 31 references to the UMWA and Arnold Miller (no BCOA negotiator was even mentioned), four Miller interview clips, and 28 rank-and-file miner interview clips. But another 14 CBS reports would pass before a BCOA member actually spoke on camera—and this only after BCOA hardline negotiators had been ousted and replaced by Nick Camicia. Following Camicia's February 25th appearance complaining about President Carter's pushing the BCOA into an agreement it did not want, the BCOA vanished for another 11 days before Camicia was drawn into conflict again with the Carter "Administration" and not with the miners. The remainder of BCOA appearances were *pro forma*—for example, ritual news conferences to reestablish "peace" in the mining industry.

CBS periodically referred to "coal companies," "companies," or the "soft coal industry," but there was virtually no mention, on any network, of the BCOA until February 20. Then, each network referred to the BCOA because public statements by Governors Carroll, Rockefeller, and Rhodes, respectively urged miners and operators to return to collective bargaining. Only because the networks were sensitive to the utterances of a political elite did they then reiterate the name "BCOA." So unfamiliar was the name "BCOA" that ABC's anchor on February 21 had to identify it for viewers: "The operators' negotiating group is known as the BCOA." Likewise, on February 25 a UPI wire story entitled, "Coal Operators a Loosely Knit Unit" (NYT, 2/25/78), started: "Besides being one party to a labor dispute that produced the nation's longest continuous coal strike, what is the Bituminous Coal Operators Association?"

CBS's Barry Serafin identified the BCOA in the barest possible terms on February 20: "It has been traditional for independent coal companies to wait for the BCOA—the Bituminous Coal Operators Association—to reach a national agreement . . ." Media attention to the BCOA was motivated by Carter's vocal displeasure with BCOA resistance to the FMCS-engineered settlement proposal between the UMWA and the Gulf coal subsidiary, Pittsburg & Midway.

Though the written press iterated the BCOA's euphemism, "labor stability," CBS never mentioned the demand. CBS occasionally referred to the union's "right to strike" demand without, however, clarifying it. Further parallelling the BCOA's invisibility was the absence of any reference to company violations of the 1974 contract. Yet, rank-and-file charges regarding contract violations lay at the heart of their rationale for wildcat strikes, and their reasoning on a "right to strike" provision. Along the same lines, CBS aired no expository reports concerning the arbitration procedure for settling grievances between miners and companies, even though a core conflict centered on the politics of that process.

Production relations

This was a story about a conflict between mine owners and coal workers, but the networks distanced it from production relations. CBS not only counterposed the hardships endured by miners against the interests of consumers/viewers, they even cast miners' hardships as simple consumption deficits resulting from "lost pay checks," the absence of cash, and the "pile up" of bills. This moment of truth in CBS's discourse about the strike could not be elaborated because the "pay check" was presumed a normal, natural, and perfectly transparent element in our lives. Accepting the "pay check" as part of the natural condition of daily life meant never tracing it to its source in production relations. Moreover, the "burden of hardship" was not framed or examined in terms of production related conditions—for example, black lung, explosions, cave-ins.

CBS periodically included production-related visual shots in reports, but not for the purpose of addressing the nature of conflicts over the labor process. Shots pertaining to coal production invariably appeared for purposes of (a) signifying the referent system of coal mining, or (b) indicating the cessation of production operations—for example, closeups of stilled wheels and empty bottoms of rail cars or the absence of motion around a tipple. Visual scenes referring to coal production focused on coal hoppers, coal bins, conveyer belts, coal cars: All shots which denote the movement (transport), or absence of movement, of coal. Production shots stressed machines. Mineworkers were rarely visible in these scenes; when a mineworker did appear adjacent to machinery, he worked alone.[6] And reporters' commentary never addressed the actual relations or conditions of producing coal. Even when showing clips of miners in work gear (with lamps, helmets, and buckets) filing into a mine, reporters spoke instead of disrupted coal supplies or the degree of support/nonsupport for the strike.

CBS translated matters pertaining to production into questions about the sphere of circulation. They drew attention to the phenomenal forms—the surface appearances of "money" and "cash"—in the sphere of circulation.

> These phenomenal forms, which arise from the relations of production themselves, provide the basis for the spontaneous forms of everyday consciousness—the set of "sedimented" typifications which form the dominant patterns of meaning in our society. (Morley, 1981, 388)

Reporters glossed over the structure of private ownership and wage labor to emphasize the effects on prices, the surface level of capitalist relations.

All manner of class conflict surrounding the strike vanished on CBS. Wildcat strikes and owners were barely mentioned. Portions of the press redbaited about communists in the Miners' Right to Strike Committee, but CBS never mentioned these matters—on February 15, CBS covered a MRTSC miners' rally without even naming the MRTSC. Was CBS

---

[6]There was one partial exception in the February 14 report on nonunion strip mining in the West. This report used a half-dozen camera angles of mammoth machines stripping coal from the surface of the earth. But even here no workers were shown, and the scenes were included to illustrate the train transport of coal to alleviate "the crisis."

unwilling to redbait, or was this another instance of not wanting to touch issues of class or class ideology?

Market relations

Though reports repeatedly alluded to matters of money and prices, they consistently averted analysis of market and commodity relations. Like the capitalist class, commodity relations are everywhere in the material world, but nowhere in the televised representations of that world. Network strike coverage presumes disputes center on money, but takes for granted the nature of the wage relation. In the spirit of Hobbes and Locke, CBS presumed market and commodity relations as the natural bedrock of a reasoned, democratic civil society. Thus, CBS had no means available to penetrate the structural sources of unreason. For instance, how can a report like that of January 31 not call to attention the apparent injustice of a man spending 33 years of his life toiling in a mine, and then in normal times getting $225/month in retirement benefits? Why mention that clinics have shut down, leaving chronically ill miners no relief, and not also ask about the merits of organizing medical care as another commodity subject to the machinations of the market? Why fail to contrast the system used to organize community clinics with corporate organization of health care? These news reports, organized and produced within a framework of commodity relations, presume commodity relations to be natural and God-given. They are beyond question.

Whose side does the State serve?

The December 8 report on miner violence illustrated a frame which is visually obvious, but not elaborated by reporters. Did police involvement in this conflict work to the advantage of one side or the other? An NBC report two months earlier brought up this issue in their coverage of an organizing battle between prounion workers and the nonunion Blue Diamond Coal Company. The company had gained a court-ordered injunction limiting the number of pickets at the mine entrance. Union miners contended that state police intervened on the coal company's side. While an angry miner declared the state was against the miners, the film showed miners and their wives with placards denouncing the court system and judges as favoring the operators. But CBS's report did not ask why Utah State patrolmen were sent in to protect "scab" workers. Similar questions fail to arise in later reports from Indiana, or in justification of Taft-Hartley court orders. CBS did not ask these questions because they presume viewers share in the normative conviction that when private property is threatened, so is the law. After all, this is the fact of the legal system's operation. This formulation, however, takes for granted precisely what requires explanation: Why and how do class interests take the form of law? and how does the form of law effect the politics of class relations?

Takeaways

Historically, the 1977-78 coal strike was among the first major collective bargaining episodes in which a corporate agenda of "takeaways" prevailed. Though CBS reporters noted the threat to UMWA survival if regional bargaining were pursued, they did not frame the strike in terms of "takeaways." Connected to this absence is another: CBS did not foreground either the ongoing struggle for union democracy, or the related pressure among rank and file workers for workplace democratization. Instead of asking questions about the extension of democratic practices into workplace relations, CBS simply characterized the turbulent process of seeking worker democracy as "anarchy" and "chaos." In February, CBS called the results of miner democracy an impediment to the consuming public's welfare. Here, as elsewhere, the broadcasting practice of achieving facticity by means of reductively recording events as sets of appearances, con cealed the sources of those appearances.

CBS coverage discouraged public debate over the meaning of democratic practices, and the tenor of their narrative commentary was antidemocratic. In the CBS lexicon, the term "democracy" has primarily symbolic meaning—akin to the platitudes of high school civics textbooks. The network loosely associated "democracy" with "free elections," "majority rule," and "representative government"—always with respect to the State, and not to Civil Society. When made synonomous with the United States, it is frequently made to signify the "free-enterprise system" as opposed to "totalitarian" communism. CBS had such trouble asking about the possibility of applying the principles of "representative government" to the workplace because, "capitalism structures practices through rights in property, to be exercised by owners . . . while liberal democracy vests rights in persons . . ." (Bowles & Gintis, 1982, p. 51).

6

Ideological Analysis

Ideological analysis of news texts examines what a text does not say, as well as what it says. News texts "represent" events which occur "out there" in the world. The gaps and silences in any news text shape these representations just as surely as the visible, hearable text. That which is absent may influence a less partial understanding of the social formation in question; it may also subvert the ideological account presented. For example, the wage contract is held to represent an equivalence exchange. Workers trade their labor power for a *fair* sum of money. Their labor power has a value (the wage represents its equivalent), while it is also a source of value and one foundation of economic enterprise. But "surplus value" over the cost of production is appropriated by the capitalist and not by the producer. Calling the wage contract an act of equivalence exchange "represents" a portion of the process, but glosses over its underlying dynamic, the alienation of labor which underwrites the private accumulation of profit, and the inequality that necessarily entails.

Ideologies cannot be separated from the structured practices which maintain and reproduce the dominance of authority/power relations. Routinized practices such as wage labor are ideological insofar as they explain, legitimate, and also reproduce relations of inequality. Though materially real and performed daily, the practice of wage labor is—both within daily life and on television—represented as something it is not. When wage labor is taken-for-granted it is considered *unproblematic* and simply presumed to be a naturally occurring—and hence, unalterable—fact of life, rather than as a historical relation constructed by humans. Television news, unreflexively reproduces this ideological stance, "representing" the wage contract as an exchange of equivalents to which each party—designated as legally free and equal subjects—

111

assents without coercion. Historically, this ideology of just exchange provided the model of social justice that legitimated the operation of labor markets, the process of appropriating surplus value, and the distribution of goods.

A parallel critique may be made of prevailing accounts of news production. Journalistic routines produce socially constituted knowledge, yet are "represented" as mirroring reality. Here, a different sort of equivalence is proclaimed between the "world out there" and the "representation on screen." The mechanical reproduction of sight and sound is held to duplicate a world out there. The ideological appeal of broadcasters' mirror metaphor enables networks to represent their journalistic routines as tailored to serve the entire public, while these routines tacitly replicate hegemonic paradigms which do not call attention to the interests of dominant groups.

The task in ideological analysis is to make explicit the social meanings of discourse: (a) flushing to the surface the claims the discourse makes by carefully distinguishing between linguistic and metalinguistic levels of media messages; (b) examining the validity of these claims as well as the validity claims made for the discourse; (c) evaluating the fit between the discourse and the referent systems which it is about; and (d) identifying and tracing out contradictions within ideological formations, in relation to contradictions in social formations and conflicts between social forces.

Events that occur in the world are bound by time and place and structure. They may be represented at another time and place but they cannot be transmitted as they are. Techniques of reproduction sever events—scenes—from surroundings, from the relational context in which they actually took place. The images, by themselves, are unmotivated in what they "tell" viewers because the act of filming plucks them out of a lifeworld in which they are meaningful. Pictures on television are rich with possible meanings but without words/concepts there is little to check our fancy. Television producers strive to compensate for this ambiguity via techniques designed to evoke a sense of realism. In television news, the soundtrack, with a voiceover narrative or a reporter speaking directly to the camera provides a means by which pictures are framed. Visual banners and captions also situate the pictures in a time and place, and guide interpretation. Realism in television news means this: turning inherently ambiguous pictures, removed from the flow of history, to appear as if they are unambiguous and natural signs. The task of reproduction is therefore an intrinsically political task, since it bears the responsibility of presenting to viewing publics the character of their history, and the range of possibilities for action that such a history may afford.

On December 5, with a UMW strike scheduled to commence "at midnight," CBS correspondent Barry Serafin situated the projected

UMWA strike in terms of other mineworkers' strikes. Using dated film with voiceover narrative, he says: "Historically, strikes by mine workers created crises so serious that Presidents Roosevelt and Truman seized the mines, sending in troops to keep the coal moving." Spotty black-and-white film captioned "1946" shows a figure which knowledgeable viewers recognize as Truman making a speech that is not heard.

CBS thus concretized an abstract issue by focusing on the actions of "known" persons (Gans, 1979). Networks commonly frame institutional relations and social forces in terms of big-name actors. But there is also an institutional slant here. These are political actors and images, not economic ones, that anchor the CBS history of mineworker strikes. This itself is an important choice of context, presupposing a way of viewing workers' struggles. The visuals appear to corroborate the narrative at every step. The fuzzy, grainy quality of black-and-white film, together with the caption and the image of a known personality, attest to the "historical" significance of coal strikes as Serafin narrates, "Historically, strikes . . . created crises so serious . . ." Frame by frame, the pictures confirm the correspondent's sober and authoritative tones. As Serafin says "sending in troops," men wearing miner's helmets walk into a coalmine tunnel; with "to keep the coal moving," coal is seen moving on a conveyer belt. The steady flow of pictures keyed to words, in conjunction with their unceasing onward movement, does not permit the viewer to pause and reflect. The narrative swept along, so that one condition of making sense of the report is to follow its flow, bracketing most questions, for the moment at least.

Serafin presents a partial "historical" account which glosses the long record of struggles between miners and mine owners in the United States He invokes the authority of history to make two claims: (a) Profound crises may occur when miners strike-indeed, strikes are made nearly synonomous with crises; (b) governmental intervention is a legitimate, perhaps, requisite means of solving such crises. This report thus previews a scenario suggested by "history"—will this strike produce a deep crisis? Will it necessitate government action?[1]

What was *not* present in this report? If the historical record is of concern, then it should be noted that miners and mine owners had been antagonists for a century. Where is the 1919 nationwide coal

---

[1]This is one of only two attempts by CBS to include a "historical" note on previous conflicts between miners and operators. CBS's presentation of "history" is static rather than dynamic or relational. In fact, CBS's view of history is to ahistorically abstract events, replacing last week's event with a more current event. CBS does not foreground history, but backgrounds it in an overarching mythology of mining.

strike, or the violence against attempts to organize the coal fields (e.g., "Bloody Harlan County"), or even a reminder of what the 1974 contract negotiations bore? The reports omit discussion of market forces and mining conditions such as mine safety or the organization of the labor process—thus suppressing possible motivating forces behind the strike. Most importantly, the report fails to note how, historically, strikes have been the means by which workers secured improvements in their working and living conditions—for example, the threat of an extended strike in 1933 induced Roosevelt to agree to the bituminous coal codes which ended child labor in the mines, created eight-hour days and five-day work weeks, established a minimum daily wage, abolished scrip pay, and put an end to company monopolies over housing and retail trade (Green, 1978). What about the legacy of company towns, inadequate housing, schools and roads, and external ownership in Appalachian coalmining areas? What about environmental problems created by decades of unregulated mining? Instead, the salient dimension of history which viewers are invited to remember is what serious crises strikes cause—although "for whom" is not explicitly specified, the message is undeniably addressed to each audience member.

HEGEMONIC ENCODINGS AND THE
PLURALITY OF DECODINGS

Narrating stories already enacted, the task of recreating the "actualness" of past events, is, then, not merely a technical task but a political process involving decisions about what constitutes the past, or rather, about what the past shall be. Reporters summon forth a vision of the "relevant" past as a template in which to fit the current strike. A form of pseudohistory is invoked not so much to restore memory, but to neatly situate events and actions within a framework that is convenient to producing network news. It provides a "backgrounding" where the struggles of the past are sanitized and freed of the contaminations of class—where worker triumphs and defeats alike are reformulated as triumphs of instrumental reason. Thus the urgency of memory is soothed, placated.

Television news is less an eye to the world than a screen on which a collage is constructed. "Gathered facts" must be processed and organized into discourses before they can be communicated over the screen. "In the moment when a historical event passes under the sign of discourse, it is subject to all the complex formal "rules" by which language signifies . . . The "message form" is the necessary "form of appearance" of the event in its passage from source to receiver" (Hall, 1980, p. 129). Televisual texts refer to the world, and embody certain significations of it (pictures, sounds, concepts used in speech), organized according to visual and verbal codes. Arrangement of "raw data" by means of communicative codes renders events meaningful. "Meaning does not occur or appear 'naturally,' but must be produced or made to appear through a particular kind of practice; the practice of *signification*" (Hall et al., 1976, p. 65).

The structuring, or encoding, of a newstext to suggest a particular interpretation draws on a conjunction of visual and verbal devices (Hall, 1980). Despite the presence of codes, the news text can yield multiple interpretations under the same rules of discourse. The news text is "the site of a plurality of meanings" which interface with a plurality of interpretive communities defined by social class and subcultural location (Hall et al., 1976, p. 53). Broadcasters, however, attempt to delimit the field of possible "decodings" by rendering a closure on the text's meanings (composed by filmed "actuality clips," interviews, and reporters' presentations), thereby making probable readings as similar as possible to their own:

> the broadcasters' objective is to have the audience reconstruct the pro-
> gramme as it has been *ideologically inflected and structured* by them . . .
> Connotational and ideological codes are therefore at work, organizing the
> elements of the message, as well as those codes which enable the broad-
> caster, literally, to "get a meaning across." (Hall et al., 1976, p. 67)

And yet, complete closure is rarely achieved or desired. More often, dispersed individuals watching alone negotiate the preferred meanings inflected by broadcasters. Though broadcasters organize and weigh the elements of messages, separated viewers decode from atomized interpretive stances. In advanced capitalist societies where mass-mediated sources of information predominate, *hegemonic* discourse no longer consists of shared, unified, coherent belief systems, but refers instead to the fact that citizen-consumers no longer share a unified discourse. Broadcast news has become hegemonic to the extent that it blocks unified public discourses from taking place?

Constructing any news text necessitates "a whole way of structuring, framing, and processing a topic" (Hall et al., 1976, p. 67; cf. Berger, 1972). The task confronting professional newspeople is how to most efficiently "get a meaning across" with minimal misinterpretation, while endeavoring to present "both sides" of an issue. Consistent with their attempts to avoid overt bias, a resolution of the different meanings of the various sides may not be attempted. This places conflicting demands on newspeople: First, the goal of "getting a meaning across" within time/space limitations propels them to overstructure and over-simplify their discourse; on the other hand, pursuit of impartiality pushes them to avoid analytic closure. Consequently, the surface features of news discourse are studiously atheoretical, while the deep structures of the discourse carry tacit, pretheoretical organizing principles.

Consider what meaning(s) David Dick tries to get across in his conclusion to a report on the coal strike on December 6, 1977:

> Even though Cannelton Hollow was peaceful today, most miners think it's going to be a long, cold winter. How bitter it becomes hinges in large part on attempts by non-union operations to stay open, and roving pickets who are committed to shutting down all coal mines in Appalachia.

Snow is blowing towards the camera (i.e., us) as we are led down a long line of standing trucks, not in use we presume, because of the strike. The first sentence, in a strict semantic sense, is a non sequitur. The "peace," however surprising, is no indication of future weather conditions. The opening phrase, "even though," seems to disavow this connection, but then offers no justification for counterposing the two phrases. One possible reading understands "the strike" to mean violence and suffering. In its projected length and unpleasantness, "winter" metaphorically exemplifies the strike, as suggested by the device of snow blowing towards the viewer. The strike, like the winter, may affect the audience/public as well. This cultivates an attitude of general concern. In the denotatively visual terms of the film clip, Cannelton Hollow appears cold, bleak, gray, and motionless. Connotatively, the present peace and quiet of Cannelton Hollow is surprising, and contrasted with what the future may bring—hardship and strife. Thus we have:

$$\text{Peace} \times \text{strife (implicit)}$$
$$\text{Strife} \rightarrow \text{strike (implicit)} = \text{bitterness} \rightarrow \text{winter}$$

The terms in the middle are absent, but the connection cannot be made without them. Peace is contrasted not with winter, but with the strike (which remains implicit). Thus the sentence is not a non sequitur at all—tacit verbal and visual codes convey an intricate chain of connections in a terse formula.

This is only one possible reading, however. Differences in structural position and interests of viewers in society—That is, class, region, race, gender—in conjunction with related differences in their communicative competences, make possible different readings. Striking miners, or other unionized workers who sympathized with them, might interpret this to resonate with the miners' situation. Indeed, miners could not but foresee troubled times ahead, having no wages with which to weather the labor stoppage. Here, the signified opposite of peace is the hardship the strike would bring. And if nonunion mines were to stay open, "it" would indeed make things more "bitter" for the miners (here, the winter is equated with a prolonged strike), since coal production would decrease the striking miners' bargaining power. Any strife would be seen as unfortunate, but necessary in the struggle to stop production. Contrast this to the first reading, where the mere hint of violence raises the question of the strike's legitimacy.

But does Dick's conclusion attempt a closure in the meaning of the passage? "How bitter it becomes hinges . . . on roving pickets who are committed to shutting down all coal mines in Appalachia." A link is indicated between possible "bitterness" and strike-enforcing, "roving pickets." "Roving" suggests a disorderly, disruptive quality: one can imagine roving tramps, or marauders, or Hell's Angels, but not, say, roving policemen, who operate on a "beat" with its connotations of order. This impression is strengthened by miners being "committed to shutting down all coal mines"—That is, challenging a shibboleth of capitalist society, the need for unceasing production. The phrase also connotes an authoritarian quality (which the media has long accustomed viewers to expect from unionized workers)—these workers intend to forcefully impose their views on others who seek to "freely," "willingly" sell their labor. While multiple decodings may be made of the text, we can perceive the effort made at limiting these, and at steering interpretations to themes consonant with a view of strikes as harmful to everyone, including the strikers themselves.

In arguing about whether or not the report is actually hostile to the strike, we risk ignoring its achievement in steering us to conceive of the strike in a particular way, framing it in terms of negative consequences (its "impact" on fuel supply) and raising fears about possibilities of violence and mayhem. The report fosters an apparently socially responsible attitude to the events. Class struggle remains absent as an analytic framework, although one group of participants appears to have socially disruptive aims. Selectively emphasising the strike's "impact" while ignoring its class dimensions, the report reiterates a way of seeing strikes: In this lies its larger ideological achievement.

FRAMING PRACTICES AND NARRATIVE CODES

Perhaps the thorniest question in studying television news and the social production of meaning is the relationship between the determinacy of the encoding process and possibility of multiple readings of a news text. All television news texts are structurally polysemic to the extent that dispersed, privatized viewers possessing varied interpretive skills and backgrounds must complete (interpret) the encoded texts.

We must not, however, confuse television's structural condition of polysemy with pluralism. The goals of maximizing audience size make it imperative that network news appear impartial—beyond ideology. One method of achieving this imperative of commodity news production is to avoid textual closure, since the inflexibility of closed texts can antagonize audience members and thus reduce potential audience size and, potential revenues. Commodified news must be rigidly enough encoded that a message gets across, but open enough that viewers do not perceive an encoding bias. Network news thus reproduces the Weberian distinction between "formal" and "substantive" rationality—the effort to establish "preferred readings" takes place almost exclusively at the format level, while substantive interpretation ostensibly remains the province of each individual viewer.

Where the determinacy of the encoding process and the indeterminacy of the decoding process meet, we echo Hall (1980, p. 129) that: "the discursive form of the message has a privileged position in the communicative exchange." It is therefore necessary to identify, not the meaning of a text, for this cannot be isolated, but the codes that produce the preferred meanings of the text. In order to pin down this discursive message form we shall abstract from the flow of the CBS news texts a series of framing devices.

1. Sequencing of topics, data, and interviewees is used in nearly all news reports to order the emphases of "facts." On network television, the anchorman's role is to frame and sequence the different parts of the story. Our basic point thus far has been that when television newscasters enact this framing and sequencing task, they construct narratives and tacitly do "social theorizing" for viewers.

Reports on the "coal shortage" frequently followed items on "coal talks," or on miners' reactions to events in Washington. Except on February 15, no substantive report on the negotiations or the fuel "crisis" was followed by a discussion of miners' grievances. The latter sequencing shifted the entire character of the report—leaving open the possibility that, despite all the trouble caused, the strike might still be worthwhile and justified.

The paired sequencing of public welfare vs. miner violence was a recurrent theme. Sometimes sequenced by the anchor relaying viewers from one report at the White House (public welfare?) to another in Indiana (site of violence?), on February 21 it was telescoped within a single report. Chris Kelley reported from Columbus, Ohio that, "In southeastern Ohio, the strike is getting rough," as 200 strikers attacked a nonunion strip mine during the night. Kelley named this "violence" and included a soundbite from an "unidentified eyewitness" who stated "they were just out to destroy property, and that's what they did." From this "violence" footage Kelly slid into tape and interview clips of striking miners who came to the Ohio state capitol to demonstrate against the independent (P&M) contract. Kelly then delegitimated the miners' political rally by sewing these scenes to yet another scenic account of trucks driving "under police escort" because of threats from striking miners.

Sequencing of interviewees may order the importance of their comments. Where there exists a clearly defined status hierarchy, deference is given to the higher-status interviewee. Network newscasters feel vulnerable to charges of "taking sides," so they compensate by sequencing speakers in a mechanical turntaking. But mechanical turntaking is not necessarily equitable, nor a guarantee of reasoned public debate. Editing and sequencing may privilege some discourses over others: e.g., on February 9th, interviews with two "defiant" miners are followed by clips from a manager and Arnold Miller predicting the region and the union will not survive if miners don't yield on penalties against work stoppages.

Sequencing the soundbite of an angry miner followed by a company official deploring the unruliness of miners and the consequent loss of profits leaves an impression that the miner's primitive anger attests to the manager's complaints. Interview sequences typically conform to a pattern of "knitting together" the "discourse of institutional voices and the contending melee of accessed voices" (Hartley, 1982, p. 115).[2]

2. Reframing the ideas, perspectives, and comments of interviewees may result in pursuing one aspect of their comments to the exclusion of

---

[2]Hartley (1982) observes that "accessed voices which take the form of interviews or on-the-spot comments are separated from the reporter's own account. There is a code of "being interviewed": The individual is filmed in closeup, but never addresses his or her remarks directly to camera; instead s/he appears to be talking to the unseen reporter, who is stationed discreetly off-camera. On the other hand, when reporters are seen on camera, it is always to address their remarks directly to "us": They don't need to be accessed through an institutional mediator" (p. 111).

others, abstracting them from their speech context. "Whatever an individual character may say, its meaning will be determined not by his or her intentions or situation, but by placing the interview in the overall context of the story" (Hartley, 1982, pp. 109-110). Interviewees may be prefaced and/or followed with comments that alter their own emphases or agendas. When a reporter's actual question is edited out (as a time-saving device), the process of reframing may become all but invisible. "Accessed voice" (Hartley, 1982, p. 111) interviews, like those with striking miners, are edited and quoted from for the purpose of illustrating the reporter's narrative choices. One recurrent method of recasting miners' comments is to frame them in terms of a reporter's assessment of their emotional state: for example, "really bothers him," "he's angry." This pattern of quotation, especially where the accessed voice is a nonelite person, takes the form of blurbs.

Reframing may simply result from positioning an image and a speech act within the narrative sequence. Whereas reporters were likely to mediate, or intervene in, miners' comments by means of editing the tape, their mediation of comments by professionals or political leaders was more verbally focused and situated. In the February 9 example mentioned above, miners' comments were severely edited, but not verbally situated by the reporter, while the reverse held for the subsequent concluding interviews with Miller and the manager.

3. Presenting a partial selection of facts—"card-stacking" (Leggett et al., 1978). For example, "As it happens, a major reason miners are striking is that companies would not agree to build a right to strike into the next contract." This does not say the "right to strike," considered almost sacred by coal miners, was their principal weapon against what they perceived as persistent coal company abuses. Nor does it address the relationship between this issue and mine safety. The BCOA demanded penalties against wildcat strikers, yet this report skips past coal companies and their agendas. The BCOA, determined to make the most of a market boom, sought to discipline miners in order to maximize production. Yet, this sentence construction suggests miners precipitated action due to rejection of a demand they had made. In context, miners were reacting to a new management initiative. Operators' initiative is blacked out and transferred to labor. While the phrase, "right to strike," may prompt positive as well as negative interpretations, positive interpretations require a prior framework of knowledge, or an alternative socialization experience. Unless viewers were already sympathetic to labor, it would be difficult to appreciate a seemingly gratuitous act that carries the threat of a fuel crisis to the public.

The term "cardstacking" may imply intent, but intent is not necessary to create the effect of cardstacking. The most vivid instance of CBS cardstacking may not have been intentional. On March 13, the first day of the back-to-work order, Ed Rabel reported from the Eastern Associated Coal Company's Keystone Mine. In all of West Virginia, only 30 out 65,000 miners reported to work and Rabel found them at this Keystone No. 1 Mine south of Charleston. Here, truly was an instance of a report which focused on the least representative moment of the day.

4. Implicitly identifying the interests of the state and capital with those of the audience (i.e., the public). The February 14 report about "Indiana's move to protect the precious commodity of coal with troops of its own" shows how the interests of state and capital are tacitly fused with those of the audience. Betty Ann Bowser reported, "It is an emergency situation, state officials say—life, property, and the safety of residents are in danger." Her awkward syntactic construction delayed attribution of the claim. In fact, Bowser's delivery made it impossible to differentiate the voice of state officials from her reportorial voice. Bowser presented no grounds for questioning this claim as fact, and the initial declarative force of the announcement followed by attribution in the passive voice suggested their assertion has credibility.

Armed with state-sanctioned alarmism as justification, Bowser naturalized the call-up of the National Guard. Then in nearly seamless fashion, Bowser concluded her narrative by echoing, without clearly acknowledging, the perspective of Whirlpool officials.

> No one knows how much the power curtailments will mean in dollars and cents; how many workers might have to be layed (sic) off from projected production shutdowns. But there is grave concern. This Whirlpool assembly plant is Evansville's major employer. Before the strike, the company was planning to hire 600 to 1000 new workers. Now, they privately concede, new jobs is not their worry—it is existing ones.

Bowser continued to pit workers (miners) against other workers and consumers, while positioning the unseen corporate employer as a model of civic responsibility and concern. The report built here on joining two propositions: "No one knows how much . . . But there is grave concern." The rhetorical force of this construction as a measure of concern dwarfs its literal meaning. She did not mean what she said, that the coal strike's effects on industry are unknown and everything said here is speculative. Who is no one? Sandwiched between the two phrases is an implicitly understood theory of the iron law of capitalist relations: Lost dollars and cents mean lost jobs. Bowser's fractured grammar suggested the "grave concern" comes from Whirlpool executives who seem neither narrow nor self-interested, but rather reflect the needs of Evansville *qua* community. Whether it is bad reporting or naivite' ("now they privately concede"), Bowser participated in their public relations scenario: If jobs should be lost, it is because of social and economic forces beyond managerial control.

5. Posing leading questions to reinforce a preferred view. For example, striking miners were asked, "What kind of Christmas do you think it's going to be if there's a strike?" In a consumer culture where festive occasions are celebrated by spending money, this question highlights the privation faced by striking workers and their families because of the strike. Reporters' questions frequently resembled pollster's inquiries about feelings and attitudes. Rarely did CBS reporters ask Why questions: Why do you feel this way? Why take this or that negotiating stance?

An unobtrusive method of posing leading questions is the clarification request. In this example from February 16, Bob Faw reported on a convoy of coal trucks moving coal with an armed state escort. The frame was miner "interference" and sabotage to keep coal from getting through to needy customers.

Trucker #1: "These are all new nails, and everybody's picking them up. Everybody's found them."

Trucker #2: "They were definitely put there."

Faw (question): "To block you guys from getting out? To make it harder?"

Trucker #2: "Roger. That'd be a, be a fact."

After noting the UMW's disclaimer, Faw returns to the allegedly guerilla nature of the struggle.

Faw: "Still, most of the drivers welcomed the armed escort, because many said they feared what might happen without it."

Trucker #3: "They would hit them if there wasn't these officers with them. No doubt they would, because they—they would be strung out too far—and they would hit them, the stragglers."

Faw (question): "The miners would hit them?"

Trucker #3: "Yeah."

Faw's clarification requests work as leading questions, each aimed at eliciting from the drivers the answers the reporter seeks about miner sabotage and violence. Faw's questions were not actually heard (only miners' answers), except when his questions were added as clarification requests. In CBS coal strike coverage, such clarification requests were heard on camera *only* when soundbites concerned themes of violence or sabotage, miner intimidation of other miners, or dissatisfaction with Arnold Miller.

6. Likewise, follow-up statements to identify unclear pronoun references in an interviewee's comments were used *only* when the subject was Arnold Miller or Jimmy Carter. For example (February 12):

> Terry Henderson [miner]: "As long as he's got that in there where it's going to fine the miners if—if they don't cross the picket line. I ain't no scab. I never was a scab. And I ain't going to be no scab now for him or nobody else."

> Ed Rabel [CBS reporter]: "He's blaming UMW President Arnold Miller for what is to the rank and file of this region the most repugnant part of the contract rejected today by the Bargaining Council."

Though ambiguous pronoun references to the coal operators were heard on 13 separate occasions in interviews with miners and Miller, reporters never sought to clarify those. Just as important as leading questions are following questions. We found that reporters never sought to keep conceptually alive, references—whether oblique or direct—to either the presence or the class interests of coal operators. Here, for example is a news conference soundbite of Douglas Fraser, head of the United Auto Workers, on the subject of a UAW donation to the UMWA and how his membership might react to giving money to support miners whose actions may trigger job layoffs in the auto industry.

> Douglas Fraser: [President, UAW]: "Oh, I think by and large our members will understand. I think the—they have insight on—the negotiations. They view the coal operators as belonging to the 19th century. I suppose there are some members of our union who might object to the contributions, but I think in overwhelming numbers that they would be in favor of it."

> Barry Serafin [CBS reporter]: "Fraser acknowledged though that a continuation of the coal strike could bring economic disaster to the auto industry."

Here, the follow-up not only detours from the coal operators and their negotiating stance ("belonging to the 19th century"?), it redirects us from class conflict between workers and owners to the possible economic damage some workers do to other workers.

7. A commonplace device involves attaching pejorative descriptions

to persons or events, for example, the "militant miners", "defiant miners," "disruption" due to the strike, "the bitterness" of the strike, the "threat" of a strike. Such "name-calling" (Leggett et al., 1978) is especially common with minority social movements where the mass media seizes on provocative images as a means of discrediting demonstrators (Gitlin, 1980).

The obvious point must be made here. The terms used by the network to indirectly capture the class character of the strike—"militant," "defiant," "disruption"—carry pejorative connotations in our culture. They all stand outside the boundaries of consensus and civility. Their descriptive accuracy turns pejorative when spoken in conjunction within a tacit cultural framework that masks and displaces the category of class.

8. Reports consistently ignored the complex relationships that constituted the event, preferring whenever possible to substitute abbreviations endowed with a thinglike character, having a simple, direct cause. Reified "walkouts" and "strikes" thus seem to occur unmotivated except by the stereotypical avarice of unions. Institutionally motivated human relations are compressed, abbreviated, and then replaced by the news-sign—"the strike," "the walkout."[3] Reified signifiers such as these may acquire either a powerful emotional valence or numbing indifference. Either way, they become informationally reductionistic, unable to stand for a complex of relations to which they refer but which are never examined. Reification means that relationships between human subjects solidify into objectlike things, and subjects forget their own active role in producing their relationships. For instance, throughout January the UMWA-BCOA strike became congealed by *CBS News'* discourse into "talks" which "broke down".[4]

---

[3]On December 6 Cronkite told of miners going "on strike." In its older forms of use, "to strike" meant to unfix, to put out of use; for example, workers would "strike tools" at the end of the day. The term used to describe labor stoppages was not a noun—laborers would strike tools or strike work. Converting this verb connected to a specified object into a noun that stands by itself, produces an ideological abbreviation that carries the aggressive connotations of its earlier forms of usage. At the same time, act and intent are congealed, frozen together into a thing that loses all traces of production, and has no roots or causes, but becomes an event with unmistakable implications. The heavy connotative weight of the preposition "on strike" could not be sustained in its verb form. Nominalized, however, it anchors an entire system of myths about organized labor.

[4]Linguistic construction in these reports is colloquial. When the verb "broke down" is not used, it is replaced with "have gone down the chute." Apart from the colloquial understandings contained in these usages, the relationship be-

Cronkite's introduction on January 31 illustrates the network's taken-for-granted reliance on reified concepts in these reports:

> Federal labor mediators spoke with both sides in the protracted coal strike today, trying to revive *the talks that broke down again* last weekend. The *walkout's* now 56 days old and assured of becoming *the longest on record.*

Here, the underlined words draw attention to how the journalistic formula used to accomodate the demands for neutrality, fairness, and brevity works within a reified jargon that cuts out the actors involved and their motivations.

9. A crucial hegemonic achievement of network television news lies in not raising strategic issues. Repetition and exclusion are closely allied features here: Recurrent themes lie within the dominant frames, while excluded themes oppose or undermine these frames. Recurrent frames included imminent fuel shortages and fears of violence by "defiant miners," while never-posed oppositional frames might have referred to the justice or injustice of wage labor or to OSHA health and safety statistics for the mining industry. The combination of repetition and exclusion formed a cogent framing pattern. The fourth report (December 6) submitted factors leading to the strike situation in terse, staccato fashion. No further discussion of the strike's etiology took place for two months. Instead, these reports consistently observed the likelihood/unlikelihood of fuel shortages and violence. Or when the first settlement proposal arose, reporters emphasized the number of days required to put the contract in place six times in three reports; this explanatory frame precluded addressing the BCOA's position and the reasons for miners' opposition to it.

These represent some recurrent framing devices in CBS's strike coverage, but there is no logical or systemic necessity for using these and no other devices. To detail framing devices is an empirical task, and at no point may the list be called complete. In the actual reports, these devices are not so artificially separated and neatly distinguished. Framing devices rarely appear in isolation, nor do they all operate at the same level. Framing devices such as the implicit equation of the interests of capital and the public are more primary than others because they help secure the field in which other devices work.

---

tween noun and verb is passive. In fact, CBS uses a verb which has many features of an adjective (their verb form draws on an adjectival term, "broken down" which means 'out of working order'). The verb refers to the noun.

FRAMES AT WORK

The first question we must address to any news report, in critical analysis, is, what gets asked? What is the scope of the report? What subjects are brought up? How are questions posed? A second level of analysis distinguishes implied as well as stated meanings. A third level examines the mode of address and the message form as a means of isolating interpretive rules. What gets asked and how it is asked determine the field in which other questions are dealt with.

Within the field created by "what gets on," the arrangement of materials via the devices of sequencing, cardstacking, reframing, and pseudobalance provide further specification of the "field" of the news report. These practices establish a field of discourse within which subsidiary practices of namecalling, leading questions, reification, and personalization may operate. The more fundamental devices of conflating private and public interests, cardstacking, reframing, sequencing, and pseudobalance may also reappear at subsidiary levels.

To illustrate how framing practices overlap and interface, we return again to the December 6 report which "explains" the focus of the dispute. As David Dick begins his report, we see and hear the gates to the mine entrance slamming shut. This is a classic shot in news on strikes used to summarize the meaning of the event—closure, stoppage of production, no work (cf. GUMG, 1976, 1980). We are shown a desolate gray scene, snow falling, and we can hear the wind blow. The machinery stands still. The camera lingers on this image as Dick begins his narration: "This morning it was peaceful up Cannelton Hollow and elsewhere in the Appalachian coal fields. Snow was falling. But nothing had changed the basic demands of the striking miners." The peace, of course, is a result of the strike; what is implied in the words, and by the film, is an absence: Silence where there should be noise, inactivity where the norm is activity. Dick enumerates the miners' "basic demands" as they are outlined across the screen:

> But nothing had changed the basic demands of the miners. They want full restoration of their medical and retirement benefits. The companies want the miners to pay part of these costs. The UMW demands a limited right to strike. The companies are bargaining for a no strike clause. More pay. That may be the easiest to resolve.

MINE WORKER DEMANDS

Full Medical and
Retirement Benefits

Right To Strike
During Contract

Increased Pay

What seems on the surface an abbreviated exercise in balanced reporting (first one side and then the other) yields neither balance nor accuracy. First, Dick cast the forces behind the strike solely in the union camp. Second, Dick failed to note that companies sought to abolish the existing system of health care. The word "restoration" suggests something was amiss, but what? Dick did not mention the crisis of the Funds or their restructuring the previous summer. By this account, the companies' stance does not seem unreasonable, surely miners can afford to pay part of their own health and retirement costs. Third, Dick substituted "no-strike clause" for the BCOA's "labor stability" demands based on penalties against miners.

Now, as the camera cuts to a man stringing up Christmas lights on a porch, Dick set the scene in terms of Christmas and miners prior knowledge that "a general strike on December 6 was all but inevitable." While Dick introduced miner Bob Pauley as being "really bothered" about how he would pay any medical bills "because he's not covered during the strike," the camera closed in on Pauley's head and shoulders, then just his extended hand holding the lights, and then his face. Now came Pauley's soundbite:

> That's the most thing—it's like me, I have a kidney stone attack every one or two years. I got to go to the hospital and stay about a week. That's about every year or so I have had it. And naturally, we want higher wages, better benefits, and better safety laws.

Why did Pauley follow his comments about kidney stones with "and naturally..?" This latter statement seems an explanation for his support of the strike, but as usual the seamless professional editing of scenes takes viewers instantaneously to another interview.[5]

Dick's introduction made it seem as if Pauley was talking about the problem of paying doctor bills during the strike, but Pauley's comments

---

[5]Network newspeople lay claim to professional superiority on the basis of their technological prowess. And certainly, their critics on the newspaper side are merciless when technical errors are made. Since their status and prestige, not to mention ratings, hinge on how seamless and invisible they are technically, network newspeople must endeavor to make each report as if it had never been assembled.

actually pertain to the miners' "basic demand" concerning medical benefits (as opposed to his paying a deductible on his hospital costs every year or so). Without breaking stride, Dick continued: "Jack Harper, who also lives up Cannelton Hollow, believes frequent wildcat strikes have not helped." With this splicing, Pauley's last sentence about wages, benefits, and safety laws is dropped and remains undeveloped. In fact, Harper's perspective on the strike is quite different than Pauley's. Yet viewers are not given a chance to dwell on this; instead Dick's phrasing in combination with the editing serializes their comments. The editorial choice of interviewee comments, although seemingly haphazard, reflects an a priori set of frames concerning the negative dimensions of strikes. Interviewed on the street in front of his house, Harper's view is that, "When the International calls a strike, that's fine, but every other two or three months you're out striking for this and that, then it really hurts everybody. I mean not only the company, but the membership as well." His point about wildcat strikes is pertinent if contextualized in the history of mineworker politics. But it is not. What comes across in the report is the common underlying frame which dictates the arrangement and tone of interviewees: Strikes are unfortunate and hurt everyone concerned.

7

Hierarchy of Access

Closely related to "what gets on" is "who gets on." In industrial news, the Glasgow Media Group found a "hierarchy of access" operating to prefer professionals, technocratic experts, and government officials over workers as interview subjects. This may be because the professionals who mediate the news prefer the elaborated codes of their own class (and educational status) over the restricted codes employed by the less educated lower classes (cf. Bernstein, 1975). Hartley (1982) and Hall et al. (1978) explain "hierarchy of access" as simply the ascendence of "institutional" voices over "accessed" voices. In this framework, the "accredited representatives of major social institutions" are permitted to play the role of "primary definers" of situations, while "accessed" voices respond and react within the field of discourse defined by "institutional voices." In the coal strike coverage, utility managers, politicians, President Carter, and energy secretary James Schlesinger were permitted to function as primary definers. Arnold Miller, as president of the Union, gained the role of primary definer when the subject was internal union conflict. More surprising, business community speakers functioned as primary definers on only one occasion.

In CBS's coal strike coverage, one telling feature of a hierarchy of access operated in reverse. Report after report, the camera remained fixed on miners, sometimes intruding through their car windows and into their homes—for example, on December 23 an older female miner allows a camera crew into her house to film her and her unemployed, ill husband on their living room couch. Many more times, miners were interviewed on the street, inside a union meeting place, or in a tavern. Meanwhile, the social and economic status of owners and managers permitted them to continually decline to appear on camera as interviewees. What's more, reporters and cameramen never intruded into their offices, homes, or cars. Several times, reporters did note that BCOA spokesmen declined comment, and let it go at that. On one occasion, however, Barry Serafin appeared on camera vainly trying to get a comment from any BCOA negotiator: One after another they file out of a hotel meeting room, each spurning Serafin's offer of the microphone as they walk past him. Otherwise, the relative privilege of the coal operators to control access was accepted without question or comment. Reporters' casual presumption of the right to enter coal miners' homes and ask them about intimate details of their lives is the reverse side of the same attitude.

Reporters conveyed different normative expectations about their— and by extension, the public's—right of access to miners as opposed to owners. CBS reporters drew direct attention to the exclusion of reporters and cameras from miners' meetings. Furtive camera shots peeking through a closed auditorium door, coupled with the reporter's comments about being denied access because of the bitterness of debate, drew attention to union efforts to shield its "backstage" region from public view (March 1). Rabel repeated this on March 12—"Anticipating bitterness over the back-to-work order, union leaders barred reporters from the meeting"—followed by the sound of a door slamming shut. In the March 19th report, Martha Teichner introduced a series of local union officers' soundbites by explaining how the media had been excluded from their meeting:

> Teichner: " . . . Three weeks ago the same group met for seven noisy hours over the last proposal. Today, reporters and camera crews were not allowed past the door. Rank-and-file miners couldn't sit in and listen. When it was over, miners said the meeting was calm and orderly, but they were divided over the contract."

But no CBS reporter was ever seen attempting to take viewers "backstage" into a stormy BCOA meeting, nor heard making inferences about the closed, secretive ways in which coal owners conducted their affairs.

Only four times did a BCOA negotiator appear on screen, and no BCOA speaker ever commented about the organization's position on the contract negotiations. On the other hand, rank-and-file members and union officers were repeatedly brought forward to "react"—117 times in 41 reports. Miners always seemed available—94 rank-and-file miner soundbites appeared, 23 union officers spoke, and Arnold Miller appeared on 17 occasions. Thus, while members of the UMWA accounted for *134* interview clips, BCOA representatives and their industrial managers were heard and seen on camera in a total of *8* clips.

One-hundred-and-thirty-four to eight seems an enormous disparity for a news program which prides itself on its "balanced" and "unbiased" reporting. Studies in Canada and Great Britain show labor speakers appear with greater frequency on television coverage of industrial news than management speakers, although the differences were far less than what we have found (GUMG, 1976; Hackett, 1985). On the surface this would appear to confirm charges that TV news is biased against business—after all, how much "balance" can there be if the ratio between labor speakers and management speakers is 17 to 1. Instead, we found the BCOA chose not to appear on television, opting for a public relations strategy of calculated invisibility to minimize possible damage to their public legitimacy. The network news media cooperated by accepting, without question, the premise that corporate employers need not justify themselves. The corollary to this was that "because the legitimacy of union activity is [tacitly] suspect, the unions are more frequently called upon by the media to account for their actions" (cited in Hackett, 1985, p. 265).

Class relations are a prime factor in assembling and producing these reports. For all their toughness and militancy in their struggle for a fair contract, the miners behaved compliantly with respect to the camera. Compliance took the form of cooperation shown by miners who let the camera into their homes to record their material deprivation; or the agreeability of a helpful miner who, thanks to a slight misediting of the clip, was revealed reacting to off-camera staging directions as he put up Christmas decorations on his front porch for the benefit of a CBS camera. Ironically, when other miners appeared on screen in their most angry and hostile displays they were no less accomodating for television news—posturing and burning contracts when they saw cameras may have gained attention, but it also positioned them precisely in terms of television's superficial stereotypes as uncouth and irrational.

The class relations of getting interviewed on video were never more evident than on January 31. When a top official of the Columbus & Southern Ohio Electric Co. speaks, he is shown at a respectable interview distance—head, shoulders, upper body. Moments later, addressing a retired miner who has been deprived of pension and medical benefits, the camera captures him at hyperintimate distance, his face occupying the whole screen. "Providing a greater distance between the camera lens (viewer) and the subject" makes that subject seem "more impartial" (Tuchman, 1978, p. 118). Conversely, the tighter closeup shot emphasizes the face, eyes, and mouth—this tends to emotionalize a person's presence and comments because they so accentuate and amplify the interviewee's expressive features. With remarkable uniformity over the entire strike coverage, CBS showed miner interviewees at either "intimate distance" or "close personal distance," while officials in interview or press conference scenes were shown at "far personal distance" (see Tuchman, 1978, pp. 116-117). The relationship between status rank, deference, and camera distance extends even among rank-and-file interviewees. The camera not only hugs the retired miner's face, we see a full-screen magnification of his hands—hand gestures comprise another expressive means of nonverbal communication. This intrusion into personal space was never shown in conjunction with a "primary definer" because it would have signified a lack of deference and respect.

That miners' were more regularly within view did not, however, give their views greater credence. "Hierarchy of access" cut in two directions in CBS's reporting. Since representatives of capital chose to avoid the camera, and because working class miners were always available (and, to a certain extent, deemed it a privilege to get on the tube), the screen registered images of strings of individual miners who spoke in an "uneducated" tongue. Via the editing process, miners' comments were turned into vox pops interviews which were splintered and deployed to affirm the acuity of professional reporters' presentations, or used as "reaction" shots. Vox pops interviews turn the interviewee into a symbolic representation of this or that "feeling" state.

But hierarchy of access also worked in the way described by the Glasgow Media Group. When available, interviews with professional administrators and government officials were accorded a preferred discursive status and permitted to speak in soundbites long enough to register a complete discursive argument or claim. Miners and retired miners were shot in tight closeups which convey their emotional involvement in the struggle. Coverage of rank-and-file rallies or meetings frequently used zoom lens to scan the faces of nonspeaking miners, before settling on the face of a speaker. Rank-and-file interviewees more often than not appeared in on-site contexts (outdoor and indoor), while "officials" were shown speaking at press conferences or from behind desks, symbolically indicating a more "rational" and dispassionate grasp of situations.[1]

Pictures of working-class miners shot at intimate distance accentuated their emotional subjectivity—permitting viewers to affectively identify with them, but also depriving their words of rational authority. Whereas interviews with "officials" were included for the facts they convey,

---

[1]"Desks are authoritative, we would argue, since in our culture for centuries authority has been found behind desks—with its knees covered. The pulpit, the judge's bench, the schoolmaster's table are prime examples of this," along with the news anchor's desk (GUMG, 1980, p. 251).

miners were interviewed to convey their feelings and attest to what has been said about them.

We have noted five dimensions of hierarchy of access: (a) number of speakers, (b) camera distance from face, (c) physical context of interview, (d) speaker as "primary definer" or as "reactor", and (e) length of soundbite. From November 25 to February 8, 23 rank-and-file miners appeared in interview clips which averaged 9 seconds. Arnold Miller appeared in 4 interviews which averaged 16 seconds in length. No BCOA interview appeared. Five interview clips of utility managers and nonelected government representatives averaged 22 seconds. From February 9 through the February 28, 25 rank-and-file miner interviewees averaged 9 seconds, while 10 union officers averaged 15 seconds. Miller averaged 19 seconds. A BCOA leader spoke once for 8 seconds; one mine manager spoke for 25 seconds; and one independent coal operator spoke for 37 seconds. Energy officials dipped slightly to 19 seconds, while politicians (excluding President Carter who had a 51 second speech) averaged over 18 seconds.

The pattern remained consistent for the remainder of CBS's strike coverage. Between March 1 and March 27, 44 miners appeared on screen for an average of 9 seconds; union officers dipped slightly to an average of 12 seconds; politicians were concentrated in a three-day period and averaged 18 seconds; and government officials or spokesmen averaged 25 seconds. BCOA representatives actually appeared four times during this period at an average of 16 seconds per soundbite.

Using length of interview as a measure, hierarchy of access runs downward from President Carter, to government officials and utility officials and politicians (all professionals), to UMW president Arnold Miller, to union officers, to rank-and-file miners. Look again at the "balance" created between February 15 and 19. On February 15 the average length of soundbites of four speakers at a rank-and-file rally was 10 seconds. On February 16, at a gathering of Governors and the President to discuss the coal crisis, the average soundbite for four speakers was 30 seconds. On February 19, at a meeting of UMW local officers, three speakers average 16 seconds apiece. Throughout CBS coverage, the relationship between speakers' social status and length of soundbite stayed consistent.

The total time given to interview clips and press conference clips in all the CBS reports was 2765 seconds (46 minutes). Rank-and-file miners spoke for 898 discontinuous seconds, or 32 percent of the total. Arnold Miller had 230 seconds and UMWA officers got 308 seconds. Though these UMWA speakers were frequently pitted against one another, they accounted for 51.5 percent of the total interview time on CBS. Meanwhile, BCOA leader spoke for a total of 72 seconds and their managers spoke for 46 seconds—barely 4 percent of the total interview time.

Miners' speech was restricted to serially edited bursts—9 second average—and pitted against fewer higher status speakers who spoke longer and more discursively. In practical terms, the ability to express a reasoned argument is the difference between a soundbite of 9 seconds and a soundbite of 18 seconds. Rank-and-file speakers were clust ered in edited strings of soundbites. The edited brevity of their soundbites, combined with tightness of camera shots, heightened the emotional flavor of miners' comments, while placing a corresponding limitation on their ability to articulate a reasoned, logical justification for their actions. Reporters reinforced this by casting miners motivations in emotional terms—for example, Don Webster calls miners' March 4 rejection of the second contract proposal a decision made in anger. On TV, miners appeared as a range of emotions, sometimes named by the reporter ("He's angry"; "He's upset"; "He's scared") and sometimes named by the camera (taciturn, bemused, belligerent, determined, gruff, laconic). As the camera scanned their faces, whatever argument could be made for the miners' side would have to be inferred by viewers from the visual documentation of the miners' material/emotional condition.

Soundbites: (in seconds)
Interviewees/Press Conference

Date	Rank & File	Arnold Miller	BCOA	Coal Managers	President Carter	Gov't Officials	Utility Managers	Union Officials	Politicians	Business	Independ. Coal Oper.	Other
Nov. 25	Schriber 3.5											
Nov. 28	Smith 15											
Dec. 4	Richards 8	Miller 15					Ludwig 28					
Dec. 5	Witherow 11	Miller 11										
	Mitchell 4											
Dec.6	Pauley 15											
Dec.8	Harper 9											
	Unnamed 7.5											
	Unnamed 9											
Dec.13	Kirkland 12											
Dec.23	Childress 9											
Dec.30	Williams 8											
Jan.2	Williams wife 15											
Jan.6												
Jan.17												
Jan.24						Schlesinger 24						
Jan.29												
Jan.30												
Jan.31	Daugherty 12						Apel 16.5		Moody 22.5			
	Huddleston 12.5											
	Huddleston 12											
	Unnamed 3											
Feb.2	Hammack 14											
Feb.3	Bower 2											
Feb.5	Hammack 7											
Feb.6	Harvey 8						Sissinger 28					
Feb.7	Grounds 5											
	Harrison 7											
	Harrison 9											
Feb.8	Ellison 12	Miller 17		Campbell 15						Costello 28		
Feb.9	Hunter 10	Miller 22		Campbell 10						Crane 14		
	Hunter 3.5											
	Walker 9.5											

135

Date	Names	Miller	Camicia	Carter	Marshall / Sorrels	Barker	Lawley	Rockefeller	Storts / Morton	Notes
Feb.10	Morris 8 Shiflett 3	Miller 33 Miller 3			Sorrels 22			Rockefeller 19		
Feb.12	Cunningham 6 Unnamed 6 Ricer 9.5 Hoskins 3.5 Unnamed 3	Miller 24 Miller 10		Carter 18			Lawley 12 Form 23			4 truckers 4 4.5 11 9
Feb.13	Henderson 9 Pugh 14									
Feb.14					Yaffe 13		Lutz 8			Mine eng 5
Feb.15	Lawson 9 Burke 5 Hirsch 11 Lane 17				Marshall 13 Watt 13					
Feb.16		Miller 10		Carter 51	**Marshall 24**		Sturgill 20 Forbes 17 Phelan 9 Forms 22	**Schapp 26 Bowen 20**		
Feb.17				Carter 37				Rockefeller 18		Auto worker 10 Persnl Dir 23
Feb.19										
Feb.20		Miller 6			Sorrels 8			Brighton 9		
Feb.21	Howard 14 Harper 8							Foley 13 Cranston 8	Storts 14	AFL Pres 27 Principal 15 Eyewitness
Feb.22	Unnamed 9	Miller 6 Miller 3			Marshall 19		Dawes 12			
Feb.23				Carter 12						
Feb.24			Camicia 13			Barker		Rockefeller 22 Baker 13		
Feb.25	Salters 13	Miller 20		**Carter 2:15**	**Marshall 20**		Lucas 17 Campbell 7	Bowen 16		
Feb.26	Bass 16									
Feb.27	Hudnall 10 Skaggs 4.5									
Feb.28	McCoy 6 Hudnall 7									
Mar.1							Roberts 11 Willis 13		Morton 37	
Mar.3	Seachrist 13 Taylor 9.5 Leach 8				Leslie					
Mar.4	Brooks 11 Rifle 8.5 Bowles 7						Hoskins			survey analyst

136

Date	Names	Miller	Camicia	Koiro	Carter	Schlesinger	Essylton	Conway	Bear	UAW
Mar.5	Unnamed 9 Jones 8 Payne 8 Rice 5 Petrus 15 Wagnild 6 Binni 13 Kenney 12.5 Unnamed 6.5 McNeal 7.5			Koiro 11		Schlesinger 27	Essylton 24 Christian 9	Conway 13 Hudnut 32		UAW pres 26
Mar.6	Prout 16 Lucido 18	Miller 5			Carter 14 17 39	Schlesinger 23	Hoskins 14	Ford 10 Hansen 16	Bear'21	
Mar.7	Prout 15		Camicia 10	Adams 10	Carter 40 12	Gentry 23	Jones 12	Brademus 19		
Mar.8	Buchanan 6 Nuccatelli 23 White 4.5 Raisovich 15 Pritt 8									
Mar.9	Lanham 8 Unnamed 12									
Mar.10	Bowyer 22						Roberts 9 Dawes Murphy			3 Natl Guard officers
Mar.11	Campbell									
Mar.12	Morris 8 Unnamed 9.5 Corris 16 R. Morris Huckleberry 12	Miller 12	Camicia 26							
Mar.13			Camicia 13				Wallace 4			
Mar.14										
Mar.17							Hayes 6 Maynard 9 Kozee 8 Belcher 12 Forms 25			
Mar.19		Miller 5	Brennan 23							
Mar.23	Ojeda 4	Miller 35								
Mar.24	Phillips 8	Miller 24								
Mar.25	Pritt Christian	Miller 26								
Mar.26	Canley Unnamed									
Mar.27	Craft									
Mar.30	Petry									

137

8

Defining the Strike Consensually

From his anchor position, Walter Cronkite announced the forthcoming news of a coal strike on November 25, 1977.

> A coal strike on December 6 now appears all but inevitable. Talks broke off today with just ten days to go on the old contract, the minimum time needed to ratify any new agreement. If a strike comes it won't affect most industries for several months. Businesses have been building up their supplies. Tens of thousands of nonunion miners will go on producing.

In this 20-second report, Cronkite established CBS's most significant and sustained frames of the strike. The coal "strike" was posed as a disruption of a societal consensus and a possible threat to public well-being. No reason was offered for the strike, merely that "talks broke off"; neither did the report indicate whose actions lay behind the coal strike. Behind Cronkite, occupying the right side of the screen, hung a squared frame containing a line drawing of a male from the shoulders up, wearing a miner's hat with lamp, in front of a loaded coal trolley. The drawing bore the legend: "Coal Strike?" In ensuing reports, variations on this drawing symbolically anchored, and designated, the story.

No mention of this impending event appeared in previous reports. Cronkite's voice and his text initially suggest a modest urgency and alarm, yet the remainder of the announcement normalizes the situation. "Businesses" obviously anticipated it, since they "have been building up their supplies." News value was located here in the near "inevitability" of the strike, although CBS chose also to lend an air of suspense—hence, the question mark on the screen. Since "minimum time" was left to ratify any agreement, the cessation of talks made the strike a virtual fait accompli. Cronkite's somber inflection signified this to be unfortunate, but the bad news was immediately followed by a reassurance about the strike's possible effects. "If a strike comes," the public would face no immediate danger because of the preparation of "businesses" and the existence of nonunion mines.

What was the relationship between the parties who have "broken off talks"? If our knowledge was confined to what *CBS News* told us, their account would be a riddle. Broadcasters assume viewers possess an extensive knowledge about society and its workings, a set of background assumptions and shared understandings that render news stories meaningful. Apparently, the term "coal strike" is sufficient to conjure up an entire picture—a map—of industrial relations. Cronkite glossed the category of "strike," assuming viewers possess enough familiarity with it to fill in an understanding that strikes designate the collective refusal of employees to work. Its opposite, "contract," is likewise glossed. Denotatively, it refers to formal/legal provisions governing the conditions and terms of employment. Its connotative weight interests us here, as a symbolic marker for the unspoken class relationship between owners and laborers. The opposition between "old contract" and "new agreement" signifies that such "agreements" require periodic renewal, and that without a contract, workers are not liable to work, thus disrupting the flow of production. The third sentence presumes viewers' background knowledge of "ripple effects" based on the interdependence of industries. Reference to "non-union mines" which will "go on producing" is an undeveloped reminder that strikes are launched by worker organizations that negotiate in behalf of their members; and that "nonunion mines" employ workers who opt not to join such organizations, and thus continue producing.

Cronkite's terse recital of "just the facts" was based on an "act of categorizing" which was an "act of theorizing" (Tuchman, 1978, p. 205). "'What is already known' is not a set of neutral facts. It is a set of common-sense constructions and ideological interpretations about the world, which holds the society together at the level of everyday beliefs . . . News values require *consensus knowledge* about the world" (Hall, 1972, p. 78). Thus far, the structure of the story presumes viewers share a body of background knowledge which does not see the contradiction of inequality in the face of apparent equality, of a sudden struggle erupting between two ostensibly equal parties. Newspeople trade on background assumptions containing unresolved contradictions, and unspoken "facts" that are unspeakable within the frameworks they have imposed on events. The unspoken relation here is that between nonunion mines and class struggle. The frame not chosen is "class relations."[1] Management hires workers under terms which are, nominally, mutually agreed upon. The subtext to this agreement is a structural constraint faced by workers who must earn a living. The term "contract" implies all this, but the coerced character of the worker's consent is not articulated within the boundaries of news talk. The "right" to hire and fire and make decisions about organization of the workplace and working conditions lies with the employer. The ability to withhold their labor enables workers to interrupt production, and therefore profits. Hence, the "agreement" the labor contract represents is a precarious one, based on mutually opposing interests. When open conflict occurs, either party is likely to use its power to renegotiate the terms of the relationship.

As in subsequent reports, the bare word "strike" stands for this entire complex of relations. It represents industrial conflict per se. Unequal power relations are presumed as the context in which labor stoppages occur, but this remains unspoken in these news reports. Network television's usual preoccupation with power in party politics and government does not carry over into relations between labor and management. The power relations which condition the dual antagonism that causes strikes cannot be spoken within the frames available to newspeople. Though CBS reporters exhibited a kind of Machiavellian interest in the question of backstage political maneuvering when the subject was internal union politics (e.g., the campaign within the UMWA to recall Arnold Miller), the political dimension between the UMWA and the BCOA remained less visible, and political machinations on the BCOA's part were invisible (with one exception on February 22). Here, again, we see that news takes shape within the ideological contours of the larger society. In decoding news messages, "ideologies are the connecting links between the so-called 'facts' of the news and the background assumptions which enable us . . . to understand those 'facts'" (Glasgow University Media Group (GUMG), 1980, p. 177). Reporting, or not reporting, on power games reveals an obverse dimension of the "hierarchy of access"—a "hierarchy of distrust"—in which the mass media maintain a wary eye and an edge of "distrust" toward unions that is absent with regard to business.[2]

---

[1]A globally alternative reading (cf. Hall, 1980) of this report would see in this tersely abbreviated account both an ideologically inflected account and the germ of an accurate appraisal of how capitalist interests have attempted to break the strength of unions. Class conflict lurks beneath the surface of the stories, there to be interpreted by those attuned to its existence.

[2]This "hierarchy of distrust" varies depending on the relationship being reported. In the 1970s, when company practices came into conflict with

"Strike" refers to workers' collective action of withholding their labor, but management may also take action by withdrawing work privileges; locking out workers; stockpiling; or taking back benefits previously given. The causes of strikes lie in structured oppositions of interest. They do not lie with workers alone, though workers perform the act of striking. Therefore, reporting the news of a strike with all its connotations of union aggression, minus an explanation of the conditions leading to it, and minus the relationality of the parties, produces ideological consequences. "The ideological reduction involved in designating a story in terms of a single protagonist when the activity by nature involves at minimum two groups, systematically structures the reporting" (GUMG, 1980, p. 178).

Newspeople portray the labor contract as a consensual one, expressing the liberal belief in a labor-management "partnership." When labor "violates" this agreement by striking work, the consensus unravels and it is "news." Owing to the structural inequality in the wage labor/private property relation, it is workers who take action, and who therefore appear to bear the onus of the "partnership." When management breaks a contract, it is less likely to be reported; since any retaliatory action labor may take is both more visible and more likely to be reported, when shown in isolation it tends to come across as unprovoked and disruptive.

The societal consensus guarded by CBS does not require a mechanical uniformity of opinion. Instead, newspeople construct stories that pivot on the tension of whether the normalcy associated with consensus will be restored or not. This model of story conceptualization and devlopment draws on tacitly shared consensual knowledge to frame the boundaries of discourse. Framing this as a 'consensual' universe is not, nor can it be, neutral, for it takes place in a class society. It works to limit the terms of debate to exclude agendas that undermine the hegemony of dominant class interests. Dissent and disruption is consistently reinterpreted, and reframed to confirm and endorse the adequacy of hegemonic representations—including the "free" labor contract, the "free" market, "free" speech, and "individual choice." The hegemonic representation is always a partial one. For example, the "freedom" to work denotes the lack of an obligation to work, but there is also no alternative but to work for a living wage. Legitimate dissent may only concern whom to work for, and for how much: This, along with freedom of

---

community interests on environmental matters, then television journalism's pendulum of 'distrust' would swing toward the companies. In fact, this was a prime reason that large corporations charged television news with being biased against business interests.

consumption, comprises the latitude of choice within a capitalist economy. Corporate news media in advanced capitalist societies rarely raise (or, permit) reflexive questions about wage labor as an activity or as a relationship. The assumption of wage labor itself is opaque and impenetrable. Where there was human history, the media invokes cliches about "human nature."

Laborers have struck work for many reasons, not solely over wages. Given the structural relationships created by commodity exchange, economic differences are obviously preeminant. But workers may also contest the right of owners to control their labor activities and impose managerial discipline and pace over their work. They sometimes seek to protect health and safety; do battle over the structuring of internal labor markets and seniority systems; contest the introduction of new technologies; and may even resist the authority by which owners constitute themselves as masters. The revolutionary element in these struggles is eclipsed when they are seen as merely pay disputes: In this way, strikes are brought back into the realm of the dominant discourse—structured by the assumption of commodity relations as natural and eternal.

The coal industry was economic and political in nature, yet questions about power and authority in the workplace remain unspoken. A pivotal framing device appears repeatedly: Political issues, involving conflicting class interests are reduced to negotiations about money. According to this crude economistic view, negotiations are automatically presumed to concern the amount paid to employees, not about the kind of authority and control exercised at work. Newstalk accomplishes this reduction by emphasizing the money wage, while scrupulously avoiding the social relations of production. Ironically, though newspeople cover strikes because they are conflictual, they assume this fundamental consensus between workers and management. When the matter is irreducibly political, such as the right to strike, it cannot be adequately encompassed by these frames of reference: hence the lack of explanation and the selective emphasis on the negative consequences of strikes. From their perspective, newspeople can only express concern at the breakdown of the (assumed) consensus and report the damage.

CONDENSATION AND FLOW

On November 28, 1977, Cronkite again addressed his audience about the impending coal strike. Flanking him on the screen is the same logo used in the first report, minus the rhetorical inscription. This squared frame encasing a miner in front of a coal trolley would alternate during

CBS's coverage with another frame of a placard reading "COAL STRIKE" beside a pickaxe lying on end. The condensed, abbreviated meanings denoted and connoted by these images form the television news-sign of the coal strike story. These static arrangements of signifiers reductively identify the coal strike story. The intent is not that viewers dwell on these iconic frames, but that they recognize them as derivative signifiers that stand for "coal strike."

As a format, this technique of photographically inserting frames on screen structures a condensation of meaning. The spatial/compositional arrangements "constitute a discourse of their own" (Hall, 1972, p. 57) which govern interpretation of this visual format. This format illustrates Barthes' argument about how myth is constructed as a "second-order semiological system." These signs (e.g., man/miners' helmet + coal trolley; or pickaxe on side + poster with words COAL STRIKE) stem from reducing images to a "pure signifying function." Drawings of a man with helmet, a coal trolley, and a pickaxe become "mere" signifiers in the format's signification process which delivers a second-order sign—a myth of "the coal strike." Look at the way the pickaxe is converted into an ideological sign. "Denotatively" the image resembles a tool used for breaking hard surfaces; one end is sharply pointed and the other end has a chisel edge. Within the frame, however, it lies on its side in a state of nonuse. This meaning is reinforced by situating it side by side with a poster bearing the phrase "Coal Strike." Now the pickaxe connotes the "absence of production" which has been made identical to the meaning of "strike." The pickaxe on its side now sybolizes the meaning of the "coal strike."

Peirce's system of semiotic classification divides signs into: (a) iconic signs which "reproduce some of the conditions of perception" (b) indexical signs which point to something else, for example, an arrow; (c) symbolic signs which stand for something else. When an image is placed inside the framebox used on television news it is made to work in all three ways. Here, the drawing of a male wearing a miner's helmet and jacket and a coal trolley resembles the objects represented—their referents. Given the function of the framebox, we may safely say the resemblance is "motivated" and "planned" (Hartley, 1982, p. 30). But it is precisely the functional aspect of the framebox which turns the image from an iconic reminder to an indexical sign—within the boundaries of the framebox, *it points to the story*. In this sense, the frame as a whole functions as a signifier. Finally, the very act of placing meaningful images in the framebox transforms them into a symbolic representation that stands for the story being presented.

Cronkite's report begins: "With a coal strike threatened for next week . . ." The subject is unnamed; viewers are not openly told who authors the threat. Instead, the emphasis is on the fact of the threat. The report is also silent regarding the object of the strike; viewers are not told who is threatened. In a conversation, we might understand a speaker to refer to himself as the threatened person, but codes of news talk are not those of conversation. Newscasters do not speak for anyone in particular, or such is their contention about addressing "the public." Because news is structured to appear as "news from nowhere," the neutrality newspeople aim at precludes acknowledgement of news as the intentional production of speaking subjects.[3] One possibility, then, is that viewers may presume the projected coal strike threatens themselves, "the public." Initiating the discourse with the preposition "with" invites viewers to join the speaker, to project themselves into the sentence. The verb "threatened" used in conjunction with this mode of address latently sets up an us/them division, implying that miners author the threat against us.

Let us return for a moment to the invisible subject. Again, we observe a shadowing of agency: A cause is implied, but obscurely. Attention is concentrated on the sudden, unexplained appearance of a coal strike, an event which apparently will affect us all. The strike is introduced, not as a set of complicated relationships arising from a series of events and institutional structures, but in isolation as a thing in itself. Reified in this way, the account naturalizes the occurrence. The strike becomes mythologized and dehistoricized. By straining to bury all signs of human agency, and all manifest evidence of class struggle, the CBS account obscures the purposive character of the ideological system. Myths "ask us to imagine that the particular inflection which has been imposed on history has always been there. They do not unveil history, they inflect it, transforming it into nature" (Hall, 1972, p. 83).

The message about a need for universal concern at the strike, however, cannot be addressed to the strikers: They are "cut out of the message and distanced from the public" (GUMG, 1980, p. 187), because they are the ones who threaten. The strikers' conflict, however, is with the coal companies; it is the latter, if anybody, whom they threaten, since fears of a fuel shortage to the public have already been allayed. What we have here, in fact, is a presumed identity of interests between the industry (private capital) and the "public." Though private accumulation has historically, on occasion, proved antagonistic to broader social interests, the mainstream media has ideologically conflated the

---

[3]In the words of Richard S. Salant, former president of *CBS News*, "Our reporters do not cover stories from their point of view. They are presenting stories from *nobody's* point of view" (in Epstein, 1973, p. ix).

interests of private ownership with those of the larger society.[4]

Look again at Cronkite's opening linguistic construction: "With a coal strike threatened for next week . . ." Newspeople construct sentences with one eye on effective rhetorical strategy and another on sequencing themes in order of importance. Here, the "peg on which to hang the message of the sentence" (Halliday, 1970, p. 256) either presumes the reasons for the strike to be common background knowledge or beside the point. We opt for the latter interpretation because a smooth, easy transition sweeps viewers along to " . . . Federal mediators have set up a meeting . . . between the union and the coal industry." Cronkite's matter-of-fact tones convey an air of normalcy surrounding the Federal mediation process and the centralization of authority it presupposes. Because a strike is implicitly presented as deviant, disruptive of production, and an unspoken consensus, the immediate concern becomes an expeditious resolution that restores consensus. Hence, Federal mediation seems an objectively natural and necessary move, an uproblematic effort at crisis management. Yet it is possible to sound as many alarms about this act as about the first. Why should the State intervene in a capital-labor dispute? How can a Federal agency fulfill the role of impartial mediator when it is in the Federal government's material interests to end the strike as soon as possible?[5] This interest entails a threat to the workers' bargaining leverage: The capacity to interrupt coal company profits, and to precipitate a fuel crisis. It may also impede the interest of coal operators to secure greater control over the work force.

Cronkite's introduction lasted 20 seconds. After delivering the item on the Federal Mediators' call for a meeting to get the "stalled" talks "moving," Cronkite shifts to a tangential frame: "Three companies have gone their *own* way", seeking their own contract with the UMW, "bypassing" the coal industry bargaining association. Cronkite's comments emphasize that strikes are undersirable, but official—That is,

---

[4]This presumed identity was less disingenuous during the ascent of the bourgeoisie, when the public sphere, limited as it was to the educated classes (who substantially coincided with the entrepreneurial classes), upheld a free market of ideas and information in order to safeguard the participants from "vested interests" of the absolutist state (Brenkman, 1979; Hohendahl, 1974).

[5]This was not an abstract issue. "The White House strategy to break the BCOA-UMWA impasse was to get one company to negotiate separately with the UMWA and use that contract as a template for the BCOA hardliners. Months before the negotiations, William Hobgood" of the Federal Mediation and Conciliation Service began the strategic manuevering that eventually produced the "P&M agreement" on February 20th. Despite serious opposition from both the UMWA and the BCOA, the Carter administration pressured both sides into it (Seltzer, 1985, p. 152).

Federal—negotiations will probably not avert this strike; hence, perhaps the unofficial talks will get things moving.

Barry Serafin's report begins with an aerial view of a coal tipple, and Serafin's voice is heard above the whirring noise of a helicopter: "As in the rest of West Virginia, coal is king in Logan County. The concern and uncertainty across the coalfields about the coming months are felt strongly here . . ." Again note the use of passive voice—by whom? The structure of the previous sentence leads us to presume "everyone" is concerned. Serafin continues:

> But while the national bargaining in Washington has reached an impasse, three local companies who have remained independent of the BCOA, today began their own talks with the UMW. The union has said an agreement might spur progress at the national level. But the betting here is, contract or no contract, the 2000 miners effected would be kept off the job by those miners taking part in the national walkout.

After this, the report shifts to two interview bites with miners about their feelings concerning a strike. The report begins with an edited sequence of seven film scenes to fit Serafin's introduction. But why these shots? Following the aerial shot is a closeup shot of a coal hopper unloading; this cuts to a shot of coal bins being lifted along a hillside. The next scene shows males seated around a table. We recognize this as a negotiating meeting. From two company representatives in coats and ties, the camera then pans to the end of the table where union representatives are clustered in their patterned shirts and workingclass haircuts. All seem grim and tight lipped. This scene gives way to a shot of six miners conversing as they mill about in front of a mine entrance. The end of the sentence about progress at the national level is keyed to a shot of a chute dumping a stream of pulverized coal into a bin. This gives way to a tighter shot of a railroad car with a mineworker holding on to the side, before the camera slowly pulls back to reveal the entire railroad car with the Chesapeake and Ohio Railroad's sleeping cat insignia on its side. These scenes parallel in structure the movement from local to national contained in the verbal narrative. The video illustrates the *transport* of coal from mine to hoppers to bins to railroads that will be affected by the walkout. The implied trajectory of this photographic narrative is the movement of coal to you the consumer.

IDEOLOGICAL CONSENSUS AND CONCEPTUAL DISARRAY

By now, the story has diverted from the initial news frame about independent negotiations to whether striking miners will prevent nonstriking miners from working. The story's tight technical organization is matched in degree by its conceptual disarray. Consider the questions left unasked and unanswered about the primary news frame? (a) Why is there an "impasse" between miners and owners? (b) what companies are referred to? (c) Why are these "local" firms "bypassing" the BCOA? (d) What differentiates their bargaining position from the BCOA's?[6] In strictly journalistic terms, why make the news frame and lead-in the independent negotiations in Logan County if no *facts* about the event are to be reported? Minimally, viewers are offered a few seconds of film of a stereotypical meeting room minus any substantive comments from, or about, those talks.

None of this can be dwelt on since the flow of the video rambles elsewhere, while Serafin's commentary shifts to miners keeping other miners off the job. Serafin's narrative then abruptly gives way to an interviewee. A miner named John Shriber appears as an accessed voice to attest to the veracity of Serafin's preceding statement about striking miners keeping other workers out with them: (Shriber) "Well, I (uh) believe we'll still be affected by the strike." The screen then cuts to another miner pictured at intimate distance—we see only his face with a chew of tobacco in his cheek—because his is an "interesting face" (Tuchman, 1978, p. 118).

> Smith: "I'd like to see more heads, not have no strike, settle it some way without a strike, as far as that goes."
>
> Serafin: "Why is that?"
>
> Smith: "Well, Christmas' comin up here, and uh every other thing and high stuff—a man get behind."
>
> Serafin: "What kind of Christmas is it going to be if it's a nationwide strike?"
>
> Smith: "Not gonna be much Christmas I wouldn't think."

---

[6]The three companies were Gilbert Imported Hardwoods, Chafin Coal Company, and Amherst Coal Company. James Harless, president of Gilbert, explained the defection from the BCOA: "I think the BCOA has made a lot of mistakes over the years. I didn't want to be a party to any more they made." These companies were unhappy with the BCOA hardline on restoration of health benefits and a limited right to strike. Both Amherst and Chafin had records of relatively harmonious labor relations. "We've always settled our grievances and we've never taken them to arbitration," said John C. Chafin, president of Chafin Coal. "Our men never go out and picket other companies. We feel like, hell's fire, a right to strike on a local issue would help Chafin, not hurt Chafin" (UPI, 11/28/77).

Serafin redirects this soundbite from miner Sherman Smith to reach a general conclusion: "While *no one* seems happy about it, there is very little chance now that *anything* that happens . . . will head off a nationwide coal strike by the United Mine Workers" (emphasis original). Serafin's words and countenance indicate concern. In this sympathetic posture he asks a leading, and gratuitous, question of Smith: "What kind of Christmas is it going to be . . . ?" Most of the interview consists of a tight closeup shot of Smith, a laconic, tobacco-chewing man, with a think mountaineer accent. A pickup truck parked behind him, Smith confirms every stereotype we might have of uneducated "hillbilly" miners. As Serafin concludes his question the camera pans back to his face and his expression of concern. Few interviews in these reports depict the correspondent's face, and when they do, there is generally minimal expression. This camera movement to Serafin helps draw the viewer into the mood evoked, of sympathy and concern for the miners' plight.

The aloof and impartial attitude correspondents normally display is dropped here, for what is, perhaps, more "effective" reporting. The sympathy shown for the miners' hardship represents a "liberal" position; a more conservative move would have condemned miners for halting production and inflicting harm on themselves at the same time. This reveals one contradiction of broadcast journalists' liberalism: While a strike is considered unfortunate, there is sympathy for the miners, who are here, also depicted as victims. The contradiction does not stand out because CBS shadows responsibility for the strike, and adopts a model that posits a disjuncture between the union and its members. It is " . . . a coal strike by the United Mine Workers," but if "no one seems happy," including the miners, then the actual forces behind the strike, and their motives, might seem mysterious or menacing were it not for the quiet distinction implied between miners and "the union." CBS tacitly questions whether the UMW *as* an institution does a disservice to both the miners and the consuming public, whether its interests are congruent with theirs.

9

Cutting Out
Capital/Foregrounding Anarchy

Over the first 66 days of the strike, CBS did not present viewers with a single interview from a BCOA representative. The BCOA position, stated in the written press, had yet to be stated on CBS.[1]

Though his comments were barely identified with management, and there was no mention of the BCOA, viewers finally saw and heard a manager during the February 9th report.

Cronkite delivered the news item: 52 presidents of union locals in one Ohio and West Virginia district had urged the union council to reject the proposed contract, partly because the new contract, if ratified, would impose penalties on wildcat strikers. Cronkite explains, "Their opposition has a lot to do with the penalties the new contract would impose on wildcat strikers. And that has a lot to do with," says Cronkite, "the powerful tradition in the coalfields." Cronkite's passive language of causation ("And that has a lot to do with") served as a lead-in to Ed Rabel's explanatory account from the field. For the first time, Cronkite stated "wildcat strikes" as having explanatory relevance. There is little hint here of management, even though the report will include our first witness of a management voice. Cronkite did not define them as a part of the story. Rabel begins:

---

[1]We have not found evidence of the BCOA voicing public displeasure with CBS strike coverage and their omission of the BCOA position. Yet, coal operators had been notoriously unhappy with what they regarded as media unfairness. Why then were they so silent about this lack of balance in network coverage?

The tradition began years ago, when the only weapon miners had to fight coal company abuse was the strike. But today, in spite of major advances in methods UMW miners can use to successfully challenge the companies, the tradition persists.

This is CBS's first reference to coal company abuse, although the unspecified abuse refers to some distant past, counterposed and unrelated to the present. When contextualized like this, "the tradition" represents an archaic anachronism. What would motivate miners to "persist" in a practice which runs counter to the efficacy of modern methods? Is the miners' behavior reasoned, is it legitimate? What were the "major advances in methods" of combatting coal company abuses? Why are these progressive factors left unspecified? What, for that matter, do coal company abuses refer to? Presumably, Rabel refers to the Arbitration Review Board created under the 1974 contract, which bureaucratically rationalized a method of working out grievances. But he crucially omits the track record of this "advance." He does not mention UMW charges that industrywide, companies violated the contract's health and safety provisions or miners' charges that companies' harassed miner safety committees. Neither does he indicate how companies like Consol Coal used the grievance procedure process to drag out disputes. What about miners' complaints about how long it took to resolve grievances via the bureaucratic review board?

The visuals shown while Rabel delivered his introduction do not enhance viewers' knowledge of the matter. The same three camera shots appeared in the January 31 story from Jacksboro, Tennessee. They've been included here for the simple iconic and indexical purpose of visually identifying and pointing to "the picket line." The shots, in order, were: (a) a handwritten placard reading "UNION on STRIKE" posted on a shed; (b) same shed from a distance across a back road, while four circled miners converse beside a pickup truck; and (c) same miners, presumably performing the task of manning the picket line, from a different angle. These shots would seem wholly discontinuous were it not for the narrator's text.

Two interview sequences follow with miners who vow they will "never cross a picket line." Their words were included to illustrate the persistence of an unreasoned tradition among the miners. Each edited interview attested to norms and sanctions regarding the picket line. A first miner recollects about transmission of the tradition as a moral imperative from father to son: "See, my daddy worked in coal mines years ago, and he said—he told me this, he said, 'Son, never cross a picket line.' Said, 'Don't you never cross a picket line.'" A second miner expresses the sentiment from the sanction viewpoint: "Well, I ain't crossing no picket line and get my head mashed in.'' Their edited comments testify to their refusal to be 'scabs' or break ranks with fellow union members but their comments do not address the reason for the strike in the first place. None of the reporter's questions are heard, but the answers suggest miners were not asked why they formed picket lines in recent years and months, but if they would cross them. This tells us something about their solidarity, but little about why they feel a need for it.

Considerable editorial effort has been expended here. The first miner spoke to viewers at head and neck distance for nearly 10 seconds, but his words have been obviously spliced together to contract his soundbite. The second miner, Oliver Hunter, was shown close up as he colorfully expressed himself in a rural Appalachian accent. We can only imagine what else he had to say because the video track remained fixed on him speaking, but his voice was cut out, superceded by Rabel's voiceover resumption of his explanatory account:

> There are charges that some forces are using the miners' almost fanatical respect for the picket line for their own purposes. They cite the time thousands honored a picket line set up by one side in the Kanawha County, West Virginia, textbook controversy, an issue that had nothing to do with conditions in the coal mines. Such work stoppages, they say, led to the controversial contract provision which would fine miners blamed for unauthorized, or wildcat, strikes.

Using this device, Rabel turned Hunter's face into a potential visual signifier of ''miner's almost fanatical respect.'' As Rabel's narrative continued, Hunter's face was replaced by a sequence of seven film scenes labeled Nov. 9, 1974, arranged in a montage to show textbook protesters. Scenes of marchers, placards and slogans offer a sense of the ideological surface of that event: for example, ''No Prayer! No Filth Either!''

Beneath this sequence lurks a deep set of ideological predispositions shared by newspeople at CBS, which they presume their audience ratifies. Their antipathy to ''Communist totalitarian'' regimes enables them to appreciate worker solidarity in Eastern-bloc countries. When reporting the Polish Solidarity movement, interviews like this came to symbolize a popular and heroic resistance to industrial oppression. But here, in a domestic situation, rank-and-file miners' vows of solidarity are turned to indict them of working class/hillbilly authoritarianism and stubborn irrationality.

With the preceding snippets of miner interviews as evidence of ''almost fanatical respect for the picket line,'' Rabel conveyed ''charges'' from unidentified sources. What initially seemed to be interviews testifying to miners' tradition-bound propensity to strike are now reframed to indicate manipulation by "some forces." Who makes these charges? "Charges" rarely come from disinterested parties. Why did Rabel avoid naming the source of these "charges"? What forces were manipulating the miners' tradition? And what were their "own purposes"?

The Kanawha County textbook case involved white, working-class parents from the Appalachian coalfields who felt power over their lives had been usurped from them, and revolted against a middle-class school board's imposition of textbooks that seemed to attack their conservative, God-fearing views. Protesters chose the symbolic focus of textbooks because they felt culturally disrespected and disempowered as to what their children would learn—their resentment was directed at middle-class educators for "talking down to the laboring class of people." However, right-wing fundamentalist leaders seized upon these anti-middle-class sentiments, and wildcat work stoppages spread in the Paint Creek and Cabin Creek districts in support of the book protest (Billings & Goldman, 1983). But the politics of work stoppages during the book protests were not straightforward: "Some miners . . . felt a wildcat strike would weaken the steel companies and utilities in the current [1974] UMWA negotiations by depleting existing stockpiles" (Seltzer, 1974, p. 433); still other miners pushed a hard line to enhance their political reputations within the union. In retrospect, miners' participation in this cultural protest hurt them in negotiations, because it undermined Miller's arguments regarding his ability to deliver a disciplined workforce.

Rabel's narrative in conjunction with file footage exemplifies a network news tendency to portray events in a fragmentary, disconnected fashion, even when there is an attempt to provide background context. Material and ideological determinations that link and unite social events are obscured. Amidst the chaos of events, newspeople do seek to exercise some discipline by ordering occurrences to let their meaning "shine forth." They point to earlier parallels, connect them with current events, suggest similarities, and thereby "explain" things. They perform pop history—a muddled "history" made up of this and that "fact" woven together into neat, but facile packages, and supported by the apparently empirical index of file film footage. No fact is wholly inaccurate, but too many are left out and the connections linking them together are haphazard at best.

Respect for a picket line is indeed a sacred and powerful tradition passed on from generation to generation in the coal fields. Why? Rabel glosses this by offering miners' testimonial of its existence. But without examining the reasons for continuing this "tradition," how can wildcat strikes, their causes, or their relationship to union politics and operator practices be understood? The problem as posed by Rabel, is the "almost fanatical" respect for a now regressive practice [compared to the unnamed "advances"] being manipulated by unnamed Machiavellian forces. As a result, and this is the report's conclusion as well, the picket line now brings trouble on the heads of all miners, the union, and the regional economy. Rooting strikes in an idealist conception of tradition mystified rather than explained the wildcat strikes.

What was Rabel's agenda here? Was he obliquely marginalizing the "right- to-strike" group as a militant hot-headed fraction of the miners: "Some forces" are using the miners "for their own purposes," to go on strike, according to "them"? His mention of the textbook controversy only makes this more mysterious—what purposes could such action serve? Why does he make fuzzy the agents/actors involved? Was Rabel cautiously and delicately echoing stories in the *Charleston Gazette-Mail* and *NY Times* reporting allegations of Communist agitators in the coalfields (see Seltzer, 1980; Clark, 1981)? If so, then the report is even more misleading, since those who took advantage of miners' respect for the picket line in the textbook protests came from the fundamentalist right. Or did these allegations come from industry spokespersons such as Cleve Campbell?

Either way, this narrative situates an abrupt break to the interview comments from Cleve Campbell, nominated on screen as "Mgr. Industrial Relations." Rabel preceded Campbell's comments by defining the primary referent of "such work stoppages" in terms of the Kanawha textbook protests. This is reinforced by the final visual scene depicting the book protests before switching to an excerpt of Campbell's interview: an image of a white, mustached male wearing a stetsonlike hat with a sign perched on the front brim: "Jesus Yes. Textbooks Nyet" (the "x" in textbooks is shaped as a Nazi swastika). Wildcat work stoppages and the practice of honoring a picket line have been defined here in terms of an exceptional event, not in the more prosaic terms of daily life in the mines and the politics of production relations. Instead of contextualizing them as episodes of class friction, wildcat strikes are cast in terms of fundamentalist, Appalachian crazies who abuse respect for picket lines.

> Campbell: We have a situation that the union will not police their own ranks. They will not hold this individual accountable for his actions. So therefore, unfortunately, it looks like we have to go to a contractual provision to start people holding them accountable for their own actions.

Positioned in response to the irrational and fanatical excesses of "such" non-coal-related work stoppages, his defense of penalties seems reason able and practical. The problem, says Campbell, lies in inadequate union policing of individuals who go too far. If the union cannot control its own men, then management must find a way to "hold people accountable for their own actions."

Speaking of accountability, let us return to the last sentence of Rabel's narrative remarks leading in to Campbell: "Such work stoppages [refers to textbook rallies], they say [his unnamed news sources], led to the controversial contract provision which would fine miners blamed for unauthorized, or wildcat strikes." The structure of sentence and verb blurs recognition of the agents involved. The pr ovision seems to have enacted itself in response to "such" stoppages. Once again, there is no attribution of operators' responsibility for this contract provision. But this was, after all, the contract provision engineered by BCOA "hardliners" Bobby Brown of Consol Coal and Bruce Johnston of U.S. Steel. Campbell is nominated on screen as an industrial relations manager for a company that remains nameless. Rabel does not verbally identify, or even refer to him, nor does his company name appear on screen.

Rabel immediately follows Campbell's words by saying, "Union President Arnold Miller is in the ironic position of agreeing with the companies on the strike issue, placing him at odds with many members of the rank and file." The scene cut to Miller wearing a dark overcoat, walking from a car in the distance towards the camera. The setting seems rustic and unpopulated, and a wall of a building to Miller's right resembles a barn. This cut to a closeup profile of an unident ified brawny male face, eyes darting one way and then another.[2] As Rabel finished this framing of Miller's position, Miller appeared at head and shoulder distance, nominated on screen:

Miller: What it says, you got a grievance, you file it properly and process it. If you got a contract violation, they'll win it. That's what it's all about.

---

[2]On February 9, there were press reports (not on CBS) about Miller and a bodyguard being involved in a "scuffle" with a critic of Miller's, Cecil Roberts, VP of District 17 (NYT, 2/9/78). Miller claimed he had received death threats. On the other hand, reports about Miller's paranoia went back several years, and he had taken to carrying a handgun under his coat.

The sequence of film shots preceding Miller's interview here is curious, especially when considered in the light of the above events. We surmise that the interview site was Miller's choice, motivated by the recent "scuffles." The burly young man is without question Miller's bodyguard. But why is there no verbal reference to these matters? Alluding to these matters with such cryptic visual scenes makes it impossible for the casual observer to decipher.

You just simply honor a contract. And if a company violates it, by God, they have to pay too.

Remember that wildcat strikes, the grievance procedure, and the nature of the grievances had put Miller in a deep bind since the 1974 contract. As UMW president he was legally obligated to enforce the contract and his statement sums up the legalistic stance he took. This, of course, did not sit well with a growing number of miners. Miller occupied the unenviable position of trying to sell penalty clauses in the contract he had helped negotiate to a constituency that strongly opposed the penalty clauses.

Though Rabel was correct about the irony, Miller's comments do not refer to the newly proposed penalties endorsed by Campbell, but to the arbitration system as an alternative to unauthorized work stoppages. In point of fact, throughout the negotiations, Miller vacillated between pressing for a right-to-strike provision (angering the BCOA on more than one occasion by reraising the issue), and conceding to BCOA demands for labor stability.

The film of Miller was sharply spliced to interview clips with two rank-and-file miners. Ripped from context, and minus specification from Rabel, the first sounded like gibberish. A young miner named Roger Ellison spoke as if the unseen reporter (and, by extension, viewers) was conversant with an insider's knowledge of the coal fields.

Ellison: Well, there's a lot of fat cats that—that run the show. It's bureaucrats and—and that's really the only thing the men have to cling to is—is striking, you know, trying to survive.

Translated, Ellison's reference to bureaucrats was his way of talking about the arbitration review process and how disputes repeatedly stalled in the bureaucratic machinery without resolution. No resolution to a dispute was as good as a win for operators, who could continue to run their mines under the status quo. Under those circumstances, miners like Ellison perceived no recourse to striking.

A second miner, Oliver Hunter, addressed the consequences for miners if they agreed to the newly proposed policing penalties.

Hunter: If they get this contract ratified here, they've—they've got us right where they want us. [An off-camera voice of a fellow miner affirms, "That's right."] If they take a notion to get rid of you, all they got to do is say, well, you're down the road, and there ain't nothing you can do about it.

Hunter's comments cut to the heart of the matter. He saw this contract in terms of operators' power and control over miners. A miner's continued employment and livelihood would become precarious, resting on currying the favor of the boss. These comments were directed against the operators, but Rabel made no effort to point this out.[3] Instead, without skipping a beat, Rabel turned our attention to the Madison Mine in Boone County. While the camera scanned the silent, snowy exterior infrastructure of the mine, Rabel explained how wildcat strikes closed down the mine for 60 days, "costing the company at least $15,000 a day. Such shutdowns bring gloomy forecasts for industry and union alike in West Virginia." This formed a lead-in to the report's closing interview clips from Campbell and Miller as voices of reason: the former prophesying economic disaster and "ghost towns in Appalachia," and the latter warning of the union's demise.

In this sequence, CBS's editing chopped striking miners' speech into briefer, more fragmented units than Miller or Campbell (manager). CBS also conveyed their speech without explanatory contextualization. Throughout CBS's strike coverage, reporters were more likely to situate the comments of higher status speakers as discursive arguments. In this report, each comment by the manager was preceded by an audiovisual narrative situating it. Differential allocation of narrative contextualization yielded an impression of the miners as incoherent and unreasoning, while the official spoke in a voice which seemed reasonable and legitimate and concerned with broader public interests.

ANARCHY VERSUS ARNOLD MILLER

When the union bargaining council rejected the first contract on February 12, Morton Dean, as anchorman, telescoped the events into a couple of sentences: "It's official. The settlement is off, the coal strike is still on, and coal supplies continue to dwindle. The rank-and-file rebellion against a tentative agreement was successful . . ." This phrasing strongly suggests a causal linkage between the "rebellion" and decreasing coal supplies, and between miners' rebelliousness and the scuttling of the settlement. In the ensuing report, the theme of dissidence and revolt was reemphasized by Barry Serafin. Again, on February

---

[3]Three days later Rabel follows a miner's unspecified pronoun reference with the clarification statement, "He's blaming UMW president Arnold Miller . . ." Yet, here no clarification is offered to identify "they" as coal operators.

13, Serafin concluded his report: " . . . Arnold Miller, who came into office promising union democracy, admits that what has developed is anarchy."

Two related frames can be seen here: characterizing the miners' collective attitude as militant and rebellious, and the union organization as chaotic. Repeated juxtaposition of reports on the energy crisis with stories on "angry miners" is significant. The strike is portrayed in terms of (a) strikers displaying militantly stubborn attitudes, and (b) its consequences, namely, the coal shortage. The link between the two was most clearly manifest in Morton Dean's February 12 announcement. There was, of course, much truth to the idea that miners were rebellious. However, what was only a partial aspect of the miners' position was made to stand for and explain their motives in general. This exaggerated the miners' militancy and made it seem aimless or greedy. But the miners' fractiousness could have been further amplified in a quite different way. It might have been specified in relational and historical terms.

West Virginia had the highest percentage of UMWA members. It was, therefore, a reasonable choice for news stories on striking miners. Of 32 reports *CBS News* made from the coalfields during the strike, 28 came from West Virginia. Representativeness alone does not explain the repeated choice of West Virginia coal towns. The majority of reports came from places within easy access (e.g., Cabin Creek) of Kanawha County airport near Charleston, rather than mining communities located in remote areas. For geographic reasons affecting access then, more reports came from UMW District 17 (which substantially overlaps Kanawha County) than any other. District 17 was also the biggest and strongest UMW district, widely reputed to have the most militant members. CBS correspondents knew this and their reports frequently emphasized it. "Militancy" is newsworthy; "Angry miners" give more interesting interviews and hold viewers' attention better than passive or apathetic miners. Thus, a multiplicity of determinations (ease of access; definitions of "newsworthiness") act to structure a particular, systematic form of representation, or in this case, overrepresentation.

Striking miners quickly learned that "fire attracts TV crews, so they would light up at the first sign of a network camera. Soon it became a ritual that trapped both miners and reporters" (Seltzer, 1985, p. 155). Strident words and raised fists drew television coverage, but they encouraged reporters to emphasize moods rather than material specifics. Though setting fire to copies of the proposed contract conveyed an unambiguous image signifying the intensity of their displeasure with it, it also signified to a watching nation their unwillingness to participate in reasonable dialogue. The absence of discursive logic on the part of miners became self-fulfilling: They reduced themselves, and were reduced by reporters, to "angry" slogan-chanting miners.[4]

News stories focus on the new and unexpected, emphasize the unusual over the usual, and controversy over consensus. Emphasis on conflict in the news helps sell the news product, while also reinforcing consensus by defining the latter against what has been isolated as deviant. Shared norms and values are stressed; opposing interests remain unelaborated. The precarious and problematic character of the consensus is exposed when something like a worker's strike occurs: there is a "crisis of consensus" in the labor-management "partnership." Network news responds to such crises by hegemonically affirming, and even enforcing, the consensus: Framing strikers as provacateurs legitimates the consensus, and even sets the stage for justifying future repressive countermeasures. Tagging the activities of some miners with the pejorative label "militant" discredits them, and by extension, makes suspect the labor organization which apparently harbors them. Such labeling exaggerates the provocation and inflates the deviance it represents, while also effectively dispensing with the need for substantive discussion of the conflicts behind such actions. Once again, an action is represented in nonrelational terms; though this depiction may have relational consequences, inflating both the "militants'" own self-image, as well as official (and public) perceptions of them.[5]

Foregrounding "threats" such as striking workers who are "militant," "violent" and "rebellious," minus background context—estranges those workers from society, which in contrast to the workers is of moderate temper and reasonable mind. Speedy termination of the strike, of course, constitutes the exercise of moderation and reason and this is the goal of the news media and the state alike. Striking workers who persist in threatening the "larger social interest" appear immoderate and unreasonable. Contrasting their refusal to work with "the larger interest" obscured the commonality of status as wage laborers that strikers proclaim to "society."

---

[4]"In noting that the media tend to focus attention on the form of the demonstration, for instance, the violent/chanting mob, one must remember that to some extent the problem is implicit in the form of mass demonstrations. By choosing to work through the medium of public spectacle, demonstrators open themselves to the possibility that they will be 'appropriated' as spectacular entertainment" (Morley, 1981, p. 386).

[5]This is akin to the process Wilkins (1967) describes as a 'deviance amplification spiral': the characterization of deviants as such leads them to internalize that definition, thus exaggerating their behavior and producing a mutual reaction and reinforcement.

The divided, anarchic state of the UMW was another frame that became prominent in February. There was substantial truth to this, as we discussed earlier. However, in CBS's reporting the "fact" becomes the explanatory framework. Union members expressed dissent at the contract negotiated for them by their union leaders, and the UMW bargaining council turned down the first contract proposal. Provisions sought by the miners had not, for the most part, been obtained; nearly all the BCOA sought, and the miners opposed, was contained in that proposal. Calling the popular vote against the proposal a "revolt," and using this to symbolize the anarchic state of the union, ignores the actual—far more complex—reasons for tensions within the UMW. Rejection of the contract and demands for Miller's resignation were tied to union negotiators' failure to deliver on their constituency's demands. Though Serafin mentions "long-standing divisions" in the UMW, he identifies neither the sources of tension nor the parties involved. Four factions were identifiable after 1975: an anti-Miller group with roots in the Boyle wing, later led by Patterson; a group to the left of Miller critical of the 1974 contract for failing to secure a right-to-strike proviso; Miller loyalists; and an unenthusiastic center that silently lent support to Miller (Seltzer, 1985, p. 135). Nonetheless, broadcast journalists repeatedly opted for a superficial description of unilinear causality—revolt leading to anarchy.

By another set of standards—indeed, by the very standards newspeople profess to honor and defend—the miners' actions seem to exemplify democracy in action, with a politically conscious electorate conveying its will to its representatives. However, because union politics are more often than not framed as authoritarian, journalists persist in defining any breakdown in internal union consensus as either rebellion or evidence of the illegitimacy of the union hierarchy vis-á-vis the rank and file. Instead of dwelling on the democratic advances within the UMWA and the struggle to extend democratic practices to the workplace, CBS conveyed images of rough-speaking, belligerent workers inclined towards anarchy.

CBS News reporters tend to reduce "democracy" to a mechanical consensus achieved via government elections. Outside, those boundaries democracy does not exist. Nor do reporters convey any notions that true democratic institutions are normally in conflict, that conflict is a necessary motor to democratic practices. Instead, reflecting a naive civics perspective, reporters equate democracy with consensus, and conflict with disruption. Apart from their attempts to reflect back to audiences populist sentiments, television reporters adopt a stance of "passive aggression" against the extension of democratic practices into daily life.

In the CBS portrayal of miners' reactions to the February 6 contract proposal, viewers are apprised of the mere fact of its rejection, with several miners' shouted "nay's" substituted for a more comprehensive account of their position. When explanation is provided, it tends to conclude with a discussion of Arnold Miller's inadequacies, and "angry miners" denouncing him. The February 12th report exemplifies CBS's approach to reporting the union's internal conflicts. Following Dean's announcement that "rank-and-file rebellion" had aborted a settlement, he sends viewers first to Serafin for a report on what the Bargaining Council did. Serafin poses the council's strong negative vote as a slap in the face of Arnold Miller: " . . . the Council turned down the settlement negotiated by union president Arnold Miller." Again, Serafin makes no reference to the coal operators in noting the council's rejection of contract provisions "that would penalize miners for wildcat strikes and affect health and pension benefits." Serafin concluded his section of the report with:

> Some calls within the union for Miller's resignation—and for regional rather than national negotiations—have emphasized the lack of unity within the union. But equally apparent is the militancy of coal miners to remain on strike until they get what they want.

On this note, the film cut to a second report from Ed Rabel "about what the dissident miners want." An abrupt visual transition took place to a closeup of a young, unidentified miner through the window of his truck cab. His 3-second interview was garbled and unsituated. He was immediately followed by another young miner, nominated as Terry Henderson, who says:

> As long as he's got that in there where it's going to fine the miners if, if they don't cross the picket line. I ain't no scab. I never was a scab. And I ain't going to be no scab for him or nobody else.

Ed Rabel's voiceover positioned this comment for viewers: "He's blaming UMW president Arnold Miller for what is to the rank and file of the region the most repugnant part of the contract rejected today by the Bargaining Council . . ." Rabel continued with a slightly more specific inventory of disagreements the miners have with the proposal,

> There is a consensus among miners here that any future contract must eliminate company-imposed penalties against those blamed for wildcat strikes. To gain acceptance here, they say, a contract must be fair to the

80,000 miners who retired under the union's 1950 pension plan, by bringing their retirement benefits in line with those who retired after 1974 under a plan providing greater benefits.

This stands significant as CBS's first acknowledgment that the contract calls for penalties which are "company-imposed." But their presence has been restricted to an adjective, and no other agents appear who might be held responsible for the unsatisfactory contract. Henderson's accusation, for want of an "other side," stands. This is reinforced by an interview clip of David Forms, President of Local 1759: "I think Arnold Miller has destroyed the credibility of this union, and I honestly believe at this time that the man should resign his position . . ." Rabel concluded by saying, "Miners in this region blame Miller for not getting them what they want. As one put it: 'If we accomplish nothing more than ousting Miller from office, we will be satisfied.'"

Depicting Miller as personally responsible for the penalty clause regarding wildcat strikes also contained an element of truth. A more savvy and assertive bargainer might not have yielded as much at such little cost. Miller came to the negotiations unprepared, with a staff in disarray, and he frequently missed negotiating meetings. A portion of the rank and file had been angry with Miller since 1974 over what they saw as "sell-out" provisions in that contract. In the summer of 1976, miners defied not only federal judges, but also Miller by persisting in a widespread "political strike" protesting the use of court injunctions against wildcats (Green, 1978, p. 11). But none of this received investigation. Miller's performance at the negotiating meetings could have been examined; the nature of previous grievances between Miller and his constituency might have been briefly delineated.

On February 13, CBS boosted concern about a possible energy crisis. Sequenced after an interview with an official at the Department of Energy, Barry Serafin turned to the problem of Arnold Miller and internal union strife.

Serafin: "Much of the controversy and the pressure during the strike has been increasingly focused on United Mine Workers president Arnold Miller. Officials of his union rejected the contract agreement he negotiated, and there have been calls for his resignation."

Arnold Miller [UMW Pres]: "Those that have been calling for my resignation—I think that the—the people that are fostering and formenting (sic) that were the ones that have tried to be disruptive and would not cooperate in the last 4 or 5 years. And we went through the electoral process last year, and when you get in an election somebody gets beat. And some of them that was in the election process last year, they fail to recognize they got beat."

Serafin: "Miller is not optimistic about starting from scratch in the negotiations, or happy about the strike dragging on."

Miller: "Well, it can't go on forever, you know, without something being done. And it's—on, on a broad spectrum, it's a case of, you know, who can stand more of what."

Serafin: "Should mine operators declare the rejected contract proposal their best, last offer, the way could be cleared for local or regional, rather than national negotiations. Miners in Illinois have expressed some sentiment for that. But their sentiment is tempered by the knowledge that the union could be irrevocably broken apart. Still, the emotions produced by the strike have reinforced long-standing divisions within the United Mine Workers, and Arnold Miller, who came into office promising union democracy, admits that what has developed is anarchy."

The primary focus on Miller's character defects minus investigation is another instance of journalists seizing on controversial and facile dimensions of an issue at the expense of a larger picture. Reporters found it easier to personalize the controversy, because conflict surrounding personalities sells. It is easier to sell to editors as a story angle, and it relieves reporters of the difficult task of disentangling a complex set of relations. But there is another factor at work here: It is safer to personalize conflict than to depict it in institutionalized terms. The latter opens a Pandora's box of legitimation problems, the former merely delegitimates an already suspect leader of a potentially "outdated" institution, labor unions. Absent in the focus on Miller are political-economic forces that shaped these events: (a) sustained conflicts between labor and management at the point of production, (b) decades of company violations of miners' rights and contract provisions, (c) the politics of an arbitration review procedure designed to avert open class hostilities over disagreements, and (d) the BCOA's desire to capitalize on the potential boom in coal, and therefore minimize production losses.

Personifying news stories is a frequently used method of reporting. Reporters and editors believe it makes stories more understandable to audiences than if they are couched in abstractions. It aids recognition by attaching the story to a well-known name and face, thereby making the story more entertaining. Something else is achieved as well by personalizing the news. The relation between social and institutional forces and the individual's actions become reversed: Occurrences appear to emanate from the individual's actions, thereby absorbing the institutional forces. In this way, personalizing stories ideologically conceals the actual context that is determinant. This pattern is not confined to reporting about labor and management, but is a recurrent and pervasive ideological frame in television news per se. Consistent with the "great man theory of history," selected subjects grow in stature to appear as the "motor force of history" (Hall, 1972, p. 78). In this instance, not only are the multiple relationships influencing the outcome of the contract condensed into individual actors, there is a further reduction of the developments, which involve at least three parties—rank-and-file UMW members, UMW leaders, and the BCOA—to a single agent, here identified in the person of Arnold Miller.

Personalizing the story had the effect of keeping the focus safely away from the BCOA and the role the organization played in these events. Once again, the most significant recurring ideological frame on the coal strike was probably an inadvertant by-product of the routines of commodified news production.

10

Formulas of Neutrality

NETWORK MEDIATION OF WORKING-CLASS SPEECH

On February 5, anchor Morton Dean began, "The coal talks have had as many ups and downs as an elevator in a mine shaft. Now it looks as if things are up . . . Ed Rabel has been talking with some striking miners in West Virginia." The subject of the talk concerns the possible ratification of a settlement proposal. Rabel commences with a voiceover about how "the record-breaking strike and the near record-breaking snow" have produced fiscal, and hence material, privation for mining communities (they are "left . . . hard hit"). This accompanies a four-shot sequence: (a) an aerial view looking down on rows of idle, empty rail cars; (b) a panoramic view of a snow-covered valley and town; (c) a lone man trudging through the snow along a roadside; (d) Rabel on "stakeout" in front of a silent coal tipple warns that "miners here are eager to see the strike end. But they say there will be no quick acceptance" of just any contract that is passed along."

Rabel then relates miners' assertions that

the biggest stumbling block to ratification will be over the issue of wildcat strikes. Sources say union negotiators have agreed that miners who are to blame for wildcats will be forced to reimburse the UMW's health and pension funds for any revenue lost during the strike.

Although Rabel's phrasing might suggest an unambiguous verdict about responsibility for who caused the problem ("miners who are to blame for wildcats . . ."), the interviews which follow may leave a different impression. Roger Hammack, a young bearded miner, speaks:

167

Well, they've always wanted to penalize us, which they have. Anytime that you sue the union for three or four million dollars you're penalizing somebody. And it's us, we're the ones that pays it. And if they put this in the contract, it will not be ratified.

Hammack's delivery and words express reasoned opposition, something which has not previously come through very often. But, because these remarks are not contextualized, a viewer would have to know about the history of company suits against the UMW for wildcat strikes, in order to fully grasp what Hammack means.

Rabel brings viewers inside the Cabin Creek Coffee Shop to get these interviews. Coffee shops and taverns in the Cabin Creek area were convenient and accessible sites for television reporters unfamiliar with sources in the region. This film sequence exemplifies the dilemma of relying on commercial television news as a forum in which to establish a democratic public sphere of debate. The coffee shop represents a social space where workers can articulate their own views in dialogue with one another. Striking miners used such coffee shops as communication centers, gathering to talk about the strike and the proposed contract, as well as passing their time. Visually the report concentrates on the latter activity, while actually disrupting the former. Bringing in the CBS camera crew made a number of miners visibly stiff and uncomfortable. Just as importantly, the report shatters their discourse into an edited series of either illustrative or unsituated comments. Here, television news colonizes this "proletarian public sphere," transforming the meaning of their discourse and their social space into materials for producing a "news product." This report shows how networks reroute local discourse into news discourse.

Rabel chose this coffee shop precisely because it is a working-class institution that affords an opportunity to hear miners' views on the proposed contract. Yet, photographically the sequence focuses on their idleness through the device of watching them shoot pool.[1]

Interview clips emphasize miners' global emotional reaction to the contract, rather than their reasons for feeling negative. In addition, camera angles and interview style serialize and individuate reactions, and deny viewers an opportunity to hear miners speaking to, and with, one another. Again, as throughout the strike, the camera hugs their somber, impassive facial expressions with one closeup photo after

---

[1]The other side of this idleness, however, is their solidarity. What Rabel does not mention, and what is not obvious to those outside of the coalfields, is that the condition which allows these men to calmly engage in games of pool is their ability to stop the production of coal without a constantly vigilant picket line.

another, as if tight facial shots will reveal some greater truth about the impasse. Despite the setting, miner interviewees are treated not as class subjects, but as a collection of individuated faces and personalities (cf. Hartley, 1982).

Editing of these interviews rarely permitted speaking miners an opportunity for discursive argument. Hammack's comments quoted above were atypical in length, taking nearly 15 seconds.[2] The format used by CBS reporters denied miners opportunities to speak discursively about the issues. Hammack's discursive foray was short-lived however, cut off by the absence of any followup clarification or discussion. Instead the camera shifts to another miner's face and another question posed—"would you ratify this contract?" To which, Jack Bower, nominated on screen as [Miner], dourly grumbled: "No way. No way." More often than not, reporters function as pollsters ("Do you agree?" "Will you vote for?" "How does it feel?") when they interview workers, more concerned to elicit attitudes and feelings than explanations.[3]

Rank-and-file miners lacked experience speaking before cameras, and had no designated spokespersons. They spoke in a regionally-inflected working-class dialect unfamiliar to a national audience, so that listeners may have been more inclined to attend to miners' unorthodox style and grammatical construction than to their thoughts. Miners' were rarely chosen for interviews according to the criterion of articulateness. In television news interviews, articulateness is generally defined in terms of a middle-class linguistic code. Bernstein (1975) identifies this as an elaborated code characterized by abstract language, lack of dependence on immediate context for meaning, verbal explicitness, and individualized response. Professional broadcast journalists' speech most closely resembles this code. Gans (1979) observes television reporters normally seek interviewees who are articulate in "standard English dialect"

---

[2]Using length of interview as a crude measure of opportunities for discursive speech, compare the length of Rabel's (Feb. 7) interview clips with local officers to the duration of Webster's (Feb. 7) interview clips with utility managers and business men in the second prong of the story. In Rabel's report, four interview clips with three local officers receive a combined 28 seconds. The longest statement is 10 seconds. In Webster's report, one utility executive and two business men receive a combined 67 seconds. The longest is 30 seconds.

[3]Hartley (1982, p. 90) calls this the vox pop interview. Such man or woman in the street interviews (a) "authenticate the coverage given to particular events by showing the concern of ordinary people in the issue," and (b) provide "potential points of identification for the audience." Newspaper reporters who covered the coal industry particularly dislike this aspect of television interviewing. The "how does it feel" questions seem to them both stupid and unnecessarily cruel.

except when it is absolutely necessary to use sources who speak in lower-class dialects. Obviously, an industrial strike is such a case. Most often, rank- and-file miners seem chosen on the basis of reporters' notions of "representativeness" and "typicality." Colorfulness—a thick Appalachian drawl or a chaw of tobacco—was systematically preferred over articulateness in selecting miner interviewees. There were, however, working miners capable of speaking articulately about the issues. Here, for example, was how Ernest Day (President of UMWA Local 1827) explained to a local reporter why wildcat strikes took place:[4]

> We can't keep a safety committee up here. They [the companies] take dead aim on the safety committee and bring charges against each miner. Then it winds up in arbitration and the men get thrown out of the mine. Somebody needs to expose what the companies are doing to block us from having any say on safety. We don't have any choice but to strike. The company won't honor the [1974] contract and our men are constantly harrassed. (interview, July 20, 1977, Ashland, Ky; cited in Maggard, 1983/84, p. 76)

Instead, miners selected to speak on screen exhibited exaggerated use of a restricted code, a working-class linguistic code "based on communal relations," which displays a greater reliance on conveying meaning through "extraverbal" channels such as intonation, wordstress, and expressive features" than through verbal planning (Bernstein, 1975, p. 151; Hartley, 1982, p. 149). Miners' speech acts show a greater rigidity of syntactic organization, reduced articulatory clues, and meanings which are often "discontinuous, condensed and local" (Bernstein, 1975, p. 146). This restricted code, in conjunction with camera placement and distance, and the edited brevity of their discursive argument, highlighted the meanings of miners' soundbites keyed to modalities of intonation, wordstress, and expressive features.

The average length of rank-and-file miners *"soundbites"* shown throughout the strike was 9 seconds. These tersely edited utterances were already densely filled with subcultural and localized referents, so that miners' comments tended toward stark brevity or incoherence. The apparent incoherence resulted from miners addressing reporters as if the

---

[4]In no instance did CBS air an interview with an articulate miner explaining why wildcat strikes occurred. A fundamental question about the CBS coverage concerns the reasons for excluding such speakers. Was selection of interviewees entirely a function of reporters' choices? Did reporters fail to seek out such articulate speakers because of their lack of familiarity with the coal fields, or did it reflect implicit ideological assumptions on their part? Did editors exclude tape of such interviewees? If so, why?

latter shared an insider's knowledge of local linguistic codes and events—but reporters did not, and rarely sought to translate or clarify these utterances for their audiences. This is especially the case where miners' comments were edited to include unspecified third-person referents ("he," "they"). Reporters consistently intervened to identify miners' references to Arnold Miller or Jimmy Carter, but on *no* occasion did a reporter intervene to specify a miner's unclear pronoun reference to coal operators. For instance, in Hammack's soundbites above, the implicit referent in his comments ("Well, *they've* always wanted to penalize us . . .") was to coal operators. But Rabel did not clarify this; in fact, positioning the soundbite immediately after Rabel's statement about union negotiators and miners being "forced to reimburse the UMW's health and pension funds," might lead viewers to infer that Hammack's comments refer to the union acting against its own rank and file.

Miners tended to speak elliptically, but not in the ellipsis of network discourse. Confronted with miners' slang, unassisted viewers could attend to miners emotional state, but not to their logic. Tuchman (1978, p. 188–89) shows that news is invariably an "indexical enterprise." Like most other forms of discourse, news is indexical in the way its units of expression "point towards larger discursive units . . . to elaborate and contextualize their meaning" (Gibson, 1980, p. 100). In the miners' strike, and with workers in general, network television prefers to edit their speech into nondiscursive units. Chanted slogans are a frequent and obvious example (Gitlin, 1980). Slogans and abbreviations without a context become reductive. Since meanings are context-dependent, "only those who possessed a shared, unspoken, implicit understanding of relevant features of the context could have access to the meanings realized by the speech" (Bernstein, 1975, p. 14).

Viewers did not hear miners in dialogue with one another. Instead of taking opportunities like the coffee shop to get a **group** of rank-and-file miners in front of the camera and **speak with them** about the contract and what they felt, Rabel and his cameramen produced an artfullycrafted montage of photos and interviews clips. Rabel prefaces the montage with an introductory description:

> Rabel: "The record-breaking strike and the near record-breaking snow in West Virginia's southern coal fields, have left these remote mining communities hard hit. Where some miners once drove to their destinations, they now walk because of the snow, and because banks are repossessing automobiles for nonpayment of loans. Long out of work and hardpressed financially, miners here are eager to see the strike end. But they say there will be no quick acceptance by the rank and file of any contract their union might agree to in Washington."

Attention then turned to the Cabin Creek Coffee Shop. Rabel finished this speech in front of a silent coal tipple, and a visual cut shifted to a brief exterior shot of the nondescript s hop. This gave way to a point-of-view shot from immediately behind a rack of pool balls, as someone prepared to "break." On that visual cut, Rabel stated "idle miners say the biggest stumbling block to ratification will be over the issue of wildcat strikes." Keyed to the phrase "stumbling block," the video cut to a closeup profile shot of a grim-faced miner (wearing a brimmed cap) sipping coffee. On the word "ratification," the scene cut to another male bent over the pool table preparing to shoot the cue ball. Rabel finished the sentence as the camera pulled back to show the same miner observing the result of his shot. A sharp film cut put viewers squarely behind the 15-ball as the cue ball rolled toward us. Rabel continued, "Sources say union negotiators have agreed that miners who are to blame for wildcat strikes will be forced to reimburse the UMW's health and pension funds for any revenue lost during the strike." Accompanying this explanation was a succession of video shots: (a) another view of a pool player following his shot, (b) a closeup profile of a grizzle-faced miner sitting quietly, (c) another young miner wearing a bent-billed baseball cap as he shoots cue ball, (d) a tight shot of ball rolling in pocket, and (e) a reaction shot from the young miner.

Ensuing interview burps with Roger Hammack and Jack Bower attest to their determined opposition to penalties. Rabel followed them with a summary of what they want: "The miners say union health and pension benefits must be fully restored and guaranteed before they'll vote for a new contract. And in spite of their strike-related hardships, the mood here is uncompromising." To capture this "mood," an edited sequence of tight closeups of miners' facial features appeared concomitantly. Another clip from Hammack's interview illustrated their mood and closes the report: "We can stay out till hell freezes over. They can't hold us out long enough. We can stay out a lot longer than they can." The camera pans across yet another still, quiet—that is, unproductive—coal tipple, which viewers may infer will not operate again until miners' "uncompromising mood" has been appeased or broken.

NARRATIVE NEUTRALITY AND BALANCE

On February 7, when it was apparent union officials had "strong doubts" about the tentative agreement, Rabel again presented a balanced view of the miners' side of the story. After several interview clips from officers of Local 6243 who indicate they could not accept penalties for wildcat strikes, Rabel said: "Mindful of the highly disputed 1974 contract they agreed to quickly, these men say they're in no hurry to approve a new contract."[5] Then, miner Carl Harrison (young and clean-shaven) was heard in sober, measured speech: "We're just now beginning to get in the ball game. They know now we're up to bat. We will hang in there. We will take a hard, long look at it." However, as Rabel brought closure to these interviews, he shifted the frame of reference: " . . . If, as some predict, the rank and file balk over a new contract, hardpressed coal users will have to wait even longer for the delivery of new supplies."

As CBS grasped at straws concerning a settlement to the dispute, their principal concern turned to the lag time before coal began flowing again. Morton Dean, as anchor on February 5, introduced Rabel's report by explaining that a settlement would take an additional 10 days for ratification and another 10 days for production to return to normal. Cronkite repeated this on February 6. Rabel began his February 7 narrative with the same "10 days" theme, and closed on the theme of "hardpressed coal users" waiting. Cronkite amplified the theme again in the studio as he fashioned a transition from Rabel's story about ratifying the contract to Don Webster's report about Columbus's fuel problems and the bad news this augured for consumers and industrial customers. Webster reiterated the message again in his conclusion on February 7, only this time "it will take about 25 days for coal to arrive. And if the strike isn't settled, industry here is in big trouble." The prominence of the "lag time" theme represents CBS's attempt to reflect and project the concerns and interests of those whom they address—their viewers, as consumers.

Reports on February 7, 10, 13, and 14 juxtaposed stories about rank and file anger with stories about coal shortages. Threats of miner violence as a means of blocking the movement of coal to fuel-starved regions became the pivot of stories on February 14 and 15. On February 16, the Carter administration and Governors of Pennsylvania and Indiana spoke about the severity and impact of coal shortages. February 17th brought a slightly different newsangle, a report on midwestern utilities "rebuilding stockpiles with coal from the West, naturally." Each report began by showing miners responding to the penalty clause; on the other hand, reports included expressions of concern at the loss of funds due to wildcat strikes, and at mounting fuel problems.

To defenders of the faith, this might appear an ideally impartial and neutral account of the event. In the reporter's smooth and competent

---

[5]This is the first reference to the 1974 contract that CBS made since they began covering the strike.

tones, moderation and neutrality expressed in his voice, viewers get "both sides" of the account: such is the miners' case; such is the fuel supply—now decide for yourself! These seem objective reports indeed, observing of both sides, and nonpartisan. But wait. Isn't something missing in these accounts, some mass of information that would tilt this delicate equipoise to one side? What about the other party to these negotiations, the BCOA? What is their case? Why do they want the penalty clause included? Why have viewers still not been treated to a chat with them in the intimacy of their offices or restaurants, to watch them partake of cocktails and cigars—just as we have seen the miners drink coffee and smoke cigarettes—and listen to them discourse about the need for higher profits and "labor stability" in the coalfields.

The fuel shortage affects the public, but it also affects capital accumulation in general. The interests of a particular group of people appear to endanger "the public" interest. In addition to considerations of balance, this is the significance of following Rabel's story on the miners with Webster's piece on the putative fuel crisis. A deeper meaning emerges: While every individual's rights are precious, the interests of the majority cannot be sacrificed to them. Following a Benthamite felicific calculus, CBS puts the public/civic interest above all else. In essence, they are rooting for a resolution to the strike, since that would mean restoration of fuel supplies—and, of the private accumulation of capital, though the latter is not indicated.

CBS showed miners expressing their reactions to a proposal negotiated by a weak union president and a relatively strong industry bargaining team, but the companies' management is nowhere to be seen. Every report focuses exlusively on the miners: Are they determined and resolved, or resentful about the strike? Are they militant and defiant, or "hurting" from loss of pay? Day after day the BCOA remained offscreen, making rare perfunctory appearances as one negotiating party, and as an apparently unwilling participant in a dispute between the weak Arnold Miller and a disruptive rank and file constituency. The Vanderbilt Archives Index to evening news broadcasts shows that of 171 reports on the strike done by CBS, NBC and ABC, the BCOA receives the barest mention in only 10 reports. CBS did finally, on February 20, explicitly identify the BCOA as the coal operators bargaining group. The BCOA remained invisible until the week of February 15-22 when they made waves by first refusing to participate in White House-sponsored talks, and then by spurning the pattern-setter agreement obtained via Federal mediation efforts. As a result, reports between February 15th and 20th included vague references to "coal operators" and "industry negotiators."

INTRODUCING THE BCOA

Finally, 86 days into the strike, CBS identified the BCOA as the coal operators bargaining association on February 20. On February 21, CBS, for the first time during the strike, put a visual frame on the screen indicating "Management." Against the frame's dark background the word "Management" appeared, written diagonally across a dark drawing of a organizational chart. Apart from a schematic line drawing of an organizational chart/ladder, apparently indicating lines of hierarchical control within corporate organizations per se, the graphic bore no content.[6]

Keyed to Serafin's mention of the BCOA, this graphic image was as murky and dark as the BCOA's public profile had been. Serafin, seated beside a framed photo of the White House, observed that Administration officials were pushing the P&M proposal "as the basis for an overall agreement between the union and the Bituminous Coal Operators Association." The White House picture shifted to the "Management" frame as Serafin stated, "The coal operators oppose some provisions of the independent agreement, which offers somewhat higher pay and fewer strike penalties." Everything here, from the visual frame to Serafin's account of the proposal, was couched in vague terms. The coal operators become totally disembodied and faceless in the murky abstracted symbolism of an organizational chart without content. Their position is stated in terms of comparatives which have been given no concrete referents (is it $.05 more or $3.00 more per hour or day or week? what is a strike penalty? And what does fewer mean?).

On February 22 and 23, the coal operators took their lumps in the news media. On February 22, referring to a proposal made by Edward Leisenring to submit the dispute to binding arbitration, Serafin reported:

---

[6]Who decides on the content of screen graphics? Is there a specialist who is given the story, and then asked to come up with an appropriate image to put in the frame beside the anchor's face?

What motivated this particular "management" graphic? A graphic is designed to foreground attention. Yet, here even the graphic buries the identity of "management". Was this an intended or an unintended consequence? Was the person assigned to come up with a graphic for "Management" unable to call to mind a single leader in the coal industry? The BCOA public relations tactic worked so well that media imagemakers could not fashion a media graphic for them.

Aesthetically, the image might actually convey a critical truth, that corporate capitalism rests on a formal bureaucratic skeletal structure.

Administration officials and industry sources describe the coal operators' binding arbitration proposal as simply a negotiating manuever, an attempt to shift the focus of negotiations away from the terms of the independent agreement, and an attempt to put the union on the defensive.

The BCOA strategy to remain outside the limelight had finally unraveled. The BCOA opposed the P&M deal, but President Carter needed a resolution quickly and wanted the BCOA to jump on the bandwagon. When they balked, it was suddenly the coal operators who appeared to stand in the way of the public welfare. Again, on February 23, CBS described a "high pressure campaign . . . to force the mine operators to accept the deal that an independent coal company made with the miners' union earlier this week, a deal that the union says it will take to end the strike." No official representative of the BCOA, nor any coal operator, actually appeared or spoke in a CBS report until February 25 when Nick Camicia (who had become chief BCOA negotiator only days earlier) complained about the federal government's role in pushing the BCOA into the P&M settlement proposal. Following this moment of BCOA displeasure with President Carter, the BCOA disappeared for another 11 days before Camicia was heard again disapproving of unspecified "Administration" comments holding out the possibility of seizure of the mines. Two more times, on March 12 and 14, Camicia appeared briefly in a nonantagonistic role along with Arnold Miller at news conferences—on the latter occasion to announce a third contract proposal. The discontinuous and sporadic presence of the BCOA was capped by a final BCOA appearance on March 25 as Joseph Brennan, BCOA President, praised the miners and the "peace treaty" just signed. The only real acrimony heard from BCOA speakers was aimed at President Carter and not the union. Only once, on March 8th, did CBS immediately juxtapose BCOA and miner interview soundbites—and, in that instance, each expressed dissatisfaction with steps taken by the Carter Administration to end the strike.

ECLIPSING CLASS WITHOUT BIAS

The strike's possible consequences were not addressed in terms of profits and losses to private capital. Instead, the potential effects on "the public" (and consumers like you) are examined, and the chances of a fuel crisis repeatedly weighed. The nature of the strike as a *capital-labor dispute* was eclipsed by projecting the strike as the *miners versus the public.* By replacing the interests of private capital with those of "the public," the assembly of news appears neutral and impartial, that is, it serves "the public interest." This sleight-of- screen surreptitiously identified Capital's interests with the general, public interest.

In an economic system where workers tend to be alienated from the fruits of their labor and subordinate to capital, how does it happen that the sole agents in this industrial news are the workers, acting and reacting all by themselves? Where are the capitalists in this picture of the world? "Nowhere and everywhere, like the sky, the horizon, an authority which at once determines and limits a condition" (Barthes, 1972, p. 51). Capitalist relations of production form the bedrock on which events occur. This ground is so thoroughly taken-for-granted as natural and inevitable that reports simply gloss over capitalist relations in framing events. Instead, viewers are shown, with carefully crafted neutrality, first the case of miners rejecting a contract, and then the consequences of this rejection, a fuel shortage. The rationale here is that viewers may determine for themselves the merits of the case, and decide where their sympathies lie. Though ostensibly impartial on the surface, the terms of presenting the issues have been stacked to privilege the interests of capital. Since capitalist social relations and market institutions predominate in the United States, any immediate disruption to them will of course have widespread consequences for "the public." But when the deeper institutional relations and forces are repressed, no particular interest group can effectively challenge private capital, since such a group then automatically imperils society at large if it proves too unyielding.

"Neutrality" and "balance" in the news are means of encompassing and accomodating different and opposing class interests. By disavowing the partisan, and upholding the "objective," newspeople seek to produce accounts acceptable to members of all classes. But there exists no absolute standard of neutrality: The "objectivity" newspeople aim for does not exist outside the realm of capitalist social relations. Journalistic "objectivity" emerged with mass audiences, signaled by the commodification of news. The rise to preeminence of a capitalist class replaced the individual capitalist interests that early newspapers represented with a more general interest in the maintenance of commodity markets and relations. The neutrality the news media seek consists not in a bias toward any particular fraction of capital, but in depending on, accepting, and promoting the interests of capital in general. In this way, class power is displaced to a neutral sphere, which, by virtue of its neutrality, secures the consent of the working classes (and equally important, of different fractions of capital).

. . . The underlying idea of the general interest, which is the most significant part of the ideological field which the media reproduces . . . is accomplished, not in spite of its rules of objectivity (i.e., by "covert or overt bias") but precisely by holding fast to the communicative forms of objectivity, neutrality, impartiality and balance. (Hall et al., 1976, p. 88)

Stories on contract negotiations, and on striking workers and their condition, are counterposed not by reports on company management, but by reports on "crises" caused by the work stoppage. Given the conventions of news reporters, we might assume "the other side" would show coal operators and their position regarding the strike. Instead there exists a pseudobalance which gives the appearance of a judicious counterposing of opposing sides of the question, while it actually substitutes for one side, the particular interests of a sector of private capital, the side of "the public interest." This effectively predetermines the outcome, since one side now clearly outweighs the other: Capitalist interests become represented as those of society at large. In reporting narrowly political news, there may actually be an accomplishment of a balanced presentation of different sides of an issue, within the circumscribed two-party framework of Congressional politics. But in industrial news, only the forms of balance and objectivity exist.

11

Pseudobalance: Carter, Taft-Hartley, and the Miners

Television news producers set up stories to pivot on the tension of two-sided contests of views. This narrative strategy boosts "news value," but also invites charges of favoritism. The pressure for fairness and impartiality has resulted in television news' rules and guidelines for presenting "both sides" in form. But "balance" does not define itself. The goal of "balance" is subverted as soon as the networks define the sides, and give a partial selection of content. Using a method we term pseudobalance, news reporters formally give each side a "hearing," thus appearing to treat the issue in a fair and impartial way. This method trades on the liberal ideal of a free contest of ideas.

There are two ideologicallycharged aspects to framing balance. First, how are the opposing "sides" conceptualized? The choices made are unavoidably politically loaded. During February, reports were thematically structured to include "angry miners" on one side and "growing crises" in fuel supply on the other. Here, "balance" was an artifact of structuring stories to maximize their newsvalue. But television journalists also allow primary institutional decisionmakers to define the sides of an issue. In the example to follow, maximizing newsvalue coincided with allowing President Carter to define the situation.

Second, the particular selections made to represent "the other side" influence the probable interpretations that may be made. Picturing rank-and-file interests in terms of interview clips with financially troubled miners who rue the very idea of a strike yields a different impression than if, say, the interview clips had been with miners' wives who delineate, point by point, their differences with the coal companies. This strike had numerous sides—the BCOA, UMWA Rank & File, Arnold Miller, President Carter, the consumer, and interested parties from shortage-affected states and utility interests. When CBS reduced these multiple sides and interests to a simple dichotomous opposition, they created a false balance by misstating the dimensions and relations of the whole.

The March 9 report illustrates the construction of "pseudobalance." The report began with the item that a federal court had granted President Carter's request for a Taft-Hartley back-to-work order.

Walter Cronkite: Good evening. Calling for reason, patience, willingness to cooperate, and obedience, uh, to the law, President Carter today obtained a federal court order for 160,000 striking coal miners to go back to work. Mr. Carter acted even as the Labor Department reported more than 250,000 [6:30] factory workers laid off last week—that's 25,000 [Cronkite corrects himself]—because of the 94 day old strike. And the nation's second largest steel firm, Bethlehem, said it plans to bank the fires at one of its major plants next week. Amid all these developments came signs and movement to resume negotiations. More on that story from Ed Bradley and Barry Serafin.

Ed Bradley [CBS]: As the President walked to his news conference, the next step in the coal dispute had already been set in motion. Earlier he had received the report of his board of inquiry and, based on their findings, directed the Attorney General to take the necessary legal steps under the Taft-Hartley law to send the miners back to work for an 80 day cooling off period. And he said that law must be obeyed and its intent carried out.

President Carter: This is a time for cooling off. We will do everything in our power to be sure that it does not become a time of confrontation. The law must be enforced. My firm commitment is that the Taft-Hartley Act will be enforced, that this will be adequate to assure supplies of coal to our country to avoid an additional crisis; and that it will also be an adequate incentive to bring the bargaining parties back to the negotiating table for a successful resolution. I have absolutely no plans to seek congressional action authorizing seizure of the coal mines.

Ed Bradley (CBS): The President said he believes the coal miners are law abiding and patriotic, and that enough of them will comply with the law to make a difference.

President Carter: I believe that—that if we can get a moderate number—hopefully all, but a moderate number—of coal miners to go back to work, that we can prevent a crisis [original emphasis] evolving in our country.

Ed Bradley: Mr. Carter feels that if only 15 to 20% of the coal now lost through the strike is brought back on line, that crisis can be averted. For coal now being mined or already above ground, transportation is the key issue. Pickets will be barred, key bridges and rail lines are now being guarded, and if necessary the National Guard will be brought out to insure the movement of coal and the protection of people.

In the first sentence containing the news item, Cronkite stressed the appeals invoked by President Carter to obtain a court order making it illegal for miners to continue striking. The appeals attributed to Carter connote calmness and order, voluntary consent and consensus. Naming "reason" and the "rule of law" as Carter's justification for using Taft-Hartley, Cronkite echoed Carter's frame—it is reason, cooperation, and obedience to the law *versus* 160,000 striking miners.

Cronkite then observed the timeliness of Carter's action by noting two economic developments. Cronkite's phrasing ("Mr. Carter acted even as . . .") suggested that cumulating evidence warranted and confirmed the urgency of Carter's move. However, neither development recounted by Cronkite held a warrant for a Taft-Hartley injunction. First, Cronkite misread the number of disemployed as 250,000 instead of 25,000, thus inflating the justification for Carter's action. Though Cronkite corrected himself a phrase later, the difference between 250,000 and 25,000 is substantial. Cronkite's delivery inferred that the statistic be taken as a measure of the crisis met by Taft-Hartley, but which number justified intervention—how shall we interpret the statistic? It doesn't matter, because the number was symbolic, its meaning conveyed in the tone and delivery of Cronkite's utterance. In retrospect, we know even the corrected number represented the peak of layoffs—that is, there was no crisis. The second item was a vivid example of cardstacking—the nation's leading steel corporations had "captive" coal mines and had taken a hard line on negotiations because they believed they could exhaust and beat the UMWA before stockpiles ran out. Bethlehem Steel had confidently gambled steel workers' job security by biding their time and taking an unyielding stance toward the UMWA. Mentioning the loss but not the gamble permits the negative consequences of the gamble to be turned to justify the exercise of a Taft-Hartley back-to-work injunction.

Before going on, we must historically situate the Taft-Hartley Act. On CBS, the meaning of Taft-Hartley was reduced to the legally prescribed "80 day cooling off period." Taft-Hartley signified the Presidential obligation to preserve the "national welfare"—to take extreme measures—when a stalemate between employers and workers threatens the greater interest. Since its passage in 1947, Taft-Hartley back-to-work orders have been rare; its most famous use involved John L. Lewis in the late 1940s. Its rare usage defined President Carter's action as having very high news value—ironically, its news value reflected the unspoken, repressed potential for the reemergence of class conflict that loomed behind the "protective" mechanism of Taft-Hartley.[1]

During the strike, President Carter often spoke in favor of the "free process of collective bargaining." Why did Carter fear a potential breakdown in the collective bargaining process? Institutionalized collective bargaining resulted from the Wagner Act and the formation of NLRB in 1935. The NLRB created an administrative apparatus and a heavily rationalized system of rules for resolving labor-management disputes. It took labor-management struggles off the shop floor and put them into the courts. Collective bargaining gave workers legal recognition of their unions and of their basic rights as workers. Though collective bargaining could settle wage and benefit disputes, the organization of the labor process lay beyond its mandate, and the principle was established that "management acts, and workers and their unions grieve" (Kochan & Piore, 1984, p. 178). Institutionalized collective bargaining also introduced a bureaucratic machinery that was unresponsive to local grievances. As a result, workers in the immediate post-World War II years resorted to so-called "quickie" strikes. After World War II, the National Association of Manufacturers and the U.S. Chamber of Commerce led an intense publicity campaign opposing the Wagner Act. They launched nearly "continuous publicity attacks. The campaigns were made not in the name of the interests of employers, so much as in the more appealing name of the interests of the public and of individual employees" (Millis & Brown, 1950, p. 290). Calling for a program that was "fair to the public" and allowed the "right to work," the nationwide antiunion campaign coalesced with Congressional political reaction against wildcat strikes and a wave of strikes in basic mass production industries such as steel, rubber, oil, coal, and railroads. Congress passed the Taft-Hartley Labor Relations Act in 1947. If ever one could speak of class-motivated legislation, this "amendment" to the Wagner Act was it.

But only the most glamorous plank of this package remained lodged in CBS's "historical memory"—namely, the power granted the President to seek a Federal restraining injunction when a strike threatens to endanger the "national welfare." CBS reified Taft-Hartley. CBS elided the right-wing origins of the Act, substituting instead the ideological

---

[1]Semiology begins with the relation between a signifier and a signified. Barthes (1972) reminds us that this relation "is not one of equality but one of equivalence." In this report, historical memory has been distilled and Taft-Hartly turned into a mere signifier—here correlated, via Cronkite's tone of voice, with a warning bell which alerts us to potential future problems.

view offered by probusiness forces back in 1947: Taft-Hartley provides a means of protecting the public from the abusive power of unions. What else was the Taft-Hartley Labor Relations Act about?

- The closed shop was declared illegal, thus diminishing the control unions exerted on hiring; and enhancing management control over the structure of labor markets.
- The Act restricted the right to strike, so that any strike during the life of a contract was illegal.
- "By making union officers vulnerable to fines and imprisonment for refusing to oppose wildcat strikes, the Congress penalized elected union officials for not acting as disciplinarians against their own rank and file" and thus effectively separated the interests of union leaders from rank and file workers" (Green, 1980, p. 198).
- It required that union officers sign an affidavit swearing they were not Communists, and outlawed political contributions by unions. This dramatically inhibited the development of effective union leadership.
- It prohibited union membership for foremen, thus giving management an edge in the struggle over shop-floor discipline.
- It made the unions subject to damage suits by employers. In fact, the Third Circuit Court of Appeals later ruled against the UMWA, making them liable to damages from companies if unauthorized strikes were not stopped (Montgomery, 1980, p. 167).
- The Act outlawed secondary boycotts and mass picketing.

In effect, the only union activity which remained legal under Taft-Hartley was that involved in direct bargaining between a certified "bargaining agent" and the employers of the workers it represented. Both actions of class solidarity and rank and file activity outside of the contractual framework were placed beyond the pale of the law. (Montgomery, 1980, p. 166)

It is not accidental that all CBS can remember is the 80-day cooling-off period. In the years following Taft-Hartley, the terms of the capital-labor accord ("a restructuring of class relations") made the state the referee in disputes and the President the ultimate guarantor of the public peace. In welfare-state capitalism the role of the President has become to block the dynamic of class struggle (Bowles & Gintis, 1982).

Now, let's return to the March 9 text as Cronkite passes us to Ed Bradley standing on stakeout outside the White House. Bradley began by retracing the line of legal protocol which led to "directing the Attorney

General to take the necessary legal steps . . ." Bradley adopted the role of official relayer of a Presidential message, unconditionally accepting the supreme authority of the Presidency. Before and after the main clip from President Carter's speech, Bradley emphatically reiterated Carter's primary point: "And he said that the law must be obeyed and its intent carried out."

Carter's delicate position was obvious—as President he had chosen to use legislation designed to handicap the side of the union, while trying to minimize his loss of support from key Labor leaders. His calm, meas ured delivery aimed at a sense of evenhandedness and distancing the forces of opposing class interests. He began with a plea for "cooling off" and assured that the power of the Presidency would be directed at preserving domestic tranquility. Carter expressed concern that "our country avoid an additional crisis," and thus pledged "my firm commit ment that the Taft-Hartey Act will be enforced."

Carter ended his announcement by seeking to put to rest rumors which had circulated through the mass media, thanks to unnamed Administration staffers, that Carter was considering seizing the mines along with invoking Taft-Hartley. Miners had been telling reporters that they would go back to work if Carter also seized the mines. But Carter also aimed this final comment at the BCOA, seeking to clarify any misunderstanding with the BCOA from the previous day when Nick Camicia (head BCOA negotiator) made a rare public appearance on CBS. Speaking as he walked away from reporters, Camicia had voiced annoy ance with a "very bad statement" which was never clearly defined ("some Administration statements that seizure of the coal mines is still possible").[2] So Mr. Carter now offered decisive reassurance, declaring that "I have absolutely no plans" to touch BCOA property. Instead, Carter acted to make illegal the union's only source of power—its collective ability to strike production. In this way, Carter took the side of Capital, but did so behind the banner of the "national welfare."

Bradley did not dwell on any of this, but recited again the key frames laid out by Carter—miners' obedience to the law vs. crisis. Bradley raised no questions about using Taft-Hartley, not even any "insider"

---

[2]Camicia [President, Pittston Coal Co.] had said on March 8: "I—I think it's a very bad statement, because it just gives encouragement to the union to not go to work under Taft-Hartley because they have seizure—which they want—to look forward to." It should be noted that Ed Bradley himself had reported three days earlier on March 6 that "Administration officials say they are not planning legislation to seize the mines. To do so, said one, would be to encourage the miners to break the Taft-Hartley law by refusing to report to work and waiting for seizure."

political analysis; instead he simulated the President's words about the miners' "law-abiding" and "patriotic" miners character as a prelude to another clip of Carter's assessment that if only a "moderate number" of miners obeyed the law, "we can prevent a crisis." Bradley repeated all this yet again, accepting without reservation the premise of "crisis" before launching into a militaristic checklist of official measures being taken to preserve the country's well-being.

Suddenly, Bradley disappeared and the story moved to Barry Serafin reporting from the Federal Courthouse in Washington where "Attorney General Griffen Bell personally went to federal district court to argue for a temporary restraining order to end the strike." Bell's taking "personal" charge presumably indicated the seriousness of the matter. Like Bradley, Serafin addressed us on stakeout at an Institutional site. As we observe the Attorney General's arrival, Serafin summarized the court proceedings. The video shifted to closeup shots of typed names on sheets of paper as Serafin said:

> 1,451 defendants were listed—individual companies plus union locals and districts. The Administration backed up its case with 11 affidavits from cabinet officers warning of extensive power cutbacks and job layoffs if the strike continues. The courtroom was jammed for today's hearing. Harrison Combs, an attorney for the Mine Workers, noted that coal is still being exported, and contended that big stockpiles remain in this country. Combs also disclosed that bargaining talks resume today between the union and the coal operators. But late today, Judge Aubrey Robinson, as expected, issued the order restraining miners from striking and companies from conducting lockouts.

An artist's courtroom sketch reminds viewers of the sacred legal context of the proceedings. In court, Serafin presents the two sides—the Administration versus the Union. "The Administration's backed up its case with 11 affidavits from cabinet officers," while the UMWA attorney "noted that coal is still being exported, and contended big stockpiles remain . . ." But why "as expected" did the Judge rule in behalf of the Administration? Serafin concluded by turning to what will happen next on the "legal" front, and how long the legal machinery will grind before "compliance" is "legally required." Because "The Law" represents the universal interest and force of our society, Serafin's Federal court angle was the longest uninterrupted speech act (1 minute and 23 seconds) in this March 9 report.

When the story returned to Cronkite at his anchor desk, he restated President Carter's primary frame, accepting it again at facevalue as he focused the question of how well the back-to-work order would work "to avoid a crisis." Cronkite framed "the other side" in terms of "the response of miners to the back-to-work order."

> Cronkite: "In expressing hope that enough miners would go back to work to avoid a crisis, Mr. Carter noted that, although 82% of miners have been on strike, coal output has been cut only in half. It's being mined by men who are either non-union or members of independent unions. Getting more coal moving, of course, depends on the response of miners to the back-to-work order. Ed Rabel in West Virginia reports that even miners who have been inclined to return may stay out."

We have already heard from Side 1—President Carter, the national interest, and the Law. The national welfare hinges on "getting more coal moving," which brings us to Side 2—miners' response to the back-to-work order. The correspondent's job is to unfold "the other side." Rabel's focus on intimidation among miners steered his selection of miner soundbites, and thereby shifted the parameters of "balance" still further.

> Rabel: "Do you welcome the prospect of the President invoking the Taft- Hartley Act? Will—will you go back to work if he does that?"

> Garry White [UMW Local 1766]: "Yes, I will, if he says go to work, I'll go to work. He's the man of the country and I'll go."

> Rabel: "But today, Garry White says he will defy the President's back-to-work order. Though he still wants to return to work, White says he fears reprisals from defiant miners,[3] and has changed his mind. While on strike, 22 year-old coal miner Debbie Raisovich took a part-time job. Now the job is ending. Still, like other miners throughout the coal fields who say they want to obey the President and go back to the mines, Raisovich says she can't."

> Debbie Raisovich [UMW Local 6025]: "The miners would probably cause a lot of trouble if you tried to go back."

> Rabel: "For example?"[4]

> Raisovich: "Cutting your tires off your cars, and—well, me being a woman, I would be especially afraid."

> Rabel: "Do you think that you would be subject to personal harm?"[5]

> Raisovich: "Yes sir. I think so."

---

[3]See Chapter 6 on pejoratives and name calling.
[4]See Chapter 6 on clarification requests.
[5]See Chapter 6 on leading questions.

"Balance" has been created by posing the "institutional voices" of the President and CBS reporters [representing television] on the one side, while "accessed voices" take the other side. Rabel defined the "other side" by assembling one ideological variable and one ideological constant. Rabel counterposed miner interviewees "who want to go back to work, but are fearful for their safety" to miner interviewees "who resent Taft-Hartley, but are fearful for their safety." Once again, working class people are classified by their emotions—fear and resentment. Let us restate the two sides as they have been framed:

President Carter	*The Miners*
Peace	Disobey or obey law?
The National Welfare	Patriotic or not?
The Law	
Reason	Fear
Patience	Resentment
Cooperation	
Obedience to Law	

Whereas Ed Bradley allowed President Carter to establish his own narrative themes, the selections of White and Raisovich were determined by the narrative preselected by Ed Rabel. How do we know this? As Garry White's image appeared on screen, a graphic in the upper-left corner of the screen read, "Last Sunday." In keeping with its own code of news ethics, CBS duly acknowledged that this question and answer was prerecorded—prior to the event to which it is being used to indicate (taken as) a response. At the conclusion of White's interview clip, his image froze on screen while Rabel's voiceover states that White has subsequently "changed his mind" because of intimidation. Rabel's comments over the frozen prerecorded image infer that Garry White has been threatened and he is now afraid even to speak. This manufactured sequence dramatically illustrates what Cronkite meant when he said that "even miners who have been inclined to return may stay out." Rabel's selection of Raisovich is equally problematic. Until now, in all of CBS's reporting, only one female miner has appeared in an interview (on December 23rd)—then for the purpose of illustrating how the union's strike was wreaking financial and material havoc on workers and their families themselves. Is it accidental that this second interview with a female rank-and-file miner is, likewise, put to the task of revealing vulnerability—here, the menace and threat of danger posed by some miners against civilized persons who seek to obey the law?

Rabel's selection of White and Raisovich influenced the probable interpretations that could be made of this report. This influence is amplified when we consider the kind of interviewees not chosen. No one from the

Miners Support Committee was heard expressing fear for their health and safety if mine operators would not comply with mine safety laws; there were no equipment operators expressing fear about being killed or maimed if the operators eliminated helpers on face equipment.

Rabel then moved from the timid to the resentful. This last sequence showed a group of older men watching President Carter's speech on television.

President Carter [on the television screen]: "The welfare of our nation requires this difficult step, and I expect that all parties will obey the law."

Rabel: "The President's comments were met by expressions of resentment and fear by miners watching his news conference—resentment of the Taft-Hartley Act, and fear of what might happen if they obey it."

Garnett Pritt [UMW Local 1766]: I believe in the right to work, and I believe in the right not to work. And—and the only way that I'll go back—I'm not going back to work up there and take a chance on getting my head blowed off up there.

Clarence Lanham [retired miner]: "If he's got the power to force these poor men back into that dark hole, why ain't he got the power to make the operators come up with what we want?"

Pritt (from off camera): "Yeah, that's right, that's right. Now that's right."

Unnamed Miner: "Now, you're right."

Unnamed Miner: "The mines, that's right . . ." [indistinct cross-talk]

Lanham: "If they can force one, why not force them, and maybe we can get some free bargaining."

President Carter [on television]: "I have absolutely no plans to seek congressional action authorizing seizure of the coal mines."

Pritt: "No you don't, brother Carter, because the—I think the coal companies is mixed—you—you're afraid—"

Unnamed Miner: "They've bought him out."

Pritt: "—you're afraid of the oil companies and the steel companies, that's what I think."

Unnamed Miner: (from off camera) "They've bought him out. They've bought him out, or they have him scared."

Pritt: "No, I don't—I don't know about that. They've got him scared to death."

Rabel: "These miners say that unless he seizes the mines President Carter should not expect miners to go back to work. Taft-Hartley, they say, has never worked here, and never will."

Here we encounter the contradictions of hegemonic frames. Rabel's voiceover framed their reactions as "fear and resentment," but these miners' voices do not match Rabel's frames. "Resenting Taft-Hartley" may capture the sentiment these men feel, but it does little to thematize the working-class perspective which lies behind the feeling. These men raise issues not otherwise addressed by CBS. They do more than resent, they question the legitimacy of government intervention on the side of the coal operators; they perceive a power alliance between corporate capital and the state. Clarence Lanham raises legitimate questions that CBS has never bothered to ask—where is the fairness or equity in this legal coercion? And, by the way, what does constitute a "free bargaining" process?

> If he's got the power to force these poor men back into that dark hole, why ain't he got the power to make the operators come up with what we want? . . . If they can force one, why not force them, and may be we can get some free bargaining.

CBS usually serialized miner interviews; rarely did they air *dialogue between miners*. Here is the exception to their rule. Though Rabel let viewers hear the miners speak about power and class inequity in the application of state force, he did not reiterate or assess the miners' claim that oil and steel companies' interests and influence may have figured in Carter's decision.

Rabel's prefatory frame emphasizes the fear of getting hurt if they cross the picket line. If we think of frames as limits or boundaries around a field of discourse, then Rabel's frame must be judged inadequate because it could not contain these men's working class rhetoric or perspective. Rabel and camera crew have made their way inside a miner's home, there to capture the reactions of a group of miners to President Carter. When Carter spoke, the camera maintained a respectful distance from his face, but here the camera scanned the miners' faces for affect, or revealed a closeup glimpse of Garnett Pritt's nervous hand fidgeting with a cigarette lighter. Inspite of all this, when Garnett Pritt angrily reacts to Jimmy Carter's television statement about having no plans to seize the mines—"No you don't, brother Carter . . . you're afraid of the oil and steel companies''—the hegemonic frames become momentarily unsettled.

But the unsettled moment is brief indeed, for Rabel turns to wrap up by reducing this dialogue to a mere signifier in yet another frame— Garnett Pritt et al are used to signify that "Taft-Hartley won't work."

SCREENING CLASS CONFLICT

Rabel's simultaneous act of visual disclosure and conceptual masking marks a recurring pattern in CBS's coverage of the strike. CBS screened class conflict in both senses—they showed it as a surface appearance while blocking out its conceptual presence. CBS reporters mechanically skirted themes of class conflict. Fourteen times during CBS strike coverage, miner interviewees referred to their conflict with coal operators, usually naming the coal operators as "they." Yet, on no occasion did a CBS reporter identify such a reference. Neither did any CBS reporter follow up or investigate the miners' claims about their conflict with operators, though twice reporters redirected and refocused miner hostility from the companies to Arnold Miller. Even when it appeared, momentarily, on screen as a visual frame, no CBS reporter explicitly formulated "class conflict" as a conceptual frame. Though CBS frequently stated "the two sides are far apart," they did not name the sides as "class" sides.

"Screening"—the visual presence of "class relations" as a variable along with its conceptual absence—can be further illuminated by visually breaking down the February 15 report. Ed Rabel followed Bob Faw's nail story (see Chapter 5) with a report on rebellious West Virginia miners. A miners' rally on the steps of the state capitol in Charleston emphasized solidarity and preventing nonunion coal from reaching power plants. A key group at this rally was the Miners' Right to Strike Committee (MRTSC). Yet, Rabel did not mention them. At least one MRTSC speaker (O.V. Hirsch) was seen and heard addressing the rally this report, but Rabel did not identify him as such (Hirsch was nominated on screen only as "miner"). And when a banner bearing the legend "We Demand the Right to Strike" appeared for an instant on screen, Rabel did *not* explain its meaning, or identify the movement organization. Why exclude this motive force in telling this story?

Whereever class conflict, or the ideological articulation of class conflict raised its spectre during the strike, CBS drew away. The class rhetoric of the BCOA was missing; also absent was the leftist language of the MRTSC. Even CBS coverage of intra-union conflict suffered from the inability to name class actors or class relationships.[6] Remember that this story is itself already situated as *the other side* of the story about coal shortages and the use of the National Guard to protect coal shipments from striking miners.

> Cronkite: "The posting of guards on coal shipments reflects the depth of feeling among the miners who've been most affected by this strike. Ed Rabel has talked to some of them in Charleston, West Virginia."

1) Closeup of a black male's face. Camera angle is low looking up. He speaks to other miners. Behind him we see others and a part of a placard. He speaks 9 secs.

2) wide angle shot of miners gathered outdoors.

3) tight profile shot of another black miner in the crowd. Behind Rabel's narration, can hear bits of a rally speaker's voice on the soundtrack.

4) Tight facial shots of 2 white miners as they lean their heads to the side to see and hear the speaker.

5) Burke speaking. Nominated on screen; has long sideburns, facial hair. A glimpse of others and signs behind him as he addresses crowd. Heavy Appalachian twang and cadence. Speaks 5 sec.

6) tight shot (angled up) of burly miner's face; wears baseball (Bb) cap. His face is framed by the shoulder and neck of two others. Long lens.

Walter Lawson [Miner]: $_1$We—we've got to stop all this nonunion coal. We've got to stop the coal in Kentucky. We've got to stop it in West Virginia. And we've got to stop it out West.

Ed Rabel: Walter Lawson's comments $_2$at this miners' rally on the state capitol steps are$_3$ symbolic of a $_4$widespread feeling among the rank-and-file of the United Mine Workers.

Lewis Burke [miner]: $_5$We need to stop that scab coal. If you don't it's going to break our backs.

Rabel:$_6$The feeling is that to achieve their contract goals of the $_7$right to strike, cost of living wage increases, $_8$and broadened medical and pension benefits, they must prevent coal now being mined in non-union mines from reaching power plants, which are $_{10}$in desperate need because of the prolonged strike.

O.V. Hirsch [Miner]: $_{11}$When we

---

[6]CBS efforts to focus on the intraunion struggle were confused, segmented and discontinuous. Reporting on internal union strife on February 19, David Dick referred to a "call for unity" at a "peaceful, orderly meeting" of UMW officials. Dick reports the meeting "was a demand for an end to unauthorized actions and speeches by those they lumped together as the union's radicals." The West Virginia UMW officials interviewed were upset about the February 15 rally on the capitol steps. Red Forbes, a local official, objects to "people running around here holding these meetings and things on the State House steps and whatnot." Though CBS had obviously covered the other rally, Dick made no effort to situate Forbes' reference.

7) large sign lettered: "We Demand the Right to Strike" draped over a wall next to the steps. Shown 3 seconds.

8) young blond miner listening to a speaker. Camera pans left to another balding miner's face.

9) closeup of young bearded, longhaired miner wearing a bent-billed Bb cap with 'CAT' insignia on it.

10) closeup of both burly bearded and unbearded miners.

11) Hirsch nominated. Head shot, bearded, wearing cap. Addresses crowd with "solidarity" rhetoric. Speaks 11 seconds.

12) closeup profile from low camera angle of bearded young miner. Pans to man behind him, wearing bent-billed Bb and t-shirt. Camera hugs his face.

13) placard held up in the crowd
    "Jimmy Carter
    John D. Rockefeller
    Puppets For The Coal Bosses"

14) another placard reads:
    Taft-Hartley Won't Work
    Soldier's Can't Mine Coal

15) Lane, speaking in front of battery of mikes. Speaks for 17 sec.

16) closeup of hands playing a guitar. Pans up to male player's face as he sings.

17) closeup of young white miner wearing Bb cap and t-shirt. Pans across to another young miner wearing same garb.

18) curly haired, bearded young miner. Seen from back wearing camouflage jacket

19) wide angle shot looking up capitol steps at back of the crowd

20) closeup of same bearded singer in front of microphone.

come out we was told how weak we were, how divided we were, how the stockpiles and the companies had us whupped. 72 days and we're whupping these big, bad rich companies, and we already done whupped their stockpiles.

Rabel: [12]Charging UMW president Arnold Miller with selling out to the coal companies, the miners renewed their calls for his resignation. [13]And there was defiance over President Carter's [14]possible use of the Taft-Hartley Act to get the miners back to work.

Bill Lane [Miner]: [15]Well, now, I'm telling him he can't break our back with that Taft-Hartley Act because we ain't going to work anyhow, are we? We're not going back to work! [cheers from assembled miners in background] We're staying out and we're going to get a good contract, that's what we're going to do! We're going to stay out and get a good contract! If they put them soldiers in there, they ain't going to move no coal away from them mines, are they? No they're not!

Unidentified Musician singing:[16] But pretty soon I won't be the only one that's cold, when those big, old power plants can't get no non-union coal.

Rabel: The consensus here is that [17]less than ten percent of the miners would go back to work if Taft-Hartley were invoked. [18]There is also the belief here that just a small number of determined miners [19]could interrupt trains and trucks delivering the badly needed coal.

Musician [singing]:[20] "I'm going to Kentucky to stop the flow of coal." Ed Rabel. CBS News. Charleston, W.V.

This event was a miners' rally—a collective action. Yet, of the 20 camera shots which visually compose the report, 12 are tight closeups of miners in the crowd or on the podium. Only two wide-angle shots denote the miners assembled on the capitol steps. The sequence contained three shots of slogan-bearing placards held aloft at the rally, and two shots of speakers addressing the audience shot at head and shoulder distance. The montage concluded with a closeup of a guitar player's hands, followed by a pan shot to his face as he sang of solidarity.

This coverage illustrates how two reportorial practices—tight closeups and sharply edited soundbites—serialized the miners' collective action. The class character of these scenes is etched in the miners' apparel, haircuts, language, and faces. The closeup profile shots include images of sideburns, beards, bent-billed baseball caps (with or without insignias, e.g., CAT), t-shirts and jacket sleeves which identify these men as workers. Though immediately recognizable as working class, these bearded and shaven, mostly burly young men, become a video string of individual portraits rather than a collectivity of faces. These scenes were shot unobtrusively with a long lens to capture closeup facial expressions unaffected by the camera's presence. This method of representation draws attention away from their collective spirit—as *classe fur siche*. Instead each face is photographically situated as an iconic representation of *classe an siche*.

We presume the many closeup shots of the male miners are intended to "reflect the depth of feeling among the miners." If facial expression is taken as a measure then the men in the crowd—the representation of the crowd—were sober, solemn, tight-lipped, and apparently unemotional. To be sure, a depth of feeling does comes across in the speakers' soundbites.

The relationship, or lack of it, between visuals of the protesters' placards and the reporter's spoken frames is also instructive. Despite including a shot of a demonstrator's sign reading "we demand the right to strike," keyed to listing it as a contract demand made by rank-and-file miners, neither Ed Rabel nor any other CBS reporter explained its meaning. Second and third placards are keyed to Rabel's statement about "defiance over President Carter's possible use of the Taft-Hartley Act . . ." The second sign reads: "Jimmy Carter, John D. Rockefeller Puppets for the Coal Bosses." The third says: "Taft-Hartley Won't Work, Soldiers Can't Mine Coal." Each sign indicated the miners' displeasure with Carter, but Rabel's narrative passes over what seems the more interesting meaning of the second placard. Why would miners perceive politicans as "puppets for the coal bosses"? Why did miners defy Jimmy Carter? By now, we should anticipate that Rabel would not pursue miners' references to coal companies. Rabel still restates the miners' antagonism toward Arnold Miller and President Carter but not that toward the coal companies.

And yet, the report's final scene includes a soundbite of a union singer's song of resistance. The lyrics undeniably convey a sense of union and class solidarity: "But pretty soon I won't be the only one that's cold, when those big old power plants can't get no nonunion coal . . . I'm goin to Kentucky to stop that flow of coal." This symbolizes miner solidarity—which translates, as Cronkite has reminded us, into discomfort for you and me at home. This last scene encompasses the uneven ideological character of television news. Even he re the hegemonic contest continues—why, after making a sustained effort to block out the class dimension, did Rabel allow the final scenic frame to include the voice of a rank-and-file "organic intellectual?" Perhaps because it emphasizes "the depth of feeling" and clearly states the agenda which flows from it—that miners intend to obstruct the flow of "badly needed coal" (Rabel). Their solidarity signals a threat to you the viewer.

CBS News' method of storytelling emphasized shot after shot of miners' faces as they attended meetings. CBS structured their reports on miners' views of the contract proposals around strategically situated soundbites and an edited succession of photographs of miners' faces (shot with long lenses so as not to bias facial expressions). Reporters used this formula to summarize what they considered the relevant facts—what we call frames. Though the setting for virtually every miner soundbite broadcast on CBS in February and early March was a union meeting, in every case, the context of such gatherings was reduced to a reporter's gloss. The solidarity or conflict expressed in such group settings was, in every case, interpreted (mediated) via the reporter's voice. This format emphasized close scrutiny of miners' expressive features, but did not allow them to speak their own story at any length— to explain their motivations.

12

Covering the Strike

We have, thus far, conducted a contextual analysis of CBS's news texts. After historically reconstructing the coal strike to produce a comparative measure of content possibilities, critical semiotic and hermeneutic analyses of the reports themselves provided a means of investigating the interpretive consequences of news form. To this, we now append an analysis of the social relations of reporting and the constraints faced by reporters in producing "news" of the strike. The specificity of our ideological critique requires a corresponding specificity of the reporting process to deepen our understanding of the relations and processes through which hegemony is reproduced.

If anything stands out about these CBS news texts, it is their reliance on format formula. We are "concerned about the way in which formats of information have been combined with unifying themes about "crises" to distort public information" (Altheide, 1987). We also recognize that these news texts were routinely produced by professional reporters who operated within overlapping sets of organizational, technological, logistical, and ideological constraints. Constructing news is an activity performed by real, living actors situated in specific social relations and determinate structural circumstances. Reporters vary in skill, background, training, personality, philosophy, and degree of commitment, the tracings of which are left across news texts. Based on interviews with journalists involved in covering the 1977–78 coal strike, we have tried to reconstruct some network practices which contributed to the form and content of the news.

1. Assignment editors shuffle reporters around. Network newsbeats correspond to regional, geographic areas ("generalist" beats). When CBS perceived the coal strike as "heating up," they temporarily brought

in reporters from the Southern and Midwest Bureaus to cover the coal "shortage" angle. Partly because of the constant demands of matching a relatively scarce number of reporters to story locations, network reporters remain generalists who lack background knowledge of particular industries or labor-management relations. No network maintains a specialist reporter covering labor relations. Moving reporters around to accomodate the daily transition in story selection and location poses additional obstacles to acquiring familiarity with the labor beat, and puts network reporters at a critical disadvantage in terms of background knowledge and access to sources. Moving reporters from story to story also promotes inconsistency in coverage. This problem is not specific to labor coverage, it influences the reporting of most topics. Tendencies toward shallowness and inconsistency in reporting labor relations are further amplified by defining news stories as immediate *events* rather than as unfolding sets of relations. Shifting reporters in response to "breaking" news items makes it difficult for reporters to be anything but reactive. Network reporters, including reporters who worked the coal strike, voiced criticism of network policies that ignore industries between crises. One network reporter observed that network coverage of industrial relations suffers because

> We offer no status reports on basic industries, whether it is steel, coal, even auto. Where does the coal industry stand today? Has the boom panned out? What has happened in the western coalfields? Where does mine safety enforcement stand?

2. Networks do not maintain stringers but rely instead on local station affiliates. Though local station affiliates are supposedly a functional equivalent of stringers, CBS's strike coverage did not visibly draw on materials provided by local Appalachian affiliates. Failure to draw on materials gathered by local television reporters resulted in (a) coverage gaps when network reporters were shuffled to other stories; (b) an absence of local knowledge in network reports; and (c) limited knowledge of, and access to, sources outside the Charleston area.

3. Reporters compete for time on the evening news, and they internalize the value of conserving time in preparing their reports. In an occupation where advancement (and by extension, salary) depends on air time, successful competition for scarce time is a means to enhancing each reporter's own commodity status—how much they get paid. By the 1970s the networks rewarded reporters who could craft narrated pictures into concise packages.

Anecdotal "horror stories" abound with regard to the time pressures imposed on network reporters. For example, a reporter might be told in the morning that s/he has 2 1/2 minutes on the evening broadcast. But by 5 P.M. in the afternoon, New York slices that to 45 seconds. What kinds of information get cut in such situations? How do "story angles" alter as a consequence?

Demands for brevity are antithetical to providing explanation, and present an obstacle to treating strike events in terms of institutional relations. Instead, abbreviation tends to favor treating events as isolated occurrences or reflections of personal conflicts. Television reporters consider the task of telling complex and complicated stories in very little time, a "frustrating fact-of-life."[1]

"Shorthanding" complex relations into terse statements simplifies matters and passes over vast areas which fall under the category of "arcane" knowledge. The tacit principle of arcane knowledge may be the most critical taken-for-granted assumption shaping labor news.[2]

Reporters define "arcane" knowledge as knowledge specific to a particular industry or occupational sector. A subject defined as involving a high degree of arcane knowledge is unlikely to be mentioned on the evening news. Hence, reporters pass over what is not common knowledge, while speaking within terms which encompass what they presume is "common knowledge" to the audience.

A self-fulfilling prophecy works itself out in reporting labor news. Network television does not cover labor relations unless there is a crisis situation. Because the networks offer no periodic status reports on the conditions and relations in basic industries, when a crisis occurs there is not enough time to do the kind of "crash" education course on the "arcane" knowledge necessary to make sense of the conflict.

4. Network television news producers construct their news product for an audience they deem to be uninterested in anything other than spectacular events or those events which immediately affect them. During the coal strike, producers apparently determined that audiences for the evening news were neither knowledgeable about relations in the coal industry nor interested except in their status as consumers. Reporters thus considered the "arcane" subject matters of the health and pension fund crisis, or the breakdown of the grievance and arbitration system beyond the realm of most viewers. Coupled with the principle of

---

[1]Reporters are aware of the dilemma, but naturalize it as a fact-of-life which the individual reporter can do little to alter. These are the 'rules of the game' if they wish to participate in the corporate world of television journalism.

[2]In interviews, reporters themselves used the name "arcane" to refer to this category of knowledge. All spoke of the category in matter-of-fact tones. None wondered at it, or questioned it as a rule of thumb.

brevity, this meant dispensing with these subjects altogether since viewers could not be informed about such issues in a matter of seconds.

5. Television news is "picture-hungry." Journalists cite this theory of technological determinism to explain the character of television news. In its most radical expression, the formula is no pictures, no news. Obvious though it may be that television news hinges on sharp visuals, this easy explanation may be partially myth. This thesis does explain why certain facets of strikes receive minor attention. For instance, the vacant coverage of bargaining negotiations between labor and management is commonly reduced to the absence of exciting visuals—it is boring. It is difficult to find dramatic visual shots in the Labor Department corridors or the Capitol Hilton negotiating site: Witness those reports that dwelt on shots of Arnold Miller walking through a corridor or that follow his car pulling out of a parking garage.

Still, close study of these tapes does not support the thesis that selection of visuals was consistently the preeminent factor determining story selection or story construction. For instance, though wildcats formed a pivotal issue in this strike, CBS did not include any file footage of wildcat strikers when such footage would seem to satisfy the criteria of exciting visuals. Similarly, though miners organized, and publicly announced, automobile "caravans" to halt the flow of nonunion coal, CBS showed no film of these events.

Conversely, a significant proportion of images used in CBS reports were mundane or technically flawed. Quantitatively, the images that appeared most frequently were included for the simple iconic purpose of indicating stoppage of production—for example, stilled wheels of railroad cars or vacant tipples. Lighting was poor at many of the sites filmed during the strike, however, so that reports contained pictorial images which were denotatively difficult to identify in the instant of their being shown.

Though television news is heavily disposed to covering violence and demonstrations, anticipating the locus of events can be a guessing game. During the coal strike, network crews were often out of position or had to rely on footage from local affiliates.[3] Because most instances of violence during the strike were unexpected, CBS frequently lacked good

---

[3]CBS relied on an affiliate for materials of a December incident in Utah, but did not make use of affiliate resources on air again during the strike. Why did CBS fail to make use of their Charleston affiliate? Also puzzling was their failure to show any film of the incidents which took place in Alabama when striking miners, reportedly, had surrounded a shed in which non-union miners had retreated. There ensued a gun battle with state police before the miners were dispersed. This would seem perfect grist for TV news' formula mill.

pictures and actually covered a relatively small proportion of violent acts during the strike.[4] To be sure, decision makers at CBS (like the other networks) did seize on "violence" as a theme when possible. For instance, CBS staked out anticipated violence on February 14, but with no visual success; nevertheless, having committed their resources to the effort they stuck with the explanatory frame of violence. When television crews had immediate access to events, then the rule of exciting visuals did prevail. Miners recognized this and burned copies of contracts when they saw television cameras.[5]

6. For reasons of geographic access CBS concentrated on the area around Charleston, West Virginia. Social proximity of sources proved to be a more important factor. Reporters' social status and background make it "easiest to make contact with sources similar to them in class position" (Gans, 1979, p. 125). This might be expected to limit reporters ability in gaining access to working-class actors like miners. However, in recent years, laborers' points of view have become more readily accessible than management's during strikes. In this strike, the numbers are shocking: CBS used interview clips of 94 miners, 23 union officers, and Miller 16 times, as opposed to 5 clips of BCOA speakers.

During the coal strike, Barry Serafin in Washington had good "backgrounding" sources among the government mediators, the BCOA, and the UMW. However, with the exception of Arnold Miller, the other participants rarely appeared on camera. Meanwhile, out in the "field" of West Virginia, Ed Rabel had apparent ease of access to rank and file miners in taverns, coffee houses, and picket lines. Yet, Rabel apparently had limited knowledge of, or access to, opposition leaders within the union. Although a few local presidents were interviewed (including

---

[4]This claim is based on comparing reported incidents of "violence" in newspapers with the CBS reports. There were some charges that television crews were involved in manufacturing scenes of "violence." On March 9, Charles Bateman, a local union officer, was arrested after attempting to confiscate equipment from a television crew. Bateman charged that a local television crew had planted spikes in the road so they could purportedly film UMW disruption of coal traffic (Kirksey, 3/10/78, p. 1).

[5]The fetish of exciting visuals is illuminated by an accident during the 1985-86 meatpackers strike against Hormel in Austin, Minnesota. ABC cameramen died in a helicopter crash while seeking pictures of a confrontation between National Guardsmen and strikers. Other reporters recalled how these ABC personnel had, on previous days, watched with disinterest from a distance. Disinclined to investigate the mundane dimensions of the strike conflict, these same men risked death (weather conditions were unsafe when they went up in the helicopter) in order to get the glitziest pictures possible.

several interviews with David Forms), prominent and colorful leader s such as Jack Perry and Cecil Roberts and Bill Lamb were rarely heard from. Local union officers available to AP and UPI reporters throughout the strike also tended to be absent from the screen in CBS coverage.

A confluence of factors conditioned the quantity and depth of coverage. The strike negotiations were a poor candidate for film coverage because they presented few arresting visual shots. They were also difficult to cover from a reporter's viewpoint because they involved an inordinate amount of waiting around—a factor which not only made the reporter's job tedious, but from the network's standpoint was an inefficient use of reportorial resources. Further, the bargaining sessions in Washington DC ended in the evening hours, too late to be included on the evening news. Therefore, much of Serafin's coverage of the negotiations appeared, buried, on the *CBS Morning News* rather than the *Evening News*. Finally, during this coal strike neither BCOA nor UMWA negotiators (except Arnold Miller on occasion) were apt to speak with reporters.

In general, television reporters simply do not know the 'territory' of industrial labor-management relations.[6] Because no network television news division allocates a specialist reporter to the beat of industrial relations, none has reporters able to grasp fundamental issues in pivotal conflicts. Ultimately, their lack of knowledge is sanctioned and justified by the system which produces it—its justification being that audiences don't have any knowledge of this area, and wouldn't understand or watch the complexities anyway.

Compared to the other television reporters covering the coal strike, Barry Serafin may have exceeded the network norm for knowledge of the coal industry. And such as they were, he obtained the only network interviews with Nick Camicia. Still, the BCOA systematically excluded him from access. Ed Rabel and the other CBS reporters who popped in and out of Appalachia (Bruce Hall, Martha Teichner, Bob Faw, Betty Ann Bowser, Don Webster) lacked familiarity with what they were covering.[7] In general, print journalists we spoke to repeatedly complained that television reporters often exhibit a disinterested attitude toward the strikes they cover.

At CBS, the principle of brevity and taken-for-granted assumptions

---

[6]Using a reputational method in interviewing, there was general unanimity among our respondents about this 'rule,' as well as on the two network reporters considered exceptions to the rule. Serafin was one of the two most frequently mentioned as exceptions to the rule.

[7]One veteran observer recalled that Rabel "never saw the ball after the kickoff."

about the nature of their audience outweighed even the reporters' lack of knowledge and television's bias for hot pictures in influencing the shape and content of coverage.[8] The latter factors undoubtedly influenced the frames of coverage, but the principle of "arcane knowledge" in conjunction with "shorthanding" (abbreviation) shaped ideological frames more profoundly.

PUBLIC RELATIONS AND CLASS RELATIONS

Prior to the 1977-78 strike, coal operators had been "unsophisticated" in their media relations. During the 1977-78 strike, BCOA public relations entered the "modern era." In April 1977, the BCOA retained Morris Feibusch as Public Affairs specialist. Previously, coal operators' public image had been coarse and unsympathetic, a result of chronic "foot in mouth syndrome"—for example, calling the Farmington mine disaster "an act of God". From their side, conservative coal operators perceived reporters as hostile and too liberal.[9]

Under Feibusch's direction, the BCOA launched a media campaign prior to the 1977-78 coal strike. In the months preceding the strike, the BCOA circulated among journalists and miners a pamphlet entitled, "Will the United Mine Workers of America Play a Major Role in the Coal's Future?" The BCOA designed the pamphlet full of charts and graphs to explain why they were demanding concessions from the UMWA, and to get their message out to rank-and-file miners about the state of the industry.

Because the BCOA was taking such a tough negotiating stance, their media agenda aimed at "backgrounding" the BCOA's quest for a "labor stability" package. With the print media, the BCOA public relations strategy worked to the extent that the BCOA's "labor stability" agenda came across without the BCOA appearing as "the moving party." But the strategy worked less well with network television, not because

---

[8]The form of journalism—the demand for a fresh daily story, a headline, a lead paragraph, the need to condense something 'new' into a minute-and-a-half television report—dictates the content. As in political reporting, this form creates an air of reportorial omniscience which further warps coverage patterns. (Ken Auletta, "How they covered the landslide," *NYT Book Review*, July 28, 1985, pp. 3, 27).

[9]Some coal operators perceived reporters as left-oriented--the reasoning being, as one reporter put it, that since reporters themselves have a union they must be biased in favor of union positions.

television reporters were more critical or hostile to BCOA interests, but because network television does not deal with labor-management disputes until they become strikes. Hence, none of the BCOA's backgrounding of the conflict, concentrated prior to the strike's start on December 6, made it to the airwaves.

Feibusch established a convivial rapport with print reporters. His success at "buddying up" with reporters may have enabled him to screen reporters away from internal BCOA conflicts. Feibusch occasionally supplied beat reporters with general tips on where to be, or when, for a story. Because most television reporters could not stay with the story, most did not have this kind of social relationship cultivated over the space of time. An apparent exception to this was Barry Serafin of CBS News. According to informants, Serafin worked the negotiation end of the strike more diligently than other network reporters. He was therefore rewarded by the BCOA (with Feibusch the moving force) with the only on-camera interview with a BCOA negotiator (Nick Camicia). Logs of other networks' coverage indicate no other network reporters gained access to BCOA executives until the very end of the strike.

From a public relations standpoint, a multiemployer bargaining unit such as the BCOA sets up a potentially "volatile" climate. In the BCOA's multiemployer bargaining situation, members compete in the market, but are allies in their labor negotiations. All members must live with a pact which is signed, and over the life of a contract some interests will fare better than others. Over a long strike like the 1977–78 coal strike, serious strains develop within the employer bargaining unit, and public pronouncements may aggravate those strains. Even with print reporters, BCOA leaders were tightlipped about their fierce behind-the-scenes political battles (Brown, 3/11/78, p. 2). The BCOA's "calculated shyness" with network television news was unquestionably influenced by the dynamic of a multi-employer bargaining unit.[10]

BCOA members were accessible to print reporters when they had something to say. Occasionally during the strike, BCOA members would perceive Arnold Miller as talking too much, and they would select a member to "shoot back against" him. But, judging by CBS's news reports, BCOA accessibility to network reporters was substantially less: On a number of occasions CBS reporters stated on-camera that BCOA spokespersons were not available or declined comment.

Gans (1979, p. 81) states conventional wisdom on hierarchy of access:

---

[10]On the other hand, the UMWA aired its dirty laundry all over the place. In late February a portion of the lower union hierarchy met to discuss the problem. CBS sent Bruce Hall to cover the story.

the economically and politically powerful can obtain easy access to, and are sought out by, journalists; those who lack power are harder to reach by journalists and are generally not sought out until their activities produce social or moral disorder news.

A corollary must be stated: The economically and politically powerful are more able to restrict or control access. The key issues here were ease of access to miners, and control over access by operators. In recent years, it has become standard operating procedure for corporate officers to "hide" behind the cloak of a public relations person (Hackett, 1985, p. 265).

Just as BCOA negotiators were rarely available to television reporters, so too, UMWA negotiators remained at a distance. Other than Miller (and late in the strike, Camicia), viewers who depended on television news could not have known the name of any other negotiators on either side. A further restriction on information flow was that the UMWA's press secretary, Paul Fortney, was apparently kept in the dark and rarely authorized to say even what he did know (Seltzer, 1985, p. 155). Throughout the strike negotiations, local union officers and rank-and-file members complained about their lack of knowledge regarding the status of negotiations and the secrecy with which Miller was proceeding (Franklin, 1/3/78).

Unlike the BCOA, the UMWA had neither a public relations strategy nor a coordinated effort to frame the conflict for the media. As a result of internal union disputes, Miller fired Bernie Aronson from his UMW public relations post in 1976. But Miller did not name a replacement. When the strike began, officials at the Federal Mediation and Conciliation Service were concerned by this deficit in staffing and encouraged the union to retain the Washington DC public relations firm of Maurer, Fleisher, Zon, and Anderson. Aside from a small handful of press releases, this public relations firm merely went through the motions and remained "almost invisible" until late February (Hughey, 2/3/78, p. 1). The firm produced a television and radio advertising campaign to sell the second contract proposal to the rank and file. Their media strategy backfired because (a) the ad campaign featured Arnold Miller, which alienated many miners against the settlement; (b) miners reasoned that if the contract had to be sold, there must be something suspicious about its content; and (c) miners' benefits were exhausted and many were hungry and cold, so when $40,000 of UMWA money was spent on the ad campaign they deeply resented it. They felt the money should go where it was needed, not to sell them a contract containing penalties. As soon as miners voted to reject the contract proposal, the union's public relations firm closed its press room at the Mayflower Hotel and quit.

"We promised them we'd stick with them through the ratification vote and ratification has just been defeated. There's nothing more that we can do for them now," said their PR man Jerry Anderson (Hughey, 3/6/78). The network television coverage that resulted from this mix was not reducible to any single set of interests. Though the BCOA sought to exert influence over the frames of network coverage, those efforts were largely dissipated by the practical routines governing network coverage. Though the BCOA's view of things never made it cleanly to the screen, network coverage coincided with BCOA interests until mid-February. The BCOA had no interest in making the strike the subject of public debate, and their strategy was aimed at keeping it off the public agenda.

Furthermore, the BCOA claimed to be relatively unconcerned with its "public image." They adopted the pragmatic stance that in a prolonged strike, public opinion will see no winners. Their public relations campaign was thus not aimed at enhancing public opinion so much as achieving their goal—a strike settlement consonant with their best interests. Toward this end, they devised a media campaign addressed to two groups: journalists and the UMWA rank and file. In each case, they saw their campaign as "educational": to "teach" from a BCOA perspective each respective audience about "the state of the industry." Though national television did not pick up on the BCOA's early campaign, its lack of attention to the BCOA effectively insured that issues of conflict between miners and coal operators did not become the subject of wider public debate.

Public relations specialists consider network television news the most difficult medium to manage during a strike. Feibusch recognized this. Further, since BCOA strategy was to achieve specific contract goals rather than a positive public image, they had no pressing need to take their case to the American public. Hence, they had no real need of the evening news. The BCOA mainly sought to shape media agendas and frames for Appalachian audiences.[11] The national audience remained relatively unimportant to the BCOA, until they began to be drawn out into public view by President Carter.

How effective was the BCOA public relations campaign with the rank and file? Some speculated that BCOA print and radio campaigns from October to December cooled out support for a right-to-strike clause in the contract. However, the BCOA campaign did nothing to dent the antipathy of miners towards the BCOA "labor stability" penalties.

By mid-February the BCOA felt burned by the national media. The

---

[11]In the local media throughout West Virginia and portions of Ohio and Pennsylvania, the BCOA frames were vigorously contested by organizations committed to rank and file miners. In Appalachia, an ideological war raged.

BCOA felt exaggerated reporting about coal shortages gave miners an unnecessary boost just when they seemed (to the operators) ready to capitulate to a strongly concessionary package. Though miners undoubtedly got a psychological boost from reports about coal shortages, it is extremely doubtful the rank and file would have accepted the February 6 contract proposal under any circumstances.

Though Feibusch masterfully steered media attention away from the BCOA until mid-February, any BCOA ability to "control" the predominant frames evaporated in February. Feibusch recalled spending hours with reporters, trying to put claims about shortages in perspective. But it was to no avail. The coal shortage story took on a life of its own. Within the national press and broadcast news community the idea of a fuel shortage was defined as being loaded with news value, and that outweighed reasoned analysis and assessment. Then President Carter pressed the political panic button and personally entered the story, creating new media problems for the BCOA. Where before the BCOA had successfully avoided public attention, Carter's attempts to leverage both sides into an agreement quickly drew attention to their presence.

Their calculated plan for avoiding the public eye unraveled, and their subsequent actions suggest, at least, a momentary concern about their public image. After rank-and-file rejection of the second contract proposal and Carter's announcement of Taft-Hartley, the BCOA reacted by taking out a full page ad in 11 newspapers on March 7, including the *New York Times*, *Wall Street Journal*, *Washington Post*, and newspapers located in the Appalachian coal fields. The ad placed blame for the impasse squarely on the union's shoulders, saying "The Bituminous Coal Operators have leaned over backwards to end the strike . . . The UMW holds the nation hostage with threats of devastating losses of power. UMWA members have openly told the American people that "We may freeze, but you will freeze with us"'' (AP, 3/8/78, p. 8B).

WHERE THEN DOES HEGEMONY COME FROM?

Where does this leave the question of hegemony and the news media? Hegemonic discourse emerges from a complex totality of contradictory relations. Hegemonic discourse on CBS news did *not* result from self-conscious, deliberate design, but from the structural constraints of the medium in combination with the specificity of the event and the actors involved. First, the unique circumstances and idiosyncratic moments of specific strikes and their key players influence reporting. During the coal strike, the erratic behavior of Arnold Miller, the disarray of the UMWA staff, the absence of a UMWA media strategy, and the mismatch between the public relations departments affected the predominant frames and lapses in the news texts. The "union divided against itself" story-line seemed self-evident to reporters because Miller was mired in conflict with the rank-and-file membership. Miller took the media stance that stopping production for every "bitch and gripe" would destroy the union. Alert to union discord, reporters foregrounded miners' efforts to launch a recall movement to oust Miller. Miller aimed at discrediting "disruptive" elements within the rank and file and he had no interest in addressing what was going on across the bargaining table. Reporters who pursued the mainstream conventions regarding news value found their primary interest lay in discrediting either the beleaguered Miller or the recall movement aimed at him.[12]

Second, because of their professional socialization reporters spoke within a taken-for-granted universe of discourse compatible with the world of capital. Taken-for-granted assumptions permeated reporters decisions about where to start stories, where to end them, what to ask and what not to ask. When these assumptions were joined with the journalistic practices of omitting arcane knowledge, abbreviation, and matching words with pictures, the substantive core of the dispute—management's reassertion of punitive control over the workplace versus miners' insistence on equity, job security, and their health—was carved out of the story.

Third, in the hierarchy of access a pivotal factor concerned control over access. The differential ability to regulate reporters access significantly affected coverage of the coal strike. Network television's ability to cover the negotiations in Washington was limited by the BCOA's strategy of calculated shyness. The CBS reporters assigned to the Appalachian coalfields did little investigative digging, but headed straight for the coffee shops where striking miners congregated. They benefitted from miners' eagerness to be on the tube, though the miners hardly benefitted from this reportorial strategy.

Rank-and-file miners, though on screen a lot, rarely spoke at enough length or depth to delineate their position. Reporters interviewed miners about Miller's leadership, and not about their problems with the operators. Reporters were unwilling to follow up any miner comments

---

[12]Evidence of Miller's alienation from the rank and file could be seen in the announcement of a second contract proposal on February 25. UPI's account of the contract's terms, taken from UMWA sources, listed none of the takeaways or penalties contained in the contract proposal. Press reliance on official UMW sources for the miners' side of the story, produced an account tailored to Miller's interests (get the contract ratified).

about conflicts with coal operators. We speculate that this was because the reporters knew that coal operators would not speak with them on camera—and from a reporter's perspective it was better to leave these matters undeveloped than to leave themselves open to charges of 'unbalanced' reporting. On the issue of wildcat strikes, miners' comments were either so carved up as to be insensible to outsiders (most of CBS's audience), or couched in relation to miners' dissatisfaction with Miller. CBS never aired an interview with an articulate miner explaining why wildcat strikes took place. Though many miners could not articulate the specific issues, there were miners capable of speaking articulately about these issues. A fundamental question about CBS coverage concerns the reasons for excluding such speakers. Was selection of interviewees a function of reporters' choices or of their ignorance? How was selection influenced by appearance/image considerations? Did story editors choose not to include interviewees who articulated such issues?

Conservative critics of television news will be delighted by our finding that CBS coverage was more "liberal" than newspaper coverage. The press's slightly more conservative bent reflected their greater access to, and familiarity with, the coal operators. But press coverage held less hegemonic potential than did the the television coverage we have described, because it more clearly stated the adversarial relation between capital and labor, and included greater detail about what was at dispute. The liberal tint to CBS coverage stemmed from an air of sympathy extended to the "common working man and family," presumably because of the network's attempt to reflect the concerns of their audience. In this sense, network "liberalism" was a stance generated by the structure of the spectacle, and its apparent "humanism" derived from the systematic occlusion of "class" as a category of analysis, while dwelling on the plight of "families" as consumption units.

Network coverage of the coal strike unfolded ironic twists at every turn. Despite network television's affirmation of liberal capitalist hegemony (the deemphasis of class and class conflict, and the unquestioning linguistic affirmation of capitalist institutions), network coverage proved to be the "factor in the media mix" which coal operators had the least success in managing. The operators' defensive March advertising campaign indicated that the BCOA perceived its public image was deteriorating. And a case can be made from the BCOA vantage point that network reporting fostered an atmosphere detrimental to the BCOA's short-term interests of negotiating the contract they wanted. We conclude by noting what seems a contradiction in terms: CBS framing of the coal strike affirmed capitalist hegemony, at the same time that it may have been detrimental to the specific capitalist interests of coal operators.

Conclusion

CBS coverage of the 1977–78 coal strike created "balance" and "neutrality" by opposing strikers, not against capital, but against the public and the state. The network defined the coal strike not in class terms, but in terms of a larger common denominator—the audience as "consuming public." Our principal finding is that *capital/management is invisible* in CBS's reporting of the coal strike. The class character of the conflict remained unspoken. Conflict in the mining industry was framed not as interrupting the accumulation of profit, but as endangering the public interest, cast as an aggregate of consumers. Defining the strike as *against the public*, CBS (and the other networks) defined the state as guardian of the public interest. Disrupted production was positioned in terms of disrupted consumption. In this context, CBS normalized state intervention, framing it as a necessary, though unfortunate, court of last resort in handling striking labor and its disruption of production.

Posing the central conflict as between striking workers and consumers, and letting slide the conflict between workers and owners, network news built its narratives around a series of tacit cultural assumptions. According to a populist mythology, which CBS perceived its audience as sharing, political and bureaucratic incumbents who staff the state are deemed potentially untrustworthy or inefficient. So the news media represent themselves as watchdogs of "the public interest," thereby guarding that the state serve the needs of citizen-consumers.

Broadcast news does not frame capital-labor relations in class terms. television news practices routinely achieve "fairness," "neutrality" and "balance" by blocking out the capital-labor dimension, and blocking out class as a conceptual category. CBS news coverage reinforced the legitimacy of Capital, *not because it was biased against labor in the*

209

traditional sense—in fact, CBS demonstrated a kind of "liberal sympathy" for the plight of striking workers and their families—but because *Capital (here, the BCOA) was systematically absent* in their reports. Because the CBS spotlight never shone on the owners, responsibility for the strike and its effects fell by default to the only participants visible on screen—the miners. Because CBS did not frame the strike in terms of class and production relations, the strike was framed *as against the audience* (positioned as the "consuming public"), and thus indirectly against the state, which CBS posed as the guardian of the social welfare and public interest. In this way, the interests of owners and management were identified with the general, public interest. Ironically, the invisibility of Capital in network news accounts such as this means the presence of Capital in our lives is not a matter for public debate.

HEGEMONY AND U.S. NETWORK NEWS— THE LATE 1970s

Empirical analysis of CBS News coal strike coverage shows how the "moving equilibrium" of hegemonic ideology in network news has shifted since the inception of the television era. Whereas in 1947, hegemony in the mass media meant that probusiness points of view were systematically privileged over labor viewpoints similarly embrace a (Ash, 1948), television network news in the late 1970s did not espouse a pro-management line. In 1947, the National Association of Manufacturers and the U.S. Chamber of Commerce maintained a vigorous public ideological presence. Their public appeal in behalf of the anti-union Taft-Hartley Bill was phrased in the name of individual rights—the "Right to Work." "The free market ideology, in which capitalist exploitation is encoded as the free interaction of free and equal individuals, rests upon the practice of this transaction between *just two* subjects" (Brenkman, 1979).

By 1977, this rhetoric was less in evidence, and corporate business interests took a low profile. During the television era, network television moved the hegemonic balance to a position which echoed and presumed the framework of the Labor-Capital Accords (cf. Bowles and Gintis, 1982). Nearly every CBS frame in 1977-78 replicated the presuppositions of that accord—(a) an "end of ideology," i.e., class conflict and class discourse are defunct (see Bell, 1960); (b) labor and management struggle primarily over distribution matters; (c) and the President plays the role of the top-ranking manager of the economy, guardian of the public interest, and referee of all public disputes.

By 1977, instead of validating a single, coherent capitalist ideology, CBS contributed to the hegemony of dominant interests by fragmenting conceptual thought and discourse. Fractured discourse was the result of sharply edited interview clips; partial and selective reporting; a persistent tendency toward abbreviation and reduction; and decontextualizing discourses from social, economic, and political experiences. Fragmented discourses produce incoherence and ideological noise, and thereby act as an obstacle to popular public debate of issues—encouraging instead apathy and passivity.[1]

In late capitalism, "it is not value-consensus which keeps the working class compliant, but rather a *lack* of consensus in the crucial area where concrete experiences and vague populism might be translated into radical politics" (Mann, 1970, p. 439).

Capital was absent in this story, and so, not judgable. Network news places questions of corporate power and control outside the boundaries of their stories about industrial relations. Because capitalists and the institutional operation of Capital were removed from the story, so too the relationship between Capital and Labor was elided. Network television news effaces class and production relations, translating these matters into non-class metaphors. Instead of appearing in the news, Capital presents its views and stylized images of its presence in our lives in advertisements, where its way of seeing (its values and frames) is uncontested. Since the mid-1970s corporate capital has escalated reliance on public relations and corporate advertising as a means of maintaining corporate legitimacy. As a result, Capital has grown faceless, seen only in their own corporate ads as global, benevolent aunts and uncles.[2]

---

[1]Held (1982, p. 190) argues that political-economic legitimacy in advanced capitalist society rests on "the 'decentring' or fragmentation of culture, the atomization of people's experiences of the social world. Fragmentation acts as a barrier to a coherent conception of the social totality." We have suggested that fragmented discourse represents a new stage of hegemonic culture, but we likewise perceive it as a response to a prolonged crisis of legitimacy.

A similar argument is voiced by Tom Bottomore in the preface to *The Dominant Ideology Thesis*. Bottomore argues for the rejection of the strong version of the dominant ideology thesis, but endorses a 'weak version' which he describes as follows: "the capacity of such an ideology, not to bring about social integration, or even to reinforce the cohesion of a dominant class, but to inhibit and confuse the development of the counter ideology of a subordinate class."

[2]See Barnouw's (1978, pp. 85-86) summary of ITT's use of television advertising to offset damage to its public image resulting from its involvement with the CIA in covert actions against the Allende regime. ITT sponsored a series of children's programs entitled "The Big Blue Marble." They then ran 44 ads on

In its earlier years, network news tended to privilege management views of conflicts, thus permitting Capital to define the situation. By the late 1970s and early 1980s, however, Capital had become as invisible as possible in stories about labor relations conflict. This did not, however, bring Labor the power to define the situation; that power instead accrued to network news itself, through its mechanical arrangement of video balance.

Public relations aim at anesthetizing and minimizing conflicts, and have become a critical resource in contests between conflicting class interests. Public relations and advertising have permitted corporations to shape public agendas and create a fundamental inequity in the sphere of public debate—treating airtime as a commodity means that access to capital makes for a lopsided advantage in defining frames of inquiry and debate. In the last decade, displacing class conflict into the arena of public relations has favored the interests of Capital. Democratic public debate has continued to seriously erode when turned into a com- modity—this effectively excludes the many from the sphere of public debate.

Though miners appeared on screen more than operators, CBS's method of presenting them did not permit miners to articulate opposi- tional attitudes or ways of seeing. Brevity of interviews and intimate camera distances emphasized workers' emotions, but not their rational arguments. While Capital remained invisible, Labor was fractured into a hundred abbreviated voices and systematically denied opportunities for discursive argument—they were never able to say, 'here is our argu- ment. Now weigh the evidence.' Hence, although CBS did not explicitly ratify a capitalist ideological agenda, alternative narratives and ways of seeing remained offstage. CBS's narrative strategies further reproduced the hegemony of dominant class interests by blocking development of any explanatory accounts of institutional relations.

In summary, then, CBS news contributed to the reproduction of hegemonic frames by omitting Capital and class relations; through a structured (format) incapacity for articulating counterideologies; and by

---

evening newscasts over a six-month period about the "warm hearted themes" of the programs. ITT's ratings in opinion polls rose again, as the "unfavorable impression of the news items had apparently been blurred and blotted out by the 'commercials'".

Our own parallel studies of corporate advertising on network television news from 1972-1982 find a significant portion of non-product corporate advertising on network news projects a 'technocratic worldview' in which corporate direction of science and technology is seen solving both individual and com- munal problems around the world and next door.

the incoherence of media explanations. Hegemony refers not only to a way of seeing, but also to a way of not seeing. While the surface of the CBS reports resolutely avoided ideological favoritism, the internal structure and flow of CBS's reports tacitly reproduced predominant definitions of social reality that reign as common sense. This is dramatized most clearly by the fact that in these news texts, capitalism—the word—is unspeakable. It is so thoroughly taken-for-granted that it need never be spoken. Capitalist institutions are beyond the realm of question, unlike Unions or even the Presidency-directed Government which must constantly strain to justify themselves.

The tacit ideological framework which defines our common sense in these CBS reports asks viewers to think of themselves not as class subjects nor as producers, but as privatized consumers bound together in their dispersed relationship to the nation-state. Stuart Hall (1977, p. 336) spells out this ideology of civil society and the state:

> In the sphere of market relations and of 'egoistic private interest' . . . the productive classes appear or are represented as (a) individual economic units driven by private and egoistic interests alone, which are (b) bound by the multitude of invisible contracts—the 'hidden hand' of capitalist exchange relations . . . this re-presentation has the effect, first of shifting emphasis and visibility from production to exchange, second of fragmenting classes into individuals, third of binding individuals into that 'passive community' of consumers. Likewise, in the sphere of the state and of juridico-political ideology, the political classes and class relations are represented as individual subjects (citizens, the voter, the sovereign individual in the eyes of the law and the representative system, etc.); and these individual political legal subjects are then 'bound together' as members of a nation, united by the 'social contract', and by their common and mutual 'general interest' . . . Once again, the class nature of the state is masked: classes are redistributed into individual subjects: and these individuals are united within the imaginary coherence of the state, the nation and the 'national interest.'

Network television coverage of industrial relations passes over the 'normal' institutional arrangements which shape the daily production and reproduction of our existence, dwelling instead on breakdowns in these arrangements. Yet, despite exclusive emphasis on disruptions to production, television reporting actually obscures the nature of conflicts and their sources. Rather than illuminate class relations and conflicts, network television reduces conflicts to stereotyped surface phenomena presented within a framework defined by the supposedly 'universal interest' of the U.S. government. Network television does so, not by resorting to bias for one side over the other, but by adhering to the logic of commodity relations. News is a commodity, and audience members are approached in terms of what is considered their most immediate self interest: their need for a stable system of consumption at reasonable prices.

ABBREVIATED INFORMATION AND PRESUMED KNOWLEDGE

As a commodity, television news is subject to both laws of production and consumption. Costs of producing network news restrict available time and place a premium on its efficient use. On the consumption side, networks strive to maximize audience size and craft the news to make it saleable. This matrix of relations overdetermines the form and content of television news. Abbreviation goes hand in hand with homogenization to eliminate specificity in reports. Time pressures promote appeals to "common knowledge," while the the quest for national audiences demands that specialized, "arcane knowledge" be evaded. Combining too much common knowledge with too little specific knowledge is a sure recipe for producing mythologies.

Network assessments of audience constituencies shape reporting strategies. Network reporters must make what they report of interest to a national audience, so they simplify and presume their audience to be uninterested in specialized details, and incapable of complex thought or sustained attention. Certainly, the formats they work with are predicated on, and reinforce, these assumptions. Because they lack sufficient background, network reporters covering wide regional beats may resort to summarizing and glossing local reporters. Finally, in the corporate political-economy of news, reporters constantly 'sell' their stories to editors. They compete for bylines and scarce air time, and learn to keep reports brief in order to compete effectively with other potential stories. Principles of brevity reinforce the pressure towards homogenized news, with its lack of specificity in the facts reported.

These mundane features of commodified news have real consequences. Repeated abbreviation of information presumes that viewers fill in, and interpretively reexpand, what has been left out. Repeatedly abbreviating social knowledge eventually results in an erosion and loss of sociocultural knowledge (as happens when traditions become discontinued over even one or two generations). The visual abbreviation practiced by television news contributes to a loss of social memory which is compunded by the fact that viewers "add details—but not necessarily those deleted in the processing of the story." Dispersed and privatized viewers "selectively attribute . . . specific details or 'particulars'" (Tuchman, 1978, p. 191). The network cuts out contexts, and then substitutes their own format/ framework for the context which has been excised. This leaves individual viewers to either resupply their own contextualization, or more likely, to rely on the interpretive procedures which go with the format. Thus, interpretation of the news becomes an increasingly rote, though subjective and privatized, act.

Socially, the conditions of reception are privatized and serialized. television news is consumed by individuals who are separated and isolated from one another in their own homes. Under such circumstances, public discourses about collective social experiences are displaced by mass processes of individuated cultural consumption. Separated viewers decipher reports on the basis of habit rather than attention—what Walter Benjamin called "distracted reception." Routinized and habituated, such distracted decoding practices discourage contemplation—"no sooner has the eye grasped a scene than it is already changed" (Benjamin, 1969).

Under such circumstances, dispersed viewers are more likely to agree upon the meaning(s) of the news format, while the realm of socially shared substantive knowledge shrinks. Network news presumes its audience shares a taken-for-granted understanding of the interpretive rules necessary to make sense of the evening news formats. Newscasters and reporters presume a consensus of grammar and vocabulary when they address mass audiences, as well as a language of daily life; and a shared sense of the boundaries of a 'moral' universe.

We have intentionally distanced ourselves in this study from the notion that hegemonic ideologies stem from conspiratorial corporate or state interests on the part of network news institutions. We have refused to consider such a thesis because we find it too facile, and too distracting from the real relations of domination. Instead, our empirical examination shows hegemonic ideology to be a consequence of the social patterns of organizing the production and consumption of the news. As we have seen, the networks labor mightily to purge themselves of overt attitudinal biases. Instead, they now permit the structural logic of commodity relations to condition the production (the encoding) of news.

TELEVISION NEWS, HEGEMONY, AND PUBLIC DISCOURSE

Two critical questions about hegemonic discourse and television news remain unresolved here. The first question concerns how different class fractions negotiate the potentially hegemonic discourses produced by the networks. Here we encounter the limits of our own methodology. Though no dialectical analysis of hegemony is complete without analysis of how subordinate groups negotiate and contest the potentially hegemonic frames, we are unable to speak directly to this. The letters to the editor in local and regional newspapers during the coal strike indicated a vigorous ideological contest within the Appalachian working class. Relying also on informal interviews, our evidence suggests that Appalachian workers were not persuaded by network accounts. So too, other major unions and farmers' groups demonstrated support for the miners. We hypothesize that the more removed people were by class, region and geography from the events taking place, the more they relied on network frames—hence, the more fragmented and displaced were their interpretations.[3]

A second obvious question after all this time and effort—whose interests did CBS aid? What impact on the events did CBS's coverage have? Here, the historical record is no easier to read than the CBS newstexts. Network coverage (or lack of it) over the first seventy days fit nicely with the BCOA interests This was, as we have shown, the outcome of an institutionally overdetermined coincidence. Noisy coverage and misinformed hyperbole about the severity of fuel shortages over the next thirty days probably weakened the BCOA negotiating strategies and bolstered the collective psychology of rank and file miners. But frankly, media coverage did not play the most important factor dictating the outcome of the strike. Political-economic forces gave the industry the upper hand in 1977-78. So, in the short run, we might hedge and say the media impact amounted to a messy draw.

If hegemonic ideology did not determine the outcome of the coal strike, then what difference does it make? The effect of this style of reporting is like 'waxy buildup'—you don't pay much attention to it until one day you can't see through the window anymore. Ten years after the coal strike, a note in the *New York Times* (1987, p. F1) stated, "Fifteen years ago, only five to ten percent of companies would have had the courage to stay in business during a strike. Now its more like 40 percent." High unemployment, Reagan's shoot-out with the air controllers, and the ability to shift production to other plants or abroad have a lot to do with this statistic. Another factor "has been a decline in public perceptions of the worth of unionism." We believe the everyday style of

---

[3]Our research has illuminated the obvious—without a Labor Party or a Labor News Network there does not exist in the U.S. any consistent vehicle for contesting hegemonic frames.

network coverage over the last decades has played a significant role in shaping this 'public perception.'

One long-term hegemonic impact of reporting characterized by the routine use of neutrality, abbreviation, and homogenization is that class issues have been neutralized and numbed away. For a major portion of our citizenry, a strike has become just another day in the life. Strikes have lost institutional mooring and meaning. In 1987, the National Football League Owners defeated the Player's Association strike by refusing to bargain in good faith. At the strike's end, Tex Schramm, President of the Dallas Cowboys, appeared on the television sports reports. Schramm was conciliatory and non-combative (much as BCOA President Brennan had been in his only CBS appearance at the end of the 1978 strike), and shrugged aside the conflict, saying simply that a strike "is just an unfortunate circumstance, that occurs."

References

Ackermann, J. A. (1979, January). The impact of the coal strike of 1977–78. *Industrial and Labor Relations Review, 32,* 175–188.

Altheide, D. L. (1985, Summer). Impact of format and ideology on TV news coverage of Iran. *Journalism Quarterly, 62 (2), 346–351.*

_____ . (1987, Fall). Formats for crises. *Phi Kappa Phi,* pp. 12–14.

Althusser, L., & Balibar, E. (1970). *Reading capital.* London: New Left Books.

Altschull, J. H. (1985). *Agents of power: The role of the news media in human affairs.* New York: Longman.

Arbitration Review Board. (1977, October 10). *ARB 108.*

Ash, P. (1948, Summer). The periodical press and the Taft–Hartley act. *Public Opinion Quarterly, 12,* 266–271.

Auletta, K. (1985, July 28). How they covered the landslide. *New York Times Book Review,* pp. 3, 27.

Bagdikian, B. (1983). *The media monopoly.* Boston: Beacon Press.

Barnouw, E. (1978). *The sponsor: Notes on a modern potentate.* New York: Oxford.

Barthes, R. (1967). *Elements of semiology.* Boston: Beacon Press.

_____ . (1972). *Mythologies.* New York: Hill & Wang.

_____ . (1977). The rhetoric of the image. *Image/Music/Text.* New York: Hill & Wang.

Bateson, G. (1972). *Steps to an ecology of the mind.* New York: Ballantine.

Bell, D. (1960). *The end of ideology: On the exhaustion of political ideas.* Glencoe, IL: Free Press.

Benjamin, W. (1969). The work of art in the age of mechanical reproduction. In H. Arendt (Ed.), *Illuminations* (pp. 21–51). New York: Schocken.

Bensman, D. (1978, Summer). Trouble in the coalfields. *Dissent, 25,* 253–60.

Berger, J. (1972). *Ways of seeing.* New York: Penguin.

_____ . (1980). *About looking.* New York: Pantheon.

Berger, J., & Mohr, J. (1982). *Another way of telling.* New York: Pantheon.

219

Bernstein, B. (1975). *Class, codes and control*. New York: Schocken.

Bethell, T. (1978, March). The UMW: Now more than ever. *Washington Monthly, 10,* 12–23.

Billings, D., & Goldman, R. (1983). Religion and class consciousness in the Kanawha County textbook controversy. In A. Batteau (Ed.), *Appalachia and America* (pp. 68–85). Lexington: University of Kentucky Press.

Bituminous Coal Operators Association (BOCA). (1977, October 6). *Will the United Mine Workers of America play a major role in coal's future?* Pamphlet.

Bluestone, B., & Harrison, B. (1982). *The deindustrialization of America*. New York: Basic Books.

Bottomore, T. (1980). Preface. In N. Abercrombie, S. Hill, & B. Turner (Eds.), *The dominant ideology* (pp. ix–x).

Bowles, S. (1982, September–October). The Post–Keynesian Capital–Labor Stalemate. *Socialist Review, 65,* 45–71.

Bowles, S., & Gintis, H. (1982). The crisis of liberal–democratic capitalism: The case of the United States. *Politics & Society, 11*(1), 51–93.

Brenkman, J. (1979). Mass media: From collective experience to culture of privatization. *Social Text, 1,* 94–109.

Brown, L. (1971). *Television: The business behind the box*. New York: Harcourt, Brace & Jovanovich.

Brunsdon, C., & Morley, D. (1978). *Everyday television: Nationwide*. London: British Film Institute.

Buck–Morss, S. (1977). *The origin of negative dialectics*. New York: Free Press.

Calavita, K. (1983, April). The demise of the occupational safety and health administration. *Social Problems, 30,* 437–48.

Caudill, H. (1977, April 23). Dead laws and dead men: Manslaughter in a coal mine: Scotia Coal Co. explosions in Oven Fork, Ky. *Nation, 224,* 492–97.

Clark, P. (1981). *The miner's fight for democracy: Arnold Miller and the reform of the United Mine Workers*. Ithaca, NY: Cornell University Press.

Connell, I. (1980). Television news and the social contract. In S. Hall, D. Hobson, A. Lowe, & P. Willis (Eds.), *Culture, media, language* (pp. 139–56). London: Hutchison.

Dahlgren, P. (1980, July). TV news and the suppression of reflexivity. *Urban Life, 9,* 201–16.

Debord, G. (1977). *Society of the spectacle*. Detroit: Black & Red.

Diamond, E. (1978). *Good news, bad news*. Cambridge: MIT Press.

Dix, K., Fuller, C., Linsky, J., & Robinson, C. (1970). *Work stoppages and the grievance procedure in the Appalachian bituminous coal industry*. Institute for Labor Studies, West Virginia University, Morgantown, WV.

Donnelly, P. (1982, October). The origins of the occupational safety and health act of 1970. *Social Problems, 30,* 13–25.

Eco, U. (1979). *A theory of semiotics*. Blooming.on: Indiana University Press.

Epstein, E. J. (1973). *News from nowhere*. New York: Random House.

Freiberg, J. W. (1981). *The French Press: Class, state, ideology*. New York: Praeger.

Gans, H. J. (1979). *Deciding what's news*. New York: Pantheon.

———. (1985, Nov.–Dec.). Are U.S. journalists dangerously liberal? *Columbia Journalism Review, 24,* 29–33.

Gibson, W. (1980, Fall). Network news: Elements of a theory. *Social Text, 3,* 88–111.

Giddens, A. (1971). *Capitalism and modern social theory.* Cambridge: Cambridge University Press.

Gitlin, T. (1979, February). Prime time ideology: The Hegemonic Process in Television Entertainment. *Social Problems, 26* (3), 251–65.

———. (1980). *The whole world is watching.* Berkeley: University of California Press.

———. (1981, March–April). Media as message: Campaign '80. *Socialist Review, 56,* 56–70.

Glasgow University Media Group (GUMG). (1976). *Bad news.* London: Routledge & Kegan Paul.

———. (1980). *More bad news.* London: Routledge & Kegan Paul.

Goffman, E. (1974). *Frame analysis.* New York: Harper & Row.

Goldman, R., & Wilson, J. (1983). Appearance and essence: the commodity form revealed in perfume advertisements. In S. McNall (Ed.), *Current perspectives in social theory* (Vol. 4, pp. 119–142). Greenwich, CT: JAI Press.

Goldman, R., & Beeker, G. (1985, August). Decoding newsphotos: an analysis of embedded ideological values. *Humanity & Society, 9,* 351–363.

Gouldner, A. (1976). *The dialectic of ideology and technology.* New York: Oxford University Press.

Gramsci, A. (1971). *Selections from the prison notebooks.* New York: International Publishers.

Green, J. (1978, May–June). Holding the Line: Miner's Militancy and the Strike of 1978. *Radical America, 12* (3), 3–27.

———. (1980). *The world of the worker: Labor in Twentieth Century America.* New York: Hill & Wang.

Guzzardi, W. (1985, August/September). The secret love affair between the press and government. *Public Opinion, 8* (4), 2–5.

Habermas, J. (1970). *Toward a rational society.* Boston: Beacon Press.

———. (1974, Fall). The public sphere. *New German Critique, 3,* 49–55.

———. (1975). *Legitimation crisis.* Boston: Beacon Press.

Hackett, R. A. (1985, Summer). A hierarchy of access: aspects of source bias in Canadian TV news. *Journalism Quarterly, 62,* 256–265, 277.

Hall, S. (1972). The determinations of newsphotographs. *Cultural Studies*, No. 3, 53–87.

———. (1973). A world at one with itself. In S. Cohen & J. Young (Eds.), *The manufacture of news* (pp. 86–93). Beverly Hills: Sage.

———. (1975). Introduction. In A. Smith, E. Immirzi, & T. Blackwell (Eds.), *Paper voices: The popular press and social change, 1935–65* (pp. 11–24). Totowa, NJ: Rowman & Littlefield.

———. (1977). Culture, the Media, and the "Ideological Effect." In J. Curran, M. Gurevitch, & J. Woollacott (Eds.), *Mass communication and society* (pp. 315–348). London: Arnold.

———. (1980). Encoding/decoding. In S. Hall, D. Hobson, A. Lowe, & P. Willis

(Eds.), *Culture, media, language* (pp. 128–38). London: Hutchison.
_____. (1982). The rediscovery of "ideology": Return of the repressed in media studies. In M. Gurevitch et al. (Eds.), *Culture, society & the media* (pp. 56–90). New York: Methuen.

Hall, S., Connell, I., & Curti, L. (1976). The "unity" of current affairs television. *Working Papers in Cultural Studies, 9,* 51–95.

Hall, S., Critcher, C., Jefferson, T., Clarke, J., & Roberts, B. (1978). *Policing the crisis: Mugging, the state and law and order.* New York: Holmes & Meier.

Halliday, M.A.K. (1970). Language structure and language function. In J. Lyons (Ed.), *New horizons in linguistics.* London: Penguin.

Hartley, J. (1982). *Understanding news.* London: Methuen.

Hebdige, D. (1979). *Subculture: The meaning of style.* London: Methuen.

Hecker, D. B. (1977, January). Internal politics splits mine workers' convention. *Monthly Labor Review,* 60.

Held, D. (1980). *Introduction to critical theory.* Berkeley: University of California Press.

_____. (1982). Crisis tendencies, legitimation and the state. In J. Thompson & D. Held (Eds.), *Habermas: Critical debates* (pp. 181–95). Cambridge, MA: MIT Press.

Hirsch, P. M. (1977). Occupational, organizational and institutional models in mass media research. In P. Hirsch et al. (Eds.) *Strategies for communications research* (Vol. 6, pp. 13–42). Beverly Hills: Sage.

Hodson, R. (1978). Labor in the monopoly, competitive and state sectors of production. *Politics & Society, 8,* 429–80.

Hohendahl, P. (1974, Fall). Jurgen Habermas: "The Public Sphere." *New German Critique, 3,* 44–48.

Horkheimer, M., & Adorno, T. (1972). *The dialectic of enlightenment.* London: Allen Lane.

Hoyt, M. (1984, Summer). Is the press anti–labor? Or just out of touch . . . *Labor Research Review, 4,* 69–80.

International Association of Machinists and Aerospace Workers. (1981). *Television: Corporate America's game.* Pamphlet.

Kellner, D. (1979, May–June). TV, ideology, and emancipatory popular culture. *Socialist Review, 45,* 13–53.

_____. (1981). Network television and American society. *Theory & Society, 10,* 31–62.

Kochan, T., & Piore, M. (1984, May). Will the new industrial relations last? Implications for the American labor movement. *The Annals of the American Academy of Political and Social Science, 473,* 177–89.

Kress, G., & Hodge, R. (1979). *Language as ideology.* London: Routledge & Kegan Paul.

Krieger, J., & Lewis, J. (1979, February). The highest stage at last. *Socialist Review, 43,* 157–70.

Lefebvre, H. (1969). *The sociology of Marx.* New York: Vintage.

Leggett, J. C. et al. (1978). *Allende, his exit, and our "times."* New Brunswick, NJ: New Brunswick Cooperative Press.

Liebling, A. J. (1961). *The press.* New York: Ballantine Books.

Maggard, S. W. (1983/4, Autumn–Winter). Cultural hegemony: The news media and Appalachia. *Appalachian Journal, 11,* 67–83.

Mann, M. (1970). The social cohesion of liberal democracy. *American Sociological Review, 35,* 423–39.

Marcuse, H. (1960). *Reason and revolution: Hegel and the rise of social theory.* Boston: Beacon Press.

Marschall, D. (1977, September). Wildcats Challenge UMW. *In These Times, 6–13,* 3,8.

————. (1978, July–October). The Miners and the UMW: Crisis in the Reform Process. *Socialist Review,* No. 40/41, 65–115.

Marx, K. (1967). *Capital.* New York: International Publishers.

Marx, K., & Engels, F. (1970). *The German ideology.* New York: International Publishers.

Millis, H., & Brown, E. C. (1950). *From the Wagner Act to Taft–Hartley.* Chicago: University of Chicago.

Mills, C. W. (1948). *The new men of power.* New York: Harcourt Brace.

Moberg, D. (1984, April). Smokestacks and Smoke Screens. *Quill, 72,* 24–30.

Molotch, H., & Lester, M. (1975, September). Accidental news: The great oil spill as local occurrence and national event. *American Journal of Sociology, 81,* 235–60.

Montgomery, D. (1980). *Workers' control in America.* Cambridge: Cambridge University Press.

Monthly Labor Review. (1978, June). *101* (6), 103. Washington, DC: Bureau of Labor Statistics.

Moody, K., & Woodward, J. (1978). *Battle line: The Coal Strike of '78.* Detroit: Sun Press.

Morley, D. (1981). Industrial conflict and the mass media. In S. Cohen & J. Young (Eds.), *The manufacture of news* (pp. 368–92) (revised edition). Beverly Hills: Sage.

Morse, M. (1986). The television news personality and credibility: Reflections on the news in transition. In T. Modleski (Ed.), *Studies in entertainment* (pp. 55–79). Bloomington: Indiana University Press.

Navarro, P. (1983, January). Union bargaining power in the coal industry, 1945–1981. *Industrial and Labor Relations Review, 36,* 214–29.

Nichols, B. (1981). *Ideology and the image.* Bloomington: Indiana University Press.

Nyden, L., & Nyden, P. (1978). *Showdown in coal: The struggle for rank and file unionism.* Pittsburgh, PA: Miner's Report Pamphlet.

O'Connor, J. (1973). *Fiscal crisis of the state.* New York: St. Martin's Press.

Paletz, D. & Entman, R. (1981). *Media, power, politics.* New York: Free Press.

Perry, C. R. (1984). *Collective bargaining and the decline of the United Mine Workers.* Philadelphia: Industrial Research Unit, The Wharton School, University of Pennsylvania.

Raskin, A. H. (1979). Double standard or double–talk. In C. Aronoff (Ed.), *Business and the Media* (pp. 249–258). Santa Monica, CA: Goodyear Publishing.

Rhodenbaugh, S.J. (1978, July–August). Death by computer and contract: The

UMWA health and retirement funds. *Crossroads,* pp. 22–26.

Rollings, J. (1983). Mass communication and the American worker. In V. Mosco & J. Wasko (Eds.), *Critical communications review: Labor, the working class, and the media* (pp. 131–52). Norwood, NJ: Ablex.

Schiller, D. (1987, December). Critical response: Evolutionary confusion. *Critical Studies in Mass Communications, 4* (4), 409–12.

Schmidt, R. A. (1979). *Coal in America, an encyclopedia of reserves, production and use.* New York: McGraw–Hill.

Schudson, M. (1978). *Discovering the news.* New York: Basic Books.

Seager, M. (1989, October). One day longer than Pittston. *Z Magazine, 2* (10), 13–24.

Seltzer, C. (1974, November). A confusion of goals. *The Nation, 219,* 430–33.

———. (1978). A strike that ended an era. *The Nation, 226,* 535–537.

———. (1980). The UMW: Need past be prologue? In R. Engler (Ed.), *America's energy* (pp. 48–51). New York: Pantheon.

———. (1977). Health care by the ton. *Health PAC Bulletin, 79,* 1–8, 25–32.

———. (1985). *Fire in the hole: Miners and managers in the American coal industry.* Lexington: University of Kentucky Press.

Simon, R. (1983, Fall). Hard times for organized labor in Appalachia. *Review of Radical Political Economy, 15*(3), 21–33.

Skornia, H. J. (1968). *Television and the news: A critical appraisal.* Palo Alto, CA: Pacific Books.

Smythe, D. (1977). Communications: Blindspot of Western Marxism. *Canadian Journal of Political & Social Theory, 1* (3). 1–27.

Sumner, C. (1979). *Reading ideologies.* London: Academic Press.

Tabb, W. (1980, Spring). Zapping labor. *Marxist Perspectives, 9, 64*–77.

Tuchman, G. (1972, January) Objectivity as strategic ritual. *American Journal of Sociology, 77* (4), 660–79.

———. (1976, November–December). Mass media values. *Society,* 51–4.

———. (1978). *Making news.* New York: The Free Press.

United Stated Department of Labor, Bureau of Labor Statistics. (1978, March 30). *Special survey on impact of coal shortages on manufacturing and trade employment in 11 Coal Dependent States, March 19–March 25, 1978.* Washington, DC: Author.

Vanderbilt Television News Archives. (1978). *Television News Index and Abstracts.* Nashville: Vanderbilt University Press.

Vietor, R. H. (1980). *Environmental politics and the coal coalition.* College Station: Texas A&M University Press.

Williams, R. (1977). *Marxism and literature.* London: Oxford University Press.

Wilkins, L. (1967). *Social policy, action and research.* London: Tavistock.

Williamson, J. (1978). *Decoding advertisements: Ideology and meaning in advertising.* London: Marion Boyars.

Winston, B. (1983). On counting the wrong things. In V. Mosco & J. Wasko (Eds.), *The critical communication review, Volume I: Labor, the working class, and the media* (pp. 167–86). Norwood, NJ: Ablex.

Yarrow, M. (1979). The labor process in coal mining: Struggle for control. In A.

Zimbalist (Ed.), *Case studies in the labor process* (pp. 170–192). New York: Monthly Review Press.

Zeitlin, M. (1980). On classes, class conflict, and the state: an introductory note. In M. Zeitlin (Ed.), *Classes, class conflict, and the State* (pp. 1–38). Cambridge: Winthrop.

Press Citations on Coal Strike 1977-1978 (organized by date)[1]

UPI, "Coal stockpiles being planned," *Charleston Gazette*, Sept 22, 1977.

"UMW, coal operators to begin labor talks," *Wall Street Journal*, Oct 3, 1977.

UPI, "Coal talks set Thursday," *Morgantown Dominion-Post*, Oct 4, 1977.

AP, "UMW funds to get $9.7 million boost," *Morgantown Dominion-Post*, Oct 6, 1977.

John P. Moody, "Coal talks stalled, union isn't ready," *Pittsburgh Post-Gazette*, Oct 7, 1977, p. 1.

Sara Fritz, "Coal strike likelihood, Miller says," *Morgantown Dominion-Post*, Oct 13, 1977.

UPI, "Coal stockpiles being planned," *Charleston Gazette*, Oct 22, 1977.

"Soft-coal operators take a tough stance," *Business Week*, Nov 7, 1977, p. 30.

UPI, "Analyst says lengthy walkout would benefit coal producers," *Morgantown Dominion Post*, Nov 10, 1977.

UPI, "Coal owners president says union not realistic," *Morgantown Morning Reporter*, Nov 12, 1977, p. 6B.

UPI, "Power firms have ample coal," *Morgantown Morning Reporter*, Nov 12, 1977.

---

[1]After the first page we have abbreviated the names of papers which recur throughout: *NYT — New York Times*

WSJ — Wall Street Journal

CG — Charleston Gazette

PPG — Pittsburgh Post-Gazette

LCJ — Louisville Courier Journal

MMR — Morgantown Morning Reporter

MDP — Morgantown Dominion-Post

BW — Business Week

WP — Washington Post

228   Citations

Andrew Gallagher, "Long miners' strike shaping up: UMW funds could die," *Morgantown Dominion-Post*, Nov 18, 1977.

UPI, "Mine strike leader linked to red party," *Morgantown Dominion Post*, Nov 18, 1977.

Strat Douthat, "Division runs deep among Appalachian coal miners," *Lexington Herald-Leader*, Nov 20, 1977, p. B7.

"Miller says RCP members may be expelled," *Clarksburg Telegram*, Nov 21, 1977, p. 1.

Ann Hughey, "UMW anti-communism reborn as party membership discovered," *CG*, Nov 21, 1977:1, 8A.

Ann Hughey, "RCP headed by former student radical," *CG*, Nov 22, 1977, pp. 1, 2A.

Ann Hughey, "Right to strike issue may be fading," *CG*, Nov 23, 1977, p. 1.

"Coal mine strike fears mounting," *CT*, Nov 23, 1977, pp. 1, 2.

Ben A. Franklin, "Activities of Maoists revive 'Red-Baiting' in coal fields," *NYT*, Nov 25, 1977, p. A18.

Ben A. Franklin, "Mine union's leader halts talks, calling a strike 'inevitable'," *NYT*, Nov 26, 1977, pp. 1, 42.

UPI, "Miller says coal strike appears inevitable," *MDP*, Nov 26, 1977.

Ben A. Franklin, "Years of conflict in coal fields set stage for a strike," *NYT*, Nov 27, 1977, p. 26.

Vartanig G. Vartan, "King coal still has its backers," *NYT*, Nov 27, 1977.

Ben A. Franklin, "Coal dispute talks resume tomorrow at urging of U.S.," *NYT*, Nov 28, 1977, p. 21.

UPI, "Three firms pull out of BCOA talks," *MDP*, Nov 28, 1977.

"Chaos in coal's labor relations," *BW*, Nov 28, 1977, p. 92.

Ben A. Franklin, "Coal bargainers promise they will resume talks," *NYT*, Nov 30, 1977, p. 16.

UPI, "Leaders drawn back to coal talks," *MDP*, Nov 30, 1977.

Ann Hughey, "Mediators take over UMW, BCOA talks," *CG*, Nov 30, 1977, pp. 1, 4A.

Ben A. Franklin, "Coal miners and industry talk, but not to each other," *NYT*, Dec 1, 1977, p. 17.

Ben A. Franklin, "Coal talks dispute focuses on leaders," *NYT*, Dec 2,1977, p. B7.

Ann Hughey, "Ouster reports 'insult' to Miller," *CG*, Dec 3, 1977, p. 1.

James Clarity, "West Virginia coal town, expecting strike, displays concern but no panic," *NYT*, Dec 3, 1977, pp. 25-26.

Evelyn Ryan, "'Nothing settled,' UMW district 31 chief reports," *Morgantown Morning Reporter*, Dec 3, 1977, p. 2B.

AP, "Coal talks proceed as walkouts begin before the deadline," *NYT*, Dec 4, 1977, p. 27.

Martha Bryson Hodel, "Strike: UMW history bares 10 production interruptions per 20 pacts," *Charleston Gazette-Mail*, Dec 4, 1977, p. 15A.

A.H. Raskin, "Arbitration in the mines has created more disputes," *NYT*, Dec 4, 1977, pp. IV 5.

UPI, "Stockpile of coal sufficient," *MMR*, Dec 4, 1977.

Ben A. Franklin, "Coal industry's troubles go beyond strike threat," *NYT*, Dec 5, 1977, p. 18.

Ben A. Franklin, "180,000 start strike in the coalfields as talks break off," *NYT*, Dec 6, 1977, pp. 1,70.

Winston Williams, "Coal labor dispute aided railroads," *NYT*, Dec 6, 1977, pp. 57-8.

Lance Gay, "Miners gird for strike's hardships," *Washington Post*, Dec 6, 1977.

"Issues in coal miners' strike," *NYT*, Dec 7, 1977, p. 12.

"Coal users start to draw down stockpiles as the expected UMW strike idles mines," *WSJ*, Dec 7, 1977.

James Branscome, "Appalachia health fears: coal miners and dependents alarmed as health care is cut," *WP*, Dec 8, 1977, pp. 1,3A.

UPI, "Isolated violence erupts at coal mine in Utah," *WP*, Dec 8, 1977, p. A3.

UPI, "Right-to-strike issue warms idle coalfields," *MDP*, Dec 8, 1977, p. 10B.

David Poling, "'Area miners informed of health fund cutoff," *MDP*, Dec 8, 1977, p. 9B.

Ben A. Franklin, "Coal talks resume but quickly recess," *NYT*, Dec 9, 1977, p. B9.

James F. Clarity, "Miners in West Virginia predict a long strike but feel that somehow they can cope," *NYT*, Dec 9, 1977, p. B9.

"Miners' benefits are cut off," *MMR*, Dec 9, 1978, p. 10B.

AP, "Union negotiator leaves coal talks," *NYT*, Dec 11, 1977, p. 24.

"Progress is reported in coal talks; fields are quiet," *NYT*, Dec 12, 1977, p. 28.

Ann Hughey, "Plans for miners' poll dropped," *CG*, Dec 12, 1977, pp. 1,4A.

Ann Hughey, "Union may drop demand for right-to-strike clause," *CG*, Dec 14, 1977, pp. 1,8A.

Ben A. Franklin, "Compromises in coal strike hinted," *NYT*, Dec 14, 1977, p. B14.

Ben A. Franklin, "Coal talks recessed until Tuesday," *NYT*, Dec 22, 1977, p. B9.

Tom N. Bethell, "UMWA and BCOA agree to fire wildcat strikers," *Whitesburg Mountain Eagle*, Dec 22, 1977, p. 1.

Ann Hughey, "Coal talks break down over fines," *CG*, Dec 31, 1977, p. 1.

Ben A. Franklin, "Operators walk out of coal negotiations," *NYT*, Dec 31, 1977, p. 5.

UPI, "Rank and file impatient with lack of data on talks," *MDP*, Jan 3, 1978.

Ben A. Franklin, "U.S. officials fear strike of coal miners could continue into February," *NYT*, Jan 9, 1978, p. A16.

John P. Moody, "Coal talks resume, individual mine strike right sought," *PPG*, Jan 13, 1978, p. 7.

"Talks resume tomorrow in coal negotiations," *NYT*, Jan 15, 1978, p. 16.

Ben A. Franklin, "No gains reported on the main issues in coal bargaining," *NYT*, Jan 20, 1978, p. 10.

UPI, "Coal session 'blows up,'" *MDP*, Jan 24, 1978.

Ben A. Franklin, "Mine union rejects wage offer, and talks break off," *NYT*, Jan 25, 1978, p. B18.

John P. Moody, "Coal firms mending fences after secret talks fail," *PPG*, Jan 27, 1978, p. 2.

UPI, "Governors issue plea in coal strike," *NYT*, Jan 28, 1978.

Ann Hughey, "Mine talks off 'indefinitely'," *CG*, Jan 30, 1978, pp. 1, 2A.

Ann Hughey, "Plight of '50s pensioners aired," *CG*, Jan 30, 1978.

Ben A. Franklin, "Walkout deepens a strain of pessimism in Appalachia," *NYT*, Jan 30, 1978.

"A coal company president discusses labor stability," *Coal Age*, Feb 1978.

Ben A. Franklin, "Coal strike perils Ohio electric power," *NYT*, Feb 2, 1978, p. A16.

Ann Hughey, "Coal settlement appears to be near," *CG*, Feb 2, 1978

Ann Hughey, "Bargaining council summoned by Miller," *CG*, Feb 3, 1978, p. 1.

Ben Franklin, "Coal talks off after raising hopes for pact," *NYT*, Feb 3, 1978, pp. 1,A16.

Steve Shapiro, "Why coal miners in W. Va. go out on wildcat strikes," *NYT*, Feb 3, 1978, p. 23.

UPI, "Police save 7 nonunion miners besieged by strikers," *NYT*, Feb 4, 1978, p. 6.

Ben A. Franklin, "Union delays parley as coal talks falter," *NYT*, Feb 4, 1978, p. 6.

Ann Hughey, "Contract talks to resume today," *CG*, Feb 6, 1978, pp. 1,2A.

"Will the coal impasse cause a power crisis?" *BW*, Feb 6, 1978, pp. 44-45.

George Getschow, "Coal industry, UMW have high hopes an accord can be reached by tomorrow," *WSJ*, Feb 6, 1978.

Ben A. Franklin, "Negotiators reach a tentative accord to end coal strike," *NYT*, Feb 7, 1978, pp. 1,5.

Ben A. Franklin, "Miners' bargaining council balks at quick approval of contract," *NYT*, Feb 8, 1978, p. 9.

Ann Hughey, "Council wants to see contract language," *CG*, Feb 8, 1978, p. 1.

UPI, "Wildcat strikes could draw fines under new pact," *CG*, Feb 8, 1978.

George Getschow, "UMW council defers contract decision until it sees full text of proposed pact," *WSJ*, Feb 8, 1978.

"Here's summary of coal wage agreement," *CG*, Feb 9, 1978, p. 12A.

Robert Morris, "Miller bodyguard, local union officer scuffle in headquarters," *CG*, Feb 9, 1978.

Ann Hughey, "UMW council summoned for meeting," *CG*, Feb 10, 1978, pp. 1,2A.

AP, "Area miners oppose contract: demonstrators in Washington force delay in balloting," *Clarksburg Telegram*, Feb 10, 1978, pp. 1,2.

Ann Hughey, "Union council votes rejection of mine pact," *CG*, Feb 11, 1978, pp. 1,2A.

John P. Moody, "UMW's council rejects contract on major points," *PPG*, Feb 13, 1978, pp. 1,6.

George Getschow and Walter Mossberg, "President moves to ease impact of coal walkout," *WSJ*, Feb 13, 1978, pp. 2,12.

"Local presidents urge adherence to '76 goals," *CG*, Feb 14, 1978, p. 14A.

UPI, "White House setting sought for coal talks," *MMR*, Mar 15, 1978.

Anthony Parisi, "Coal industry faces record quarter loss," *NYT*, Feb 16, 1978, p. D-1, 13.

Martin Tolchin, "Coal owners renew talks with miners," *NYT*, Feb 16, 1978, pp. 1,D-13.

Ben A. Franklin, "UMW president a target of both sides," *NYT*, Feb 17, 197, p. D-11.

"Miners call for solidarity," *MDP*, Feb 17, 1978.

UPI, "UMW council cool to industry's offer," *MMR*, Feb 18, 1978.

UPI, "Talks stall, proposal is rejected," *MDP*, Feb 19, 1978.

UPI, "Miners continue to hold meets shaping strategy," *MDP*, Feb 19, 1978.

Ben A. Franklin, "White House postpones any action to force an end to miners' strike." *NYT*, Feb 19, 1978, pp. 1,19.

UPI, "What the miners want," *MDP*, Feb 19, 1978, p. 2A.

UPI, "State labor backs UMW: BCOA charged with 'stall'," Feb 21, 1978.

John P. Moody, "BCOA requests arbitration in pact snag with UMW," *PPG*, Feb 22, 1978, p. 1.

Ben Franklin, "Coal operators refuse to accept pact as model," *NYT*, Feb 22, 1978, p. 1.

Seth King, "Mediators turned to Miller opponents in reaching separate pact," *NYT*, Feb 22, 1978, p. A14.

UPI, "Arbitration asked by coal operators," *MDP*, Feb 23, 1978.

David Ignatius and George Getschow, "The coal war," *WSJ*, Feb 24, 1978, pp. 1,28.

UPI, "Coal operators a loosely knit unit," *NYT*, 2/25/78, p. 9.

UPI, "Contents of new miners' pact listed," *MDP*, Feb 26, 1977, p. 3A.

William Robbins, "West Virginia miners criticize pension plan in proposed contract," *NYT*, Feb 26, 1978, p. 1.

District president opposed contract," *MDP*, Feb 26, 1978.

"Coal agreement faces uphill battle for ratification; similar pact at Pittsburg & Midway soundly rejected," *WSJ*, Feb 27, 1978.

Gay Sands Miller, "Accuracy of figures on coal stockpiles is open to question," *WSJ*, Feb 27, 1978.

"UMW leaders start drive for approval of coal labor pact," *WSJ*, Feb 28, 1978.

UPI, "Ohio locals shun proposed contract," *MDP*, Feb 28, 1978:

David Poling, "Local presidents to meet," *MDP*, Feb 28, 1978, p. 1B,2B.

David Poling, "Miners are warned union in jeopardy," *MDP*, Mar 1, 1978.

UPI, "Retirees ponder contract," *MDP*, Mar 1, 1978.

UPI, "Miners, industry agree—to blast pact," *MDP*, Mar 1, 1978.

UPI, "Dissident miners rally to blast new contract," *MDP*, Mar 1, 1978, p. 16A.

UPI, "Divided union wrangles over contract offer," *MDP*, Mar 1, 1978, pp. 1,2A.

UPI, "Fists fly over contract," *MDP*, Mar 2, 1978.

Ann Hughey, "Close vote and trouble predicted as thousands discuss UMW pact," *CG*, Mar 3, 1978, pp. 1,2A.

David Poling, "Miners divided on new contract," *MDP*, Mar 3, 1978.

Mark Dodosh, "Coal-dependent utilities are scrambling to find fuel and maintain their services," *WSJ*, Mar 3, 1978, p. 30.

UPI, "They can take this contract and shove it," *MDP*, Mar 3, 1978.

UPI, "Miners prepare to cast votes on contract," *MMR*, Mar 3, 1978.

"District 4 priorities missing," *MDP*, Mar 4, 1978, p. 1,15.

Helen Dewar, "In early returns miners are voting against coal contract," *WP*, Mar 4, 1978.

Helen Dewar, "Striking miners are voting 2 to 1 against contract," *WP*, Mar 5, 1978, pp. 1,4A.

Ann Hughey, "Defiant coal miners vote down pact," *CG*, Mar 6, 1978, pp. 1,2A.

Ann Hughey, "Coal miners pondering wh at's next," *CG*, Mar 6, 1978.

Urban Lehner and George Getschow, "Coal miner vote runs against pact as Carter plans to act to end strike," *WSJ*, Mar 6, 1978.

"Coal's bungled negotiations," *BW*, Mar 6, 1978 pp. 94-95.

David Poling, "District rejects contract by 4-1," *MDP*, Mar 6, 1978.

UPI, "Large local favored pact," *MDP*, Mar 6, 1978, p. 3A.

Strat Douthat, "Survival of union seen regardless of Carter's action," *CG*, Mar 6, 1978, p. 1B.

"Carter invokes Taft-Hartley act," *MDP*, Mar 6, 1978, p. 1.

AP, "'Holding nation hostage,' BCOA ad accuses UMW," *CG*, Mar 8, 1978, pp. 8B.

David L. Langford, "Miners foresee trouble," *MMR*, Mar 8, 1978.

Ann Hughey, "Injunction inquiry opens," *CG*, Mar 8, 1978, p. 1.

Robert Morris, "Striking miners confront Rockefeller: protest use of Taft Hartley," *CG*, Mar 8, 1978, pp. 1,2A.

Edward Peeks, "Inequality of pensions threatens settlement," *CG*, Mar 8, 1978, p. 10D.

Joseph Kraft, "Coal talks on a different level," *MMR,* Mar 8, 1978.

UPI, "Carter not planning mine seizure," *MMR*, Mar 8, 1978.

Urban Lehner, "Carter may yet order coal mines seized, despite effort to play down that option," *WSJ*, Mar 8, 1978.

Ann Hughey, "Both factions criticize Carter in coal strike," *CG*, Mar 9, 1978.

John P. Moody, "US goes to court today for T-H order," *PPG*, Mar 9, 1978, pp. 1,2.

UPI, "Auto Workers Back Coal Miner Strike," *Times West Virginian*, Mar 9, 1978, p. 16.

David Langford, "America may get to know the dark and cold of mines," *Times-West Virginian*, Mar 9, 1978, pp. 1,10A.

UPI, "Board backs Taft-Hartley action," *MDP*, Mar 9, 1978, p. 14A.

UPI, "Injunction try 'mistake,'" *MDP*, Mar 9, 1978.

Ann Hughey, "Strikers ordered to return to the mines," *CG*, Mar 10, 1978, p. 1

"Coal miners told to return to job by federal judge," *WSJ*, Mar 10, 1978.

UPI, "Taft-Hartley law invoked," *Kingsport News*, Mar 10, 1978.

Ron Kirksey, "Union leader arrested after scuffle with television crew," *Times-News*, Mar 10, 1978, pp. 1,14A.

UPI, "Recall miners claim victory," *MDP*, Mar 10, 1978.

Stuart Brown, "'Low profile' BCOA: like UMW, internal conflicts," *PPG*, Mar 11, 1978, p. 2.

John P. Moody, "Coal talks resumed, U.S. eyes TH impact," *PPG*, Mar 11, 1978, pp. 1,2.

Alvin Rosensweet, "Miners await T-H papers, resolving they won't work," *PPG*, Mar 11, 1978.

Bob Minnocci, "March shows Taft-Hartley opposition," *CG*, Mar 12, 1978.

UPI, "A human side of miners and strike," *Wheeling News-Register*, Mar 12, 1978.

UPI, "Coal dumped at White House," *MDP*, Mar 12, 1978.

Ann Hughey, "Main coal negotiations recessed," *CG*, Mar 13, 1978, pp. 1,2A.

AP, "Mining veterans' experience makes 'difference' in coal talks," *CG*, Mar 13, 1978, p. 12A.

George Getschow and Walter Mossberg, "President moves to ease impact of coal walkout," *WSJ*, Feb 13, 1978, pp. 2,13.

William Robbins, "Miners, after union meeting, vow 'no contract, no work,'" *NYT*, Mar 14, 1978, p. 26.

William Claiborne, "Coal operators ready for production but mood of miners is quiet defiance," *WP*, Mar 14, 1978.

Ben A. Franklin, "Coal miners ignore back-to-work writ; pact reported near," *NYT*, Mar 14, 1978, pp. 1,26.

UPI, "Nation selling miners short?" *MDP*, Mar 14, 1978.

George Getschow, "Coal firms, UMW reach tentative pact; union panel to take up sweetened offer," *WSJ*, Mar 15, 1978.

John P. Moody, "UMW to call panel to vote on proposal," *PPG*, Mar 15, 1978, pp. 1,20.

UPI, "Council eyes coal pact," *MDP*, Mar 15, 1978.

Charles Spencer, "UMW pensioners, widows vow to picket mines," *Register*, Mar 15, 1978, p. 1,2.

Ann Hughey, "Optimism colors 3rd tentative strike pact," *CG*, Mar 15, 1978, p. 1.

Terry Wimmer, "Determined miners continue to ignore order to work," *CG*, Mar 15, 1978.

"Phone poll of miners had the wrong number," *MMR*, Mar 15, 1978, p. 10A.

Ben A. Franklin, "Spur-of-moment meeting led to tentative coal accord," *NYT*, Mar 16, 1978.

Ann Hughey, "Bargainers approve new mine contract," *CG*, Mar 16, 1978, pp. 1, 2A.

Rob Morris, "All sides anxious to see new pact," *CG*, Mar 16, 1978:

UPI, "UMW leaders fan out with third coal contract," *MDP*, Mar 16, 1978.

Barbara Rasmussen, "Miller recall signatures gathered at miner rally," *MDP*, Feb 17, 1978.

UPI, "Third contract may be miners' charm: district 6 leader sees passage," Mar 17, 1978.

UPI, "Coal Dumped at White House," Mar 17, 1978.

"Coal firms made sizeable concessions in nonwage areas of latest contract," *WSJ*, Mar 17, 1978.

Helen Dewar, "UMW unit approves pact: 22-17 vote not encouraging," *WP*, Mar 17, 1978, pp. 1,A8.

"Growing coal output of non-UMW mines may undercut strike," *WSJ*, Mar 17, 1978.

"UMW council's close vote on coal pact casts shadow over rank-and-file ballot," *WSJ*, Mar 17, 1978,

AP, "Miller blames contract woes on Gazette, *CG*, Mar 18, 1978, pp. 1,4A.

"Taft-Hartley balk praised as 'correct,'" *Charleston Daily Mail*, Mar 18, 1978, pp. 1,6A.

AP, "Judge won't extend back-to-work order," *CG*, Mar 18, 1978.

David Green, "Pensioners: influential undercurrent will be felt by miners voting Friday on contract," *Charleston Gazette-Mail*, Mar 19, 1978, p. 1B.

Ben A. Franklin, "Doubts about contract linger in coalfields," *CG*, Mar 19, 1978, pp. 1,6A.

John P. Moody, "Latest coal offer criticized by officers of UMW locals," *PPG*, Mar 19, 1978, p. 1.

Charles A. Mason, "Local Miners Rally, Farmers' Support," *Beckley Register*, Mar 19, 1978.

David L. Langford, "Some miners are turning anger toward leaders," *Times-West Virginian*, Mar 19, 1978, p. 5B.

David L. Langford, "Is nation's longest coal strike running out of steam," *Times-West Virginian*, Mar 19, 1978, pp. 1,3A.

Johanna Maurice, "Industry source explains: pensions, benefits," *Beckley Post-Herald*, Mar 19, 1978.

"Trying to thaw the coal talks," *BW*, Mar 20, 1978. p. 32-3.

"Unionists resigned to terms, with fiery exceptions," *NYT*, Mar 20, 1978, p. D10.

James Clarity, ""Officials of a large union district predict ratification of coal pact," *NYT*, Mar 20, 1978, p. D10.

Vartanig Vartan, "Digging into coal industry's outlook," *NYT*, Mar 20, 1978.

Ann Hughey, "Pact ratification uncertain as miners get review copies," *CG*, Mar 21, 1978.

Evelyn Ryan, "UMW vice president reviews negotiations," *MMP*, Mar 21, 1978, p.. 1B,2B.

David Singleton, "Contract good one—Church," *MMP*, Mar 21, 1978, p. 1B,5B.

William Robbins, "In militant Harlan County, Ky., miners vow to reject new settlement," *NYT*, Mar 21, 1978, p. 10.

George Getschow, "The mood of miners mellows on the eve of latest coal vote," *WSJ*, Mar 23, 1978, pp. 1,32.

UPI, "Ohio coal miners accuse UMW of withholding funds," Mar 23, 1978.

UPI, "Communications workers pledge $1 million for striking miners," Mar 23, 1978.

Ben A. Franklin, "Miners to vote today on new pact; union denies withholding relief," *NYT*, Mar 24, 1978, p. A12.

UPI, "Coal miners voting today on contract," *MDP*, Mar 24, 1978.

UPI, "Patrick fears rejection effect," *MDP*, Mar 24, 1978.

Ann Hughey, "They may say yes, but solution missing," *CG*, Mar 24, 1978.

Ben A. Franklin, "Miners ratify contract to end longest strike; work to resume Monday," *NYT*, Mar 25, 197, pp. :1,7.
William Robbins, "Miners gloomy as they vote on new contract," *NYT*, Mar 25, 1978, p. 12.
Al Moran and Dave Weymiller, "Local miners nixed pact," *MMP*, Mar 25, 1978, pp. 1,10.
Thomas Grubisich, "Mine workers in southwest Virginia switch stand, vote to accept contract," *WP*, Mar 25, 1978.
Helen Dewar, "New contract is winning, UMW says," *WP*, Mar 25, 1978, pp. 1,A6.
David Langford, "Miners' need for paychecks helped contract win okay," *MMR*, Mar 25, 1978.
Evelyn Ryan, "Delay in UMW benefits hit," *MMR*, Mar 25, 1978.
Ben A. Franklin, "In the bitter aftermath: whither the UMW?" *NYT*, Mar 26, 1978.
Jerry Flint, "Bigger concessions from unions sought," *NYT*, Mar 26, 1978, pp. 1,14.
William Robbins, "Coal settlement cheers some miners and vexes others," *NYT*, Mar 26, 1978, p. 12.
Steve Rattner, "Coal industry problems expected to persist long after mines open," *NYT*, Mar 26, 1978, pp. 1,13.
Helen Dewar, "Relieved Carter hails coal settlement," *WP*, Mar 26, 1978.
William Robbins, "Reporter's notebook: mines still bristle with distrust," *NYT*, Mar 27, 1978.
Urban C. Lehner, "Coal strike: a needless panic?" *WSJ*, Mar 28, 1978.
Strat Douthat, "Mellow mood prevails at coal mines after strike, officials say," *Louisville Courier-Journal*, June 25, 1978, p. B5.
AP, "Coal association cuts '78 production estimate," *LCJ*, Sept 24, 1978.
Howard Fineman, " Some say mining panel lacks direction," *LCJ*, Sept 24, 1978, p. 1.
Jim Parks, "Coal industry future cloudy, though not entirely dark," *LCJ*, Sept 24, 1978, pp. E1,6.
AP, "Regulations hurt coal production, operators say," *LCJ*, Nov 14, 1978, p. B2.
Howard Fineman, "Mining, pollution controls targets in war on inflation," *LCJ*, Nov 14, 1978, p. 1.
Howard Fineman, " Congressional study lambasts US role during coal strike," *LCJ*, Nov 16, 1978:1.
Howard Fineman, "Two U.S. officials known for tough stand on mining are fired," *LCJ*, Aug 4, 1978.
Jane Mayer, "How Reagan Staff Manages News: best 'spin-control' ever," *WSJ*, Oct 12, 1984, p. 64.
"On Strike, In Business," *NYT*, April 5, 1987, p. 1F.
"A Generation of Couch Potatoes Looms," *Library Hotline*, v.XVII, no.23, June 13, 1988, p. 3.

Appendix I
Reading the Wider
Political-Economic Framework

To more fully contextualize the social location and significance of the coal strike we must touch at least on the history of relations between capital, labor and the state from the late 1940s through the mid-1970s. The political compromise between capital and labor after World War II in the United States has been called "the labor-capital accords" (Bowles & Gintis, 1982). In conjunction with Keynsian "pump-priming" logic and currency manipulations, these Accords underlay "corporate liberalism" as the dominant political agenda at the national level. An understanding of the rise and fall of corporate liberalism and the capital-labor accords reveals much about the dominant ideological frames which structure CBS reporting of the strike.

By 1977, the labor-capital accords were unraveling because the United States' economic hegemony over the World Capitalist System had begun to ebb. An ascendent stage of United States capitalism followed World War II and lasted through the early 1970s, until the internal contradictions and the crisis tendencies of state-steered and -managed corporate capitalism could no longer be supressed. Declining rates of productivity and profit for first-generation corporate capitalist firms accompanied increasing costs of policing the American world-system, even while U.S. corporate control over the world-system shrank. In addition, pressures to extend civil rights and to regulate (civilize) class conflict pressed the state to intervene in markets in ways which reduced rates of profitability. Likewise, victories by the labor movement in the late 1960s in securing health and safety legislation and bureaucratically mandated COLAs created workplace disadvantages to employers who sought lower labor costs without the "shackles" of safety and environmental regulations in Third World nations. By the

237

early 1970s, the "fiscal crisis of the State" was unfolding, the product of asking the state to assume too many of the social costs necessary for capital to reproduce itself. Budget deficits continued to grow—the price of the thousands of political compromises which were business-as-usual in post-war Pork-Barrel Congresses.

Organized working-class opposition to capitalist social relations and economic inequality in the 1930s and 1940s initiated a path toward the labor-capital accords which characterized the United States after World War II. Corporate liberalism developed into a politics of cooptation, institutionalizing a political style designed to deflect conflict away from the nexus between capital and labor and make the state/law the problem solver. Corporate liberalism demonstrated a practical method for displacing conflicts surrounding the production and distribution of surplus value. Under "corporate liberalism" organized labor became a junior partner in the governing process (cf. Mills, 1948).

The CBS portrayal of labor in 1977 reflected a media image that had initially been composed in the early 1950s when "the new men of power" from major industrial unions agreed to the accords. In the early 1950s, major corporations compromised on redistribution issues because they wanted labor peace and control over the labor process. Meanwhile, communist leaders were purged from the unions and supplanted by the "crusty but pragmatic" new men of power. This paradigm and the imagery that went with it continued to dominate CBS coverage during the coal strike, as they used George Meany to symbolize the crusty, irascible, institutional voice of labor which must be duly consulted.

In a climate of growing union power, corporate leaders recognized the unions and relented in their opposition to State intervention into the allocation of surplus value and the reproduction of labor-processes. State intervention in the 1930s took forms such as Social Security and the National Labor Relations Board, each structured by a bureaucratic-legal framework. In the post-World War II period, union policies and objectives were limited by a framework defined in terms of corporate accumulation interests—as steady growth of GNP and minimal disruptions in the labor process. In this context, a centralized bureaucratic union movement sought "to realize its class interests through state policy, such as social welfare, full employment programs, public health and medical services, low cost housing, and redistributive policy in general" (Zeitlin, 1980, p. 29).

Reliance on the State as an agent in the accumulation process continued to grow, as did expanded State responsibility for transfer payments and income redistribution policies as a means of reproducing labor markets and legitimating the unequal social relations which are both precondition and means of private capital accumulation. The State grew also to meet the costs of reproducing the conditions necessary for private accumulation.

The post-World War II restructuring of capital-labor relations built around a pattern of State intervention which altered both the "distribution of the social product" (Bowles, 1982, p. 49) and the structure of the accumulation process. Keynesian policies allowed the State to become an agency for the systematic promotion and facilitation of private capital accumulation. The goal was to stimulate economic growth (pump-priming), control the severity of business cycle fluctuations, and manage unemployment. Forms of State intervention included monetary and fiscal controls, investment in economic infrastructure, finance of new technologies, stimulation and support of transportation (e.g., highway expenditures) and housing industries and absorption of costs for education and labor-training programs. The State also acquired formal responsibility for both the "social costs of production" such as environmental protection, and expenses of "stabilizing the world capitalist social order" so a favorable climate for capital accumulation could be maintained (O'Connor, 1973). Corporately oriented Keynsian policies redirected the accumulation process toward a "demand-constrained" accumulation process in which workers' expanded consumption power fueled growth.

The regulation of class conflicts between capital and labor led, by the 1960s, to a bureaucratically elaborate State apparatus providing welfare benefits and public services. Social movements organized by labor and poor people and blacks prompted programs to ameliorate the living conditions of those ill-served by market forces. "The expansion of the state is also conditioned by demands from the working class for the state to provide public services and welfare as family and community structures are destroyed by the growth of universal wage labor and universal commodity production and consumption" (Hodson, 1978, p. 431). By 1979, 29 percent of workers' living standards in the United States was "acquired not through the exchange of labor power for a wage, but through claims on the state made quite independently of the sale of labor power" (Bowles, 1982, p. 52).

Rank-and-file initiatives combined with corporate elites' interest in minimizing disharmony led to the creation of agencies like as OSHA (Donnelly, 1982). Such agencies established rationalized conflict-resolution mechanisms that cooled out overt class conflicts by rerouting them into the arena of juridical proceedings. Though Presidents like Nixon staffed these organizations to their own advantage, and gains made by labor were "incremental" at best, the very fact that labor acquired limited access to these organizational structures proved costly to Capital (Calavita, 1983). Just as Keynesian policies precipitated a wage-price spiral, so too, rationalized conflict-resolution mechanisms and institutionalized collective-bargaining procedures designed to avert class conflicts were leading to a Capital-Labor stalemate (Bluestone & Harrison, 1982).

The prosperity of corporate capitalism in the 1950s and 1960s was "predicated on the complementarity of domestic redistribution and international expansion" (Bowles, 1982, p. 55). But while short-term outcomes were favorable to both organized labor and capital, "the end result of these two interconnected social processes—the demands by capital that the state underwrite monopoly accumulation and the demands by labor that the State deal with the consequences of accumulation on the lives of workers—is a systematic tendency for the state to expand in the course of capitalist development" (Hodson, 1978, p. 431).

As it turned out, the "big fix' displaced capitalism's crisis tendencies from the economic to the political sphere. The postwar labor-capital accords brought piecemeal reforms to implement an unevenly rationalized state apparatus to contain the contradictions of capitalist development. Yet efforts at balancing accumulation and legitimation demands led to a continuous expansion of state expenditures for the socialization of production costs (particularly for the monopoly sector) and the socialization of costs of reproducing labor power and consumption. The Federal Reserve Board continued to grow in institutional prominence in the effort to stabilize and insure the reproduction of capital, labor and consumption power. The Fed's policy aimed to steer between inflation and recession (and later, stagflation) by intervening into the circulatory process of money. But this did not heal the basic contradiction between the "socialization of costs and the private appropriation of profits [which] creates a fiscal crisis, or "structural gap," between state expenditures and state revenues" (O'Connor, 1973, p. 9).

To aid the goals of corporate accumulation, the State intervened to absorb the costs of legitimation and reproduction. By the 1970s, these costs had become a fetter on aggregate accumulation. Even State expenditures to stimulate accumulation in the monopoly sector boomeranged—resulting in intensified environmental destruction and increased surplus population which, in turn, necessitated increased state expenditures for the "social expenses" of cleaning up the dumps and giving minimum care to those unfit for labor markets. This became an unending political hot potato because the socialization of costs of reproducing labor power was increasingly shouldered by a middle class who viewed escalating tax bites as anathema. And so it went, state expenditures escalating along with the political consequences. The price of crisis displacement—the negation of corporate liberalism—began to be realized by the early 1970s, as the state "expanded social revenues to the breaking point, wearily juggling political demands with the persistent requirements" imposed by the practice of continuous accumulation (Krieger & Lewis, 1979, p. 1678).

Concessions made to working-class demands from the 1930s through the early 1970s contributed to the steady expansion of the state, and hence, to a now chronic tendency toward fiscal crisis and inflation. Many of these concessions involved creation of new state agencies—endowed with a sphere of influence and a set of regulations—to protect people from the consequences of unregulated private capital accumulation. Capital responded both at the level of the firm and the state to reverse this process.

In the short term, organized labor realized gains in employment security and income redistribution. However, in the long run, the corporate liberal accords between labor and capital have led to a fragmented, internally divided union movement with diminished political power. Labor's acquiescence to the economistic definitions imposed by capital led to their failure to contest either the arrangement of the labor process or the growing international mobility of investment, goods, and now infrastructure. By the mid-1970s, corporate capital was bogged down, and it struck back first in labor markets—exporting jobs to low-wage countries and demanding benefit and wage concessions from unions. Labor firmly wed itself to the Keynesian policies of income redistribution and international expansion which premised their postwar prosperity, but by the mid-1970s these placed the union movement in a defensive posture. The union movement was ill-prepared to respond. Not only leaders, but union workers as well, had developed fragmented interests over the years. Labor market segmentation, in conjunction with once-protective mechanisms such as unemployment insurance and multiyear contracts, created divergent interests among workers.

> Since the 1930s big capital has come to accept the inevitability of unions and has worked to turn them into institutions to control and discipline labor. The 'productivity deal' called for multiyear contracts to promote labor peace, security of seniority, and retirement benefits. The company retained control of the production process and was generally free to introduce labor-saving technology. The workers who continued on the job would share in the gains through higher wages. In consequence, a decreasing proportion of the workforce belongs to the unions. The multidivision corporations moved first to subcontracting parts to non-union shops and finally to moving their plants into nonunion areas, where they actively fight unionization efforts. The union today is paying the price of its earlier accomodation. (Tabb, 1980, pp. 67–8)

Labor leaders who had benefitted from the capital-labor accords were unprepared to contest the new corporate strategies. In addition, the internal rigidity of unions alienated rank-and-file members. Hence, organized labor found itself declining in numbers and power by the mid-1970s. Not only were they outflanked at the political-economic level, these same labor leaders were wholly unprepared for the ideological struggles which would be waged through the mass media.

Appendix 2
CBS News Dates

		Start	End	Length	Location
1)	11/25/77	5:41:10	5:41:30	0:20	
2)	11/28/77	5:45:20	5:47:00	1:40	
3)	12/4/77	5:12:30	5:15:00	2:30	
4)	12/5/77	5:37:10	5:40:50	3:40	
5)	12/6/77	5:36:20	5:38:30	2:10	
6)	12/8/77	5:42:10	5:44:10	2:00	
7)	12/13/77	5:48:00	5:48:50	0:50	
8)	12/23/77	5:49:20	5:51:40	2:20	
9)	12/30/77	5:52:20	5:52:30	0:10	
10)	1/2/78	5:48:30	5:50:20	1:50	
11)	1/6/78	5:49:00	5:49:20	0:20	
12)	1/17/78	5:53:10	5:53:40	0:30	
13)	1/24/78	5:49:40	5:50:00	0:20	
14)	1/29/78	5:09:10	5:09:30	0:20	
15)	1/29/78	5:09:30	5:10:10	0:40	
16)	1/30/78	5:37:20	5:37:40	0:20	
17)	1/31/78	5:38:20	5:43:20	5:00	
18)	2/2/78	5:43:50	5:44:10	0:20	
19)	2/3/78	5:38:50	5:40:20	1:30	
20)	2/5/78	5:05:30	5:07:30	2:00	
21)	2/6/78	5:30:10	5:32:40	2:30	1st
22)	2/7/78	5:30:10	5:35:20	5:10	1st
23)	2/8/78	5:51:00	5:51:10	0:10	

	Start	End	Length	Location
24) 2/9/78	5:36:00	5:39:30	3:10	
25) 2/10/78	5:30:10	5:35:20	5:10	1st
26) 2/12/78	5:15:20	5:19:10	3:50	
27) 2/13/78	5:30:10	5:35:30	5:20	1st
28) 2/14/78	5:41:00	5:45:50	4:50	
29) 2/15/78	5:30:20	5:36:50	6:30	1st
30) 2/16/78	5:38:20	5:44:00	4:40	
31) 2/17/78	5:30:10	5:35:40	5:30	1st
32) 2/19/78	5:10:30	5:14:50	4:20	
33) 2/20/78	5:37:00	5:43:00	6:00	
34) 2/21/78	5:30:10	5:34:20	4:10	1st
35) 2/22/78	5:35:30	5:38:10	2:40	
36) 2/23/78	5:30:10	5:34:30	4:20	1st
37) 2/24/78	5:31:00	5:33:10	2:10	1st*
38) 2/26/78	5:15:40	5:19:40	4:00	
39) 2/27/78	5:35:50	5:37:40	1:50	
40) 2/28/78	5:42:20	5:45:00	2:40	
41) 3/1/78	5:41:20	5:43:40	2:10	
42) 3/3/78	5:41:10	5:44:00	2:50	
43) 3/5/78	5:00:10	5:08:50	8:40	1st
44) 3/5/78	5:21:10	5:23:00	1:50	
45) 3/6/78	5:30:10	5:37:00	6:50	1st
46) 3/7/78	5:30:10	5:36:40	6:30	1st
47) 3/8/78	5:36:40	5:41:20	4:40	
48) 3/9/78	5:30:10	5:36:40	6:30	1st
49) 3/10/78	5:30:10	5:34:20	4:20	1st
50) 3/12/78	5:07:40	5:13:20	5:40	
51) 3/13/78	5:40:10	5:43:10	3:00	
52) 3/14/78	5:37:10	5:40:00	2:50	
53) 3/15/78	5:45:10	5:45:30	0:20	
54) 3/16/78	5:49:40	5:50:00	0:10	
55) 3/17/78	5:40:40	5:42:20	1:40	
56) 3/19/78	5:21:30	5:23:10	1:40	
57) 3/23/78	5:40:00	5:43:50	3:50	
58) 3/24/78	5:30:10	5:34:30	4:20	
59) 3/26/78	5:03:40	5:06:20	2:40	1st
60) 3/27/78	5:30:10	5:32:40	2:30	
61) 3/28/78	5:36:20	5:36:40	0:20	1st
62) 3/29/78	5:41:40	5:44:10	1:00*	
63) 3/30/78	5:44:50	5:45:10	0:20	

Appendix 3
Framebox Symbols

245

Feb 8, 1978	—none
Feb 9, 1978	miner/helmet/trolley
Feb 10, 1978	pickaxe & placard
Feb 12, 1978	pickaxe & placard
Feb 13, 1978	pickaxe & placard
	coal trolley
Feb 14, 1978	pickaxe & placard
	coal trolley
Feb 15, 1978	pickaxe & placard
	coal trolley
	miner/helmet/trolley
Feb 16, 1978	pickaxe & placard
	coal trolley
Feb 17, 1978	pickaxe & placard
Feb 19, 1978	railroad cars/'coal strike'
	W. Va. map/pickax/helmet
Feb 20, 1978	miner's helmet/'coal strike'
	Indiana map
Feb 21, 1978	miner's helmet
	'Management' logo
	UMWA official seal
Feb 22, 1978	miner's helmet
Feb 23, 1978	miner's helmet
	miner/helmet/trolley
	coal seam/'coal strike'
	Ray Marshall photo
Feb 24, 1978	coal seam/'coal strike'
	George Meany photo
	Presidential seal
Feb 25, 1978	—NA (not available)
Feb 26, 1978	UMWA official seal
	Ray Marshall photo
	coal seam/'coal strike'
	Pres. Carter photo
Feb 27, 1978	miner's helmet/'coal strike'
	miner/helmet/trolley
Feb 28, 1978	miner's helmet/'coal strike'
Mar 1, 1978	pickaxe & placard
Mar 3, 1978	miner/helmet/trolley
Mar 4, 1978	–NA
Mar 5, 1978	ratification ballot/'Rejection'
	map of mideast region
	Arnold Miller photo
	miner/helmet/trolley
	coal trolley
	'coal strike'

Mar 6, 1978	miner helmet/'Taft-Hartley Act'/'coal strike
	miner/helmet/trolley
Mar 7, 1978	miner's helmet/'coal strike'
	miner/helmet/trolley
	coal bin
Mar 8, 1978	–none
Mar 9, 1978	helmet/'coal strike'
	miner/helmet/trolley
	coal trolley
	West Virginia map
Mar 10, 1978	helmet/'coal strike'
	Arnold Miller photo
	pickaxe & placard
	Department of Justice seal
	UMWA seal
	Arnold Miller photo
	photo of food coupons
	piece of steel industry equipment
Mar 12, 1978	photo of Arnold Miller and UMWA attorney Harrison
	Combs (not nominated)/'Coal Talks'
	'Taft-Hartley'
	miner/helmet trolley
Mar 13, 1978	miner/helmet/trolley
Mar 14, 1978	photo of miners/'tentative agreement'
	'Coal Strike'/'Negotiations'/silhouettes face to face
	miner/helmet/trolley
Mar 15, 1978	miner/helmet/'trolley
Mar 16, 1978	–none
Mar 17, 1978	miner helmet/trolley
	seal/'coal strike'
Mar 19, 1978	pickaxe/'coal strike'/'104 days'

Author Index

Subject Index

252